ISLAMIC
CIVILIZATION

CW01497007

ISLAMIC CIVILIZATION

CIVILIZATION

Its Foundational Beliefs and Principles

Sayyid Abul A 'lā Mawdūdī

Translated by
Syed Akif

THE ISLAMIC FOUNDATION

Islamic Civilization: Its Foundational Beliefs and Principles

Published by
THE ISLAMIC FOUNDATION,
Markfield Conference Centre,
Ratby Lane, Markfield, Leicestershire
LE67 9SY, United Kingdom
E-mail: publications@islamic-foundation.com
Website: www.islamic-foundation.com

Quran House, PO Box 30611, Nairobi, Kenya

PMB 3193, Kano, Nigeria

Distributed by
KUBE PUBLISHING LTD.
Tel: +44(0)1530 249230, Fax: +44(0)1530 249656
E-mail: info@kubepublishing.com

Cataloguing-in-Publication Data is available
from the British Library

ISBN: 978-0-86037-479-4 *casebound*
ISBN: 978-0-86037-474-9 *paperback*

Typeset by: N.A.Qaddoura
Cover design by: Nasir Cadir

Printed by: Imak Ofset - Turkey

Contents

Translator's Note

Sayyid Abul A'lā Mawdūdī (1903-79) is undoubtedly one of the greatest Islamic scholars produced by Muslim South Asia throughout its 1200 year-long history. With the launch of the Jamā'at-i-Islāmī in 1941, he not only joined the ranks of leading Muslim reformers, but became the torch bearer of a new Muslim political awareness being born out of the demise of Western colonialism and imperialism. He was one of the progenitors of the people called by the rather new term 'public intellectuals' – the rare breed of people who not only sit behind their desks or search the deep recesses of libraries to produce new epistemological views and scholarship but also have the vigour and the vision to combine social and political activism with their intellectualism – persons who, to borrow a modern management phrase, 'walk the talk'. Coming in the wake of the epochal work of South Asia's all-time intellectual giant Muḥammad Iqbāl and his reformation of classical Muslim thought, Sayyid Mawdūdī joined other modern Muslim public intellectuals, like Muḥammad Rashīd Riḍā, to inspire three generations of twentieth-century Muslims on to the path of Muslim rethinking, reformation, and revolution.

Sayyid Mawdūdī's political thoughts, chiefly the essential requirement of a vanguardist movement that was not just Islamic and revolutionary but one which also believed in the theo-intellectual basis of a state, which inspired reformist intellectuals like Sayyid Quṭb and numerous others throughout the Muslim world. Sayyid Mawdūdī's influence on Muslim youth and intellectuals was very significant – so significant that Pakistan's military and political elite saw him as a threat strong enough to be locked up and even sentenced to death!

The present work *Islāmī Tahdhīb awr uske, Uṣūl-o-Mabādī* is one of the few works of Sayyid Mawdūdī which has remained untranslated in a complete modern version, even though parts of the work have found their way to Western readers though other works of the author. I am grateful to two colleagues of my late father, Dr Zafar Ishaq Ansari and Professor Khurshid Ahmad, for reposing their confidence in me in giving me the chance to translate this work.

May God bless Sayyid Mawdūdī for his seminal works – and the team that has made this translation possible, which will help to bring the work of this great scholar to a new audience. I seek your prayers for my own forgiveness (*maghfirah*) as well as for that of my family, my late parents and for all Muslims.

Makkah al-Mukarramah   **Syed Akif**
Rabī' al-Awwal 1432
February 2011

Foreword

Sayyid Abul Aʿlā Mawdūdī (1903-1979), one of the twentieth-century's leading Muslim intellectuals and revivalists, wrote *Islāmī Tahdhīb awr Uske Uṣūl-o Mabādī*, which was published in 1933. This book, written during the last period of colonial rule in British India and at a time when the momentum for independence was growing, attempts to bring out the vital relationship between a civilization and its underlying worldview and vision of life, with particular attention to the case of Islamic civilization.

Now civilization is one of the major ideas of the modern age. To stress its importance it would suffice to say that Arnold Toynbee, the towering historian of the twentieth century, regards it as the proper unit of historical inquiry.[1] At the opposite end of the spectrum, we find the late Samuel Huntington, the well-known prophet of gloom, predicting a global future defined by a 'clash of civilizations'.[2] Be that as it may, the term has come to denote a community or society with a developed state of intellectual, cultural and material development, an improved state of moral conduct, an extensive use of record-keeping, including writing, and the appearance of complex political and social institutions. Civilization is associated with a whole range of factors such as an intense urbanisation leading to the emergence of huge cosmopolitan cities, the establishment of the writ of the state over its citizens, the rise of capitalism, the emergence of occupational specialisation and the existence of a variety of socio-political institutions. In short, the word signifies an ordered society that has far outgrown

---

[1] Arnold J. Toynbee, *A Study of History* (Oxford: Oxford University Press, 1934-1961), 12 vols.

[2] Samuel P. Huntington, *Clash of Civilizations and the Remaking of World Order* (New York: Simon & Schuster, 1996).

the primitive conditions of existence in which, to borrow Hobbes' words, 'life was nasty, brutish and short'.[3]

A civilization understandably has a time and space dimension. Hence we speak of entities such as the Indus Valley civilization, the Babylonian civilization, the civilization of ancient Rome, or modern European civilization. Are civilizations, however, also related to the ideas and ideals cherished by those who live under their shadows?

In the present work Mawdūdī focuses his attention on the relationship between a civilization and its worldview, or the vision of life and the religious outlook that inspires and permeates it. His concern is to explore the relationship between Islam and civilization, and he sets out to examine how, in what ways, and to what extent Islam gives shape and direction to the civilization of Muslims. If Islam's role in this regard is considered to be crucial, then how is Islam related to the temporal and spatial contexts of civilization itself?

Mawdudi notes with displeasure the trend among contemporary scholars of his day to regard Islamic civilization as an outgrowth and continuation of previous Middle Eastern and Greek and Roman civilizations. These scholars strove to prove that the constituent elements of Islamic civilization were derived from the civilizations that preceded it. As for the distinctive aspects of Islamic civilization, they tended to attribute them to the characteristics of the Arabs' 'mindset' which prompted them to make some adjustments while using the building blocks of other civilizations in erecting the edifice of their own civilization.[4]

Mawdudi altogether denies the validity of this whole approach. He is at odds with the attitude of equating civilization with a nation's cumulative 'knowledge, literature and fine arts, its literary and rhetorical devices, modes of social life, style of refined living and system of governance'. He does not consider these to be the equivalent of 'civilization'. In his view, they are the end results and manifestations rather than the essence of a civilization; they are not the root of a

---

[3] Thomas Hobbes, *Leviathan* (London, 1651), Part 1: Of Man, Chap. 13, para. 9.

[4] See *Tahdhīb-i Islāmī awr Uske Uṣūl-o Mabādī*, 27th edn. (Lahore: Islamic Publications, 2100), "Muqaddimah", pp. 9 ff.

civilization's tree but only its leaves and fruit. The true understanding of a civilization is possible only by having access to the soul of that civilization and its underlying fundamental principles.[5]

There are good reasons why civilizations should be viewed in terms of the basic ideas and ideals underlying them. Yet while many changes have taken place over the millennia, humanity continues to be perennially confronted with the same basic questions: Is the existence of the universe and of humankind simply the result of a fortuitous combination of circumstances or does it represent the decision of an All-Wise and All-Powerful Creator? If the latter is the case, then what are His basic attributes and how is humanity expected to relate to Him? What is the position of the human being in the overall scheme of the universe and what is the purpose and mission of his life? Is the physical death of the human individual tantamount to his total extinction or does his life continue even after he has been subjected to biological death? Does God expect human beings to act in a particular manner to achieve self-fulfilment and abiding success and felicity? If so, has God provided any guidance to that effect and how can humanity find out what that guidance consists of?

These questions would seem quite remote from the day-to-day concerns and pursuits that inform the lives of most men and women. This, however, does not detract in the least from the fact that unless these questions are clearly answered and a definite position is taken with regard to them, then a person's life will remain devoid of proper direction. By evading these questions, humanity is likely to continue to stumble. This might give rise to a lot of frenzied activity only to discover from time to time that – thanks mainly to a lack of clarity about his worldview – the life of the human individual keeps going around aimlessly in circles without making any true headway.

The present book raises these profound questions and attempts to answer them candidly, an attempt that leads in this book to the fleshing out the essentials of the Islamic worldview. In addressing this task, the author mainly draws upon the rich reservoir of the Qur'ān and does so with admirable resourcefulness and insight. Thus the

<hr>

[5] Ibid.

teachings pertaining to the fundamental tenets of belief in Islam – God, the angels, the Prophets, the Revealed Books and the Last Day – have been clearly expounded. Thanks to a very systematic exposition, three salient features emerge very prominently. Firstly, that the basic doctrines of Islamic belief are cohesive and organically interrelated. Secondly, that these doctrines are in harmony with human nature and appeal to human reason as being innately sensible and judicious. Thirdly, that these doctrines are capable of serving as the foundation of a civilization that says 'yes' to the human urge to satisfy his legitimate biological drives without going to the extreme of Epicureanism, in which the chief goal of existence is the pursuit of individual pleasure.

In any case, as far as Muslims are concerned, they have been committed from the very beginning to fashion their individual and collective lives according to the worldview and principles and values derived from Islam, a fact which has given their culture and civilization a flair and flavour all of its own. Whatever is distinctive about Islamic civilization stems from the distinctiveness of the foundations upon which it rests. This is why Islamic civilization can only be adequately appreciated by grasping the constitutive concepts of its worldview such as its concepts of God, Prophethood, the Afterlife, and the aim and purpose of human life.

In sum, the book brings into sharp relief the concepts as well as the ethos of Islamic civilization. It is the characteristic paradigm of this civilization that needs to be grasped in order to understand the Muslim psyche and the 'venture of Islam' in history. This is true not only for Islam's bygone ages, but it is equally true for Islam in the second decade of the twenty-first century.

The book is characterized by some of the qualities for which Mawdūdī's writings have been known throughout his long and distinguished literary career: His discourse is supported by an impressive degree of knowledge of the subject in hand which he presents logically and persuasively. Additionally, even in this early work, Mawdūdī's literary style displays its distinctive charm and elegance.

It is presumably not insignificant that in this relatively early part of his life Mawdūdī set out to articulate Islam's worldview before embarking on his lifelong task of elucidating the details of the Islamic way of life. This seems, in my opinion, to reflect Islam's inherent scheme of priorities in which the essentials take precedence over the subsidiary details. Quite obviously, unless there is a clear concept of Islam's basics, it would be meaningless and sterile to strive for the establishment of an Islamic order of life with all of its ramifications. In this sense the book might be seen to represent the early Mawdūdī's clarion call towards 'first things first'. As Mawdūdī has observed elsewhere, anyone seriously concerned with the operationalization of Islam should start with its ABCs, with understanding the basic tenets of Islamic belief. This first step should be to know well the meaning of *lā ilāha illallāh* ('There is no deity except the One True God') to be followed by translating its implications in terms of practice. All else follows from this.

This work has been ably rendered into English by the gifted writer and intellectual, Syed Akif. Akif has admirably acquitted himself in expressing Islamic religious ideas in chaste English, at a stage when English as a vehicle for articulating some of the finest and subtlest of ideas and emotions related to Islam is still in its early stages of development. What made Akif's task even more difficult was that apart from being a great scholar and thinker, Mawdūdī had a highly-regarded and distinctive literary style all of his own. In my opinion, Akif's success speaks volumes about his deep familiarity with the universe of Islamic lore and his outstanding ability to write felicitously in English.

It is to be hoped that this contribution will serve to further enrich the growing body of Islamic literature in the English language and lead to a deeper and better grasp of the Islamic worldview, thereby promoting mutual understanding and friendship among human beings belonging to a variety of civilizations, religious faiths, and ideologies. I would also like to acknowledge the editorial support extended by the able team of the Islamic Foundation, particularly Dr M.M. Ahsan and Dr A.R. Kidwai, and the logistic and financial support given by the World of Islam Trust, Islamabad, the Institute of Policy Studies, Islamabad, and the Madina Trust, Peterborough, U.K.

Islamabad
Rajab 1432 H
June 2011

Zafar Ishaq Ansari

Transliteration Table

Arabic Consonants

Initial, unexpressed medial and final:

ء	ʾ	د	d	ض	ḍ	ك	k
ب	b	ذ	dh	ط	ṭ	ل	l
ت	t	ر	r	ظ	ẓ	م	m
ث	th	ز	z	ع	ʿ	ن	n
ج	j	س	s	غ	gh	هـ	h
ح	ḥ	ش	sh	ف	f	و	w
خ	kh	ص	ṣ	ق	q	ي	y

Vowels, diphthongs, etc.

Short: ـَ a   ـِ i   ـُ u

Long: ـَا ā   ـِي ī   ـُو ū

Diphthongs: ـَوْ aw

ـَىْ ay

Preface

Western authors on Islam – and through their influence a great majority of our own scholars – are of the opinion that 'Islamic Civilization' is derived directly from the civilizations that preceded Islam, especially the Greek and Roman civilizations. In their view, the fact that Islam developed its own characteristic civilization can mostly be attributed to the Arab mindset that altered the pre-existing corpus of knowledge and cultural wealth in a way that its form was changed without any substantial transformation of the content. It is because of this outlook that these people attempt to trace the constituent elements of Islamic civilization in the ancient Persian, Babylonian, Sumerian, Phoenician, Egyptian, Greek and Roman civilizations. Furthermore, they then proceed to investigate the mental processes in the Arab ethos that, so of to say, rebuilt a new edifice from the old building blocks by merely reapplying its own fresh mortar without necessarily having a worldview of its own.

A Misconception

This line of thought is, however, a great misconception. While I do not deny that the human condition, not only in its present form but in every time and age and in every walk of life, has been influenced by the past and that, in a way, every new construction employs the building material of pre-existing structures, I wish to state unequivocally that the Islamic civilization is, in its very existence and essence, purely Islamic. No non-Islamic factor has had the least bit of influence in shaping the core of Islamic civilization. All the same, it is in the expression or manifestation of certain issues that Arab customs and elements of the Arab mindset, as well as extraneous influences from both pre- and post-Islamic cultural traditions, have entered its folds.

Undoubtedly, for any building, the particular architectural style, the construction plans, the proposed use and the appropriateness of the structure for the designated purpose are fundamental considerations, while its paint and surface coverings, façade and beautification elements, fixtures and furniture comprise elements that are only superficial and not of fundamental importance.

Thus, as far as the origins and fundamentals are concerned, the citadel of Islamic civilization is the product of its own genius. The building plans are original and nothing has been borrowed from any other plan. The architectural style has also been invented and developed indigenously with no imitation of foreign forms. The purpose of the construction is also unique; no building either before it or since has ever been built with this aim in mind. Similarly, the type of structure required to achieve the purpose behind the creation of this edifice is also original and fully conforms to the architectural considerations.

The building that now appears as the Islamic civilization is truly purpose-built and complete; no external architect or engineer holds the power to add to it or alter it in any way. As far as the marginal elements are concerned, here too Islam has borrowed very little from others; it can very well be said that most of these marginal factors are Islam's own. On the contrary, Muslims took the decorative elements from others and proceeded to develop and embellish these to such a point of excellence that superficial observers see the whole building as one whose plan has been totally or extensively borrowed from outside.

The Meaning of Civilization
Before proceeding towards a conclusion about the debate on original and borrowed civilizational factors any further, it is important to answer the question, 'What is a civilization?'

Generally, people believe that 'civilization' is a term that stands for the totality of a nation's knowledge and wisdom, literature and fine arts, its inventions and products, economic pursuits, living styles and cultural traditions, socio-political norms, and the like. However, the fact of the matter is that these aspects are not the essence of a civilization but only its end results and manifestations, not the stem-root system of civilization's tree but only its leaves and fruit. The significance and worth of any civilization cannot be assessed on the basis of such appearances and decorative body coverings. Instead, we should attempt to reach the soul of a civilization and explore its underlying, fundamental principles.

The Structural Elements of Civilization

From this latter approach towards studying civilizations, it is important to determine a given civilization's conceptual view towards temporal existence. What does it have to say about man's place in this world? How does it regard the world itself? What, according to this civilization, is the relationship of man with this world? And what does it say about man's interaction with this world – that is, if man were to interact with the world how must he regard this world? These fundamental questions relating to a civilization's worldview have an extremely profound impact on all other aspects of human life, so much so that any change in the foundations of such concepts totally transforms the nature of the civilization itself.

The second set of questions having a central relationship with the concept of human life in any given civilization deals with the end purpose of life itself; these include questions like these: What, according to this civilization, is the whole object of human life in this world? What is the purpose of all our incessant endeavours, struggles, labours, trials and tribulations? What is that ultimate object of our desire towards which we must move forward – and rapidly so? What is the worldview that we should attempt to strive for? What is that end, consideration of which must always be foremost in each and every one of our actions and efforts? This set of core questions relating to our final destination determines all practical aspects of human life and the pace of the journey. From the answers to such questions follow the choices relating to all human actions and the adoption of successful strategies for meeting the stated objectives.

The third group of questions that constitutes our analysis relates to the manner in which the civilization under study deals with the character building of its individuals as well as the fundamental beliefs and philosophical concepts on which such human development takes place. In what mould does the civilization shape the mentality of its members? What thoughts and feelings does it inspire in the minds and hearts of human beings? What are the motivations that encourage and drive the members of a civilization to act in a certain way, which itself leads to the grand objective that the civilization has set for itself? The fact that the power of human action is subservient to the power of human thought can hardly be debated. The spirit that moves the body into action emanates from the 'heart' and mind. The mindset and belief system that a person espouses and the philosophy that rules the 'heart' naturally govern all forces geared towards concrete action. The dye in which a mind is set determines all the sensibilities and incentives of the individual who possesses these and all bodily actions that follow also adhere to the individual's mindset. Indeed, no civilization can come into existence without a fundamental belief system and a conceptual foundation upon which its worldview is based. It is because of this core concept that it is absolutely essential to understand the set of beliefs and worldviews that comprise a civilization's ethos in order to determine its merit. To use the building metaphor once again, such an analysis of a civilization's highs and lows is as important as inquiring about the depth and strength of a structure's foundation when one is determining its strength and durability.

Coming to the fourth level of inquiry, we need to ask, 'What kind of human beings does the civilization aim to make out of its constituent members?' Or in other words, 'How will the group conscience act to transform the mere physical and animal entities of men and women into humans?' This is also to ask, 'What kind of moral and ethical training does the civilization provide its people with whereby they are able to prepare themselves for leading successful lives within the ideology that the said civilization has stated for itself?' What are the states, traits and characteristics that it aims to inculcate and develop at both individual and group levels and what kind of human beings are actually produced as a result of the particular moral training that is imparted?

The intellectual basis of this level of analysis should be quite clear, especially in the light of the widespread recognition that human beings are the single most important asset for any and every collective human entity from small groups and organizations to nations. While all civilizations aim at developing and strengthening collective social organizations, individuals are the mortar with which the bricks of the organizational edifice are put together. The strength of the structure is dependent upon the manner and level to which each brick has been baked, the finesse with which every stone has been shaped, the strength of each wooden beam (to ensure that it is not termite infested), and the quality of the mortar and implements that hold all the elements together.

The fifth array of questions relates to the ways and means with which the civilization establishes interpersonal relationships – that is how individual members of this civilization connect with each other and form appropriate relationships corresponding to their social roles. What are the relationships that individuals form and maintain with their family members, neighbours, friends, superiors and subordinates, and others with whom they relate and live? What are the actions and associations that the civilization mandates upon its followers, both individually and collectively, as well as upon those groups who do not subscribe to its particular ethos (i.e. ethnic and religious minorities)? What is the structure of rights and duties between individuals – rights due unto others and others' duties due unto them? What are the limits of action that have been imposed upon individuals and the extent of freedoms given to them? Within this fold of analysis come all issues relating to ethical behaviour, social interaction, law, politics, and even international relations. Briefly, such a study should shed ample light on the manner in which the said civilization organizes family, social and governance structures. From this analysis, it can be seen that the totality that we call civilization is built with five essential elements:

(i)   The worldview relating to temporal life
(ii)   The ultimate aim of life
(iii) Fundamental beliefs and philosophy
(iv) The mechanism for the training of individuals
(v)   The social system for collective organization

Every civilization in the world has been built upon these five principal elements; Islamic civilization is no exception. In this work, I have surveyed the first three elements with respect to Islamic civilization. I have presented herein Islamic civilization's particular worldview relating to temporal life, its ultimate aim of life and the fundamental belief system and philosophy on which it has been established, all of which have given it a character distinct from all the other civilizations of the world. The remaining two elements have not been taken up in this book. As far as the theme of 'training of individuals' is concerned, a study of my book *Islāmī 'Ibādāt par aik Taḥqīqī Naẓar*[1] (*An Analytical View of Islamic Worship*) and *Khuṭubāt*[2] (*Let Us Be Muslims*) [*Chapter Nos. 20–28*] would be useful. An overall view of the Islamic collective social system may be found in my speeches that have been published under the title *Islām ka Niẓām-i-Ḥayāt*[3] (*The Islamic Way of Life*).

[1] Mawdūdī, Sayyid Abul A'lā, *Islāmī 'Ibādāt par aik Taḥqīqī Naẓar* (Lahore: Islamic Publications, Ltd., 1991).

[2] Mawdūdī, Sayyid Abul A'lā, *Khuṭubāt* (Lahore, 2012), English translation *Let Us Be Muslims* (Markfield: The Islamic Foundation, 2011).

[3] Mawdūdī, Sayyid Abul A'lā, *Islām ka Niẓām-i-Ḥayāt*. English translation *Islamic Way of Life* ((Markfield: The Islamic Foundation, 2011).

Publisher's Note

It gives me immense pleasure to publish the English translation of Sayyid Abul A'lā Mawdūdī's scholarly and thought-provoking work originally in Urdu, *Islāmī Tahdhīb awr Uske Uṣūl-o-Mabādī*, under the present title, *Islamic Civilization: Its Foundational Beliefs and Principles*. This work, like all other valuable writings of Sayyid Mawdudi, brings out the distinctive features of the Islamic worldview. Since the present work focuses on the Islamic concept of civilization, rather than Muslims' contribution to culture and civilization, it delves deep into the philosophical underpinnings of the Islamic belief system. Since the doctrine of the Hereafter is central to the Islamic worldview, it receives the author's due attention. Sayyid Mawdūdī's works are deeply rooted in the Qur'ān, a feature which is to the fore in this present work. In the light of scores of Qur'ānic passages Mawdūdī has elucidated a wide range of concepts, themes and issues such as man's place in the universe, the ideal way of life, man's accountability, concept of life in major world faiths and the outstanding features of the Islamic viewpoint. The author, nonetheless, appears at his sharpest in the exposition of the Islamic belief system, especially its stance on life after death. Equally illuminating is his discussion on the great questions of the Being. He succeeds remarkably in presenting a cogent account of the Islamic position on these and related issues.

The Islamic Foundation is grateful to the renowned scholar of Islamic Studies, Professor Zafar Ishaq Ansari for his insightful "Foreword" to this work. Brother Syed Akif deserves every credit for translating Sayyid Mawdūdī's Urdu original into English. This is one of the earliest books of Sayyid Mawdūdī which was first published in 1933. It is also one of the most difficult books to translate as it tackles a frofound and complex subject. This made the task of the translator very arduous. The Foundation is especially thankful to Dr. A.R. Kidwai for not only comparing the translation with the Urdu text but also undertaking extensive copyediting as required. Credit is also due to the Foundation research staff, especially Brother Sadiq Khokhar, who have painstakingly ensured the accuracy of the Qur'ānic passages cited in this work. Brothers Abdur Rashid Siddiqui and Faiyazuddin Ahmad also read the translation and suggested some minor changes. These and others, too many to mention specifically, for whose assistance we are deeply grateful.

Last, but by no means least, we will be failing in our duty if we do not express our thanks and appreciation for the generous support and encouragement of the Madina Trust, especially its Chairman, Br Zia-ul Hassan, as well as the World of Islam Trust and the Institute of Policy Studies, Islamabad.

We pray to Allah *subḥānahū wa ta'ālā* to reward all those associated with the publication of this work. May Allah accept our efforts for communicating the message of Islam through the publication of such literature and forgive our lapses.

We will be grateful to receive comments and suggestions from our readers and well-wishers.

Rabī' al-Awwal 1433H
February 2012

Dr. M. Manazir Ahsan
Director General

1 The Islamic Concept of Temporal Life

From the very beginning, man has had great misconceptions about his place in life, and the mistaken notions that have emerged from this state persist to the present. When man is in the ascendant, he considers himself as the highest creature on earth; delusions of pride, arrogance and rebellion fill his mind. He does not deem any power to be his equal. In the words of the Qur'ān, he proclaims: "*Who is greater than us in strength?*" [*Fuṣṣilat* 41: 15], and "*I am the supreme deity*" [*al-Nāziʿāt* 79: 24].

It is on such occasions that man discards all notions of responsibility and accountability to a higher authority and incarnates himself as a god of evil and injustice spreading inequity and wickedness. When, on the other hand, he is inclined towards debasing his status, he regards himself as the lowest of the lowly. He prostrates himself in front of trees, rocks, mountains, animals, wind and fire, clouds and thunder, sun, moon and stars, and, indeed, before any object that to his mind has the least power to affect him negatively or beneficially. In fact, he has no hesitation in submitting to human beings like himself, making them supernatural deities.

The Reality of Man

Rejecting these two extreme positions, Islam presents man in his true status. At various points, the Qur'ān presents this real human state in the following words:

> So let man consider of what he was created. He was created of a gushing fluid, emanating from between the loins and the ribs.
>
> [*al-Ṭāriq* 86: 5-7]

1

Does man not see that We created him of a sperm-drop, and lo! he is flagrantly contentious. He strikes for Us a similitude and forgot his own creation.

[*Yā Sīn* 36: 77-78]

He originated the creation of man from clay, then made his progeny from the extract of a mean fluid, then He duly proportioned him, and breathed into him of His spirit.

[*al-Sajdah* 32:7-9]

It is surely We Who created you from dust, then from a drop of sperm, then from a clot of blood, then from a little lump of flesh, some of it shapely and other shapeless. (We are rehearsing this) that We may make the reality clear to you. We cause (the drop of sperm) that We please to remain in the wombs till an appointed time. We bring you forth as infants (and nurture you) that you may come of age. Among you is he that dies (at a young age) and he who is kept back to the most abject age so that after once having known, he reaches a stage when he knows nothing.

[*al-Ḥajj* 22: 5]

O man! What has deceived you about your generous Lord? Who created you, shaped you, and made you well-proportioned, and set you in whatever form He pleased?

[*al-Infiṭār* 82: 6-8]

Allah has brought you forth from your mothers' wombs when you knew nothing, and then gave you hearing, and sight and thinking hearts so that you may give thanks.

[*al-Naḥl* 16: 78]

Did you ever consider the sperm that you emit? Do you create a child out of it, or are We its Creators? It is We Who ordained death upon you and We are not to be frustrated. Had We so wished, nothing could have hindered Us from replacing you by others like yourselves, or transforming you into beings you know nothing about. You are well aware of the first creation; then, do you learn no lesson from it? Have you considered the seeds you till? Is it you or We Who make them grow? If We so wished, We could have reduced your harvest to rubble, and you would have been left wonder-struck to exclaim: "We have been penalised; nay; we have been undone!" Did you cast a good look at the water that you drink? Is it you who brought it down from the clouds or is it We Who brought it down? If We had so pleased, We could have made it bitter. So why would you not give thanks? Did you consider the fire which you kindle? Did you make its tree grow or was it We Who made it grow? We made it a reminder and a provision for the needy. Glorify, then, (O Prophet), the name of your Great Lord.

[*al-Wāqiʿah* 56: 58-74]

When a calamity befalls you on the sea, all those whom you invoke forsake you except Him. But when He delivers you safely to the shore you turn away from Him, for man is indeed most thankless. Do you, then, feel secure against His causing you to be swallowed up by a tract of the earth, or letting loose a deadly whirlwind charged with stones towards you, and there you will find none to protect you? Or do you feel secure that He will not cause you to revert to the sea, and let a tempest loose upon you and then drown you for your ingratitude whereupon you will find none even to inquire of Us what happened to you?

[*Banī Isrā'īl* 17: 67-69]

All these verses address and negate the twin issues of human pride and arrogance. Man's attention is invited (in a mocking way) to his true state: 'Look at yourself, created out of a totally inconsequential drop issuing forth from a rather unbecoming aperture into another vessel considered unspeakable (in polite conversation) wherein it undergoes so many unsightly transformations only to emerge as a messy piece of meat. It is only God's power that enables life to enter this fistful of meat lest it passes out in this incomplete and insignificant state. It is by His Divine Power that God bestows life to this mass of cells, creates in it a mind with intellect and senses and equips it with the tools and forces essential for worldly life'

It is in this rather unbecoming manner that man comes into this world. The initial state of this being is that of a totally helpless and dependent infant without any ability even to carry out essential tasks. God Almighty arranges for his upbringing in a way that he grows, becomes strong and acquires mastery over the affairs of life. Then, slowly but surely, comes about a decline in the powers as youth turns into old age, so much so that a time comes when the same feebleness that characterized the early years returns. The energies dissipate and the forces degenerate, mental sharpness begins to fail and the once formidable knowledge starts diminishing. Finally the light goes away from the 'flickering candle of life'. Thus man departs for the grave, bereft of all material possessions, relatives and friends.

At no point during his rather brief existence is man fully capable of ensuring the continuation of his lease on life. There is a Power, higher than man, which keeps him alive – and which can force him to depart from the world at a time of Its own choosing. Indeed, throughout the period that man is alive, his life is bound by the strict laws of nature and requirements of (at appropriate levels) air, water, food, light, and temperature. The earthly produce, natural resources, and environmental conditions on which he is dependent do not submit to his absolute control; neither does he bring them into existence nor do they take orders from him.

And when the forces of nature begin to act against man, how powerless does he seem? A blast of wind can decimate his settlements, a tidal wave of water washes away all his significance, and a few tremors of the earth unite him with the dust. Irrespective of the tools with which he arms himself, notwithstanding the techniques that he devises from his knowledge (which also is not of his own creation), whatever be the inventions that his intellect (which again is not of his own acquisition) enables him to come up with, all seem insignificant in the face of nature's adverse forces. How imprudent – even ludicrous –

is it of man to act arrogantly (on the basis of his trivial abilities and inventions) becoming haughty and heartless as he spreads mischief throughout God's kingdom, raises the banner of rebellion against the Almighty, and sets himself up as a false deity over God's people?

Man's Place in the Universe

So much then for battering man's false pride, which is just a small aspect of the Qur'ān's challenge. In turn, the Qur'ān also addresses mankind with a message that it should not consider itself as lowly as it occasionally does.

> Indeed, We honoured the progeny of Adam, and bore them across land and sea and provided them with good things for their sustenance, and exalted them above many of Our creatures.
>
> [*Banī Isrā'īl* 17: 70]

> Have you not seen how Allah has subjected to you all that is in the earth.
>
> [*al-Ḥajj* 22: 65]

> He created the cattle. They are a source of clothing and food and also a variety of other benefits for you. And you find beauty in them as you drive them to pasture in the morning and as you drive them back home in the evening; and they carry your loads to many a place which you would be unable to reach without much hardship. Surely your Lord is Intensely Loving, Most Merciful. And He created horses and mules and asses for you to ride, and also for your adornment. And He creates many things (for you) that you do not even know about. It rests with Allah alone to show you the Right Way, even when there are many crooked ways. Had He so willed, He would have (perforce) guided you all aright. He it is Who sends down water for you from the sky out of which you drink and out of which grow the plants on which you pasture your cattle, and by

virtue of which He causes crops and olives and date-palms and grapes and all kinds of fruit to grow for you. Surely in this there is a great Sign for those who reflect. He has subjected for you the night and the day and the sun and the moon and the stars have also been made subservient by His command. Surely there are Signs in this for those who use their reason. And there are also Signs for those who take heed in the numerous things of various colours that He has created for you on earth. And He it is Who has subjected the sea that you may eat fresh fish from it and bring forth ornaments from it that you can wear. And you see ships ploughing their course through it so that you may go forth seeking His Bounty and be grateful to Him. And He has placed firm mountains on the earth lest it should move away from you, and has made rivers and tracks that you may find your way, and He has set other landmarks in the earth. And by the stars too do people find their way. ... For, were you to count the favours of Allah, you will not be able to count them.

[al-Naḥl 16: 5-18]

These verses narrate to us humans the fact that all natural resources on and within the earth, as well as many in the atmosphere, have been subjugated for our benefit and placed at our service – the rivers and seas, the trees and animals, the stars and the moon, the day and night, light and darkness – all have been made of service to man. Human beings enjoy superiority over all of these. They have been bestowed with the greatest honour and dignity and made masters over these.

Why, then, does man bow before such [powerless objects], considering them capable of answering their wants and desires? Why is man afraid of their (supposed) powers, and why does he spread his hands before these material objects, make supplications, and sing songs of praise for their greatness? In this way, by becoming a slave of slaves, man only debases himself and engineers his own fall from grace.

Man is God's Vicegerent

From the foregoing, it is clear that human beings are neither as supreme as they occasionally consider themselves nor so lowly and insignificant as they often make themselves out to be. We, thus, come to the question: 'What is the true status of human beings in this temporal world?' Islam's response to this query is as follows:

> Just think when your Lord said to the angels: 'Lo! I am about to place a Vicegerent on earth,' they said: 'Will You place on it one who will spread mischief and shed blood while we celebrate Your glory and extol Your holiness?' He said: 'Surely I know what you do not know.' Then Allah taught Adam the names of all things and presented them to the angels and said: 'If you are right (that the appointment of a Vicegerent will cause mischief) then tell Me the names of these things.' They said. 'Glory to You! We have no knowledge except what You taught us. You, only You, are All-Knowing, All-Wise.' Then Allah said to Adam: 'Tell them the names of these things.' And when he had told them the names of all things, Allah said: 'Did I not say to you that I know everything about the heavens and the earth which are beyond your range of knowledge and I know all that you disclose and also all that you hide?' And when We ordered the angels: 'Prostrate yourselves before Adam,' all of them fell prostrate, except *Iblīs*. He refused, and gloried in his arrogance and became one of the defiers. And We said: 'O Adam, live in the Garden, you and your wife, and eat abundantly of whatever you wish but do not approach this tree or else you will be counted among the wrong-doers.' But Satan caused both of them to deflect from obeying Our command by tempting them to the tree and brought them out of the state they were in
>
> [*al-Baqarah* 2: 30-36]

Recall when your Lord said to the angels: 'I will indeed bring into being a human being out of dry ringing clay wrought from black mud. When I have completed shaping him and have breathed into him of My Spirit, then fall you down before him in prostration.' So, the angels – all of them – fell down in prostration, except *Iblīs*; he refused to join those who prostrated. The Lord inquired: '*Iblīs*! What is the matter with you that you did not join those who prostrated?' He said: 'It does not behove of me to prostrate myself before a human being whom You have created out of dry ringing clay wrought from black mud.' The Lord said: 'Then get out of here; you are rejected, and there shall be a curse upon you till the Day of Recompense.'

[al-Ḥijr 15: 28-35]

The same subject is addressed by the Qur'ān at numerous places in different ways. The gist of this discourse is that God has made human beings his Vicegerents – in modern parlance, a representative plenipotentiary – and granted them greater knowledge than the angels. It is because of that status that God has given human beings preference over the angels in spite of their constant remembrance of and practice of paying homage to Him. Indeed, God ordered the angels to prostrate themselves before this Divine representative. Having so carried out the Divine command, the angelic assembly accepted man's newly designated status – all except Satan[1] who thus raised the flag of rebellion and refused to bow before the human race.

Indeed, man was nothing but a lump of clay into which a Divine spirit had been blown. It was rather man's higher state of knowledge that had made him fit for Divine representation on earth. Satan, however, who did not follow all the other angels in submitting to Divine command, and who thereby earned eternal damnation, nonetheless sought and received Divine permission to lead human beings astray from the Divine path [by way of a rhetorical challenge]. Carrying out

---

[1] Satan, according to the Qur'ān (18:50), was a *jinn*, another category of beings specifically mentioned in the Qur'ān as being distinct from humans and angels – Translator.

his evil promise, Satan deceived the first couple and this led to the human expulsion from Paradise. From that day onwards, there has been an unceasing and eternal struggle between human beings and Satan. God has clearly communicated to human beings that they will be saved and led to Paradise if they follow Divine guidance. Yet if they listen to God's sworn enemy, Satan, their destination will surely be Hell.

An Explanation of Vicegerency

From the above discussion we further understand that the human race (both jointly and severally) has been granted the status of God's caliph. A caliph is the term used for an assistant or 'a second in command'. Naturally, it goes without saying that it is the responsibility of the immediate subordinate – in modern legal parlance 'an agent' – to carry out the commands of the superior or 'principal'. The representative can neither follow the dictates of someone other than his principal or superior, for that would be insubordination – if not outright rebellion – nor is he authorized to act independently as by way of considering the subjects, servants and slaves of the lord as his own servants and slaves. In the latter situation he would also be considered a rebel and in either case would be liable to punishment.

In this position as the Lord's representatives, human beings are free to use the Principal's properties and possessions, rule over His subjects, acquire beneficial servitude from them, and generally manage or organize them, but not in a way that the action is deemed as that of the Principal. Moreover, no human being may act in a manner that can be construed as if he is acting as the agent of someone other than his true Master. Man's only appropriate manner of action is that of a Divine representative, one who is a custodian of the Lord's temporal possessions. Accordingly, a human being can be a true, well-liked, and praiseworthy representative only if s/he does not betray any of the trusts placed in herself or himself, follows the given guidelines and does not go beyond any explicit orders. Moreover, the representative should adhere to the set of rules that the Master has laid down in terms of the utilization of His properties and the governance of His subjects. If a representative or agent does not act in a manner that is envisaged in the Principal-Agent relationship, s/he shall cease to be

9

a representative and instead become a rebel, one who far from being appreciated and deemed worthy of reward shall actually be subject to punishment and damnation:

> Whoever will follow My guidance need have no fear, nor shall they grieve. But those who refuse to accept this (guidance) and reject Our Signs as false are destined for the Fire where they shall abide forever.
>
> [al-Baqarah 2: 38-39]

Agents or a trustees are neither free to act according to their free will in terms of the principal's material and human resources, nor are they free of accountability for their actions. In fact, an agent is fully answerable before his principal who may not only seek an explanation from him about any and every one of his actions regarding the utilization of physical assets and treatment of human resources, but may also hold him responsible for any credits or debits in the matters entrusted to him and then reward or punish him accordingly.

The first duty of the subordinate representative is to fully accept the complete sovereignty and superiority of the principal whom s/he represents. If s/he fails to do so, then it is apparent that s/he has not understood the basis of her/his status as a subordinate, nor has s/he been able to internalize the correct conceptual framework of being a trustee, cognizant of the responsibility and accountability that s/he owes to the Trust-giver. Thus, finally s/he would simply render her/himself incapable of carrying out her/his duties in the appropriate way.

First and foremost, it is simply not possible for any human being to adopt an attitude compliant with the mission of upholding a trust without then fully developing and achieving the necessary state of mind required for becoming a trustee. Even if, for argument's sake, a person claims to have upheld his trusteeship while having declined to accept the master's dominion, the very fact of refusal is enough to denigrate the value of his actions. If the person has carried out ethically superior actions, whether by following an internal sense of uprightness or through the guidance of any other power source, the reward for the same can only be sought from the force or authority whose orders he has carried out. Such actions cannot earn any reward from a principal who has not been a party to his actions.

As regards his origin, man is a lowly creature. The approbation that he has acquired is merely on account of his having been the recipient of the Divine Spirit blown unto him and his having been granted the status of God's vicegerency. The preservation of that status is contingent upon his refusal to accept Satan's guidance for that can only corrupt his spirit and degrade him from the high status of a Divine trustee to one of a renegade who shall once again be reduced to his original lowly state.

While the angelic forces have accepted man's status as God's temporal representative, it is the Satanic forces that question this relationship and openly avow to challenge it by making man one of their own: a supporter and an associate. If man were to carry out his duties as God's representative faithfully and follow Divine guidelines well, the angelic forces would support him. Indeed, he would not find the angels at odds with himself and would be able to defeat Satanic forces with the help of what one may – in the absence of a better term – call the 'angelic troops'. However, were man to fail in his duties as God's representative on earth and not follow the given guidelines, he would find himself deprived of the angelic force's support – simply because by that time he himself would have abandoned his mission. And when man finds himself without the help and support of such other Divine forces, he will be relegated back to the mere lump of clay that he essentially is. In this state he would easily be overcome by Satanic forces. Thereupon, only Satan and his supporters would be his allies and he would be forced to follow them.

By virtue of being God's vicegerent, man's status is superior to and above everything else in the universe. Everything in the material world has been made subordinate to him and exists so that he may put these to use according to the manner that his Master has taught. Man submitting to such subordinate entities is, therefore, a matter of disgrace. If he does so, this amounts to subjecting himself to injustice (*zulm*). Moreover, by so doing he voluntarily abdicates from the high status of God's trusteeship.

There is but one Being whose commands human beings must obey. It is only before this Supreme Being that they may supplicate. Prostrating before this Being and this Being alone is an honour for humankind. Who is this Being? Naturally, the Lord Who is man's Creator and Master.

No one particular person or group can exclusively claim to be God's representative. Rather, this honour has been bestowed upon humanity as a whole. By virtue of being God's trustee, every human being is equal to all others. Thus, it is not becoming of any human being to bow before another, nor is it rightful for any human to demand that another human prostrate in submission before him. The only thing that one human being may demand from another of his kind is the obligation to follows the writ and guidance of their common Lord. In this context, a person who follows the Lord's writ is superior to the one who does not accept the Divine dictates just as the trustworthy person who fulfills his trusts is better than a person who does not. Yet this superiority cannot be interpreted to mean that the better human being has become or can become the master of the others. The status of true representation and trusteeship is available to every human being in his own personal capacity. This is not a responsibility that may be held collectively. Every individual is personally answerable in respect of his status as God's representative. Just as no responsibility accrues upon one person for actions of others, no benefit may be reaped by one person on account of someone else's actions. No human being can allow another to relinquish his responsibilities. Nor can the burden of actions of one person be placed upon another.

For as long as human beings live upon earth and until the time that there remains any connection between what would otherwise be inert masses of clay and the Spirit that God has blown into them, they shall remain God's trustees and representatives. Man loses the honour of enjoying the stature of temporal high office as soon as the connection between body and spirit is severed. It is, therefore, appropriate that his record from the period that he was a Divine trustee be examined with a view to accounting for the trust with which he was entrusted. It must be investigated as to how successfully he carried out duties assigned to him as a subordinate. If he was guilty of any embezzlement, dishonesty, insubordination, or dereliction of duty he must be punished. On the contrary, if he acted with honesty, devotion, and conduct in becoming a trustee, he should be duly rewarded.

The Islamic Concept of Life

Arising directly from the very conceptual basis of the terms 'trustee' and 'representative' is an important feature of the relationship between the 'principal' and the 'agent'. The true merit of a representative lies in his making efforts to fully protect and improve the assets of the principal. In fact, as far as possible, the representative should display the same manner of thought and action that the true owner is likely to possess and demonstrate. If a king were to appoint a deputy to look after his subjects, the only befitting manner in which the appointee should discharge his duties would be one that emulates the king's own conduct. He should keep himself informed of subjects' welfare and dispense the same thoughtfulness, kindness, protection, justice, and when required disciplining, as done by the king himself. Similarly, he should deal with the king's properties and affairs with the same wisdom, pragmatism and care as is expected of the king himself.

Thus, when man has been made God's Vicegerent, this means that man can only do full justice to the duty of guardianship if he treats God's subjects in the same way as God is expected to. This means that the human representative should look after God's creatures with the same grace and benevolence as the Lord does – naturally, keeping in view human limitations and the extent of resources that God may have placed at his disposal.

God's human representatives should display the same mercy and benevolence, dispense the same justice, and act with similar restraint even when manifesting annoyance or letting loose their fury over God's creatures as God Himself does and can be expected to. In short, those whom God has favoured with power over His subjects should conduct themselves in every act, large and small, with a grace similar to God's own. This is the wisdom reflected in the Prophet's saying (*ḥadīth*): *takhallaqū bi akhlāq Allāh* ('Adorn yourselves with the code of conduct laid down by Allah').

13

However, this high ethical state can only be achieved if man fully understands the fact that he is not [totally] free to act as he pleases in this world. Rather, he is only a trustee of the true owner, the Lord of the Universes. It is this status of representation that establishes man's relationship with every single object in this world, even including his own body, and determines the boundaries of that relationship.

Details of all these features of vicegerency occur in the Qur'ān. It is through these passages that every aspect of man's existence in this temporal world is amply clarified and illuminated.

Man is subordinate, not the master
Regarding man's status the Qur'ān declares:

> For He it is Who has appointed you vicegerent over the earth, and has exalted some of you over others in rank that He may try you in what He has bestowed upon you.
>
> [*al-An'ām* 6: 165]

> Moses said: 'Your Lord will soon destroy your enemy and make you rulers in the land. Then He will see how you act.'
>
> [*al-A'rāf* 7: 129]

> (We said to him): 'O David, We have appointed you vicegerent on earth. Therefore, rule among people and do not follow (your) desire lest it should lead you astray from Allah's Path.' Allah's severe chastisement awaits those who stray away from Allah's Path, for they have forgotten the Day of Reckoning.
>
> [*Ṣād* 38: 26]

> Is not Allah the Greatest of all Sovereigns?
>
> [*al-Tīn* 95: 8]

> Judgement lies with Allah alone.
>
> [*al-An'ām* 6: 57]

Say: 'O Allah, Lord of all dominion! You bestow dominion on whomever You please, and take away dominion from whomever You please, and You exalt whom You please, and abase whom You please.'

[*Āl ʿImrān* 3: 26]

(O people), follow what has been revealed to you from your Lord and follow no masters other than Him.

[*al-Aʿrāf* 7: 3]

Say: 'Surely my Prayer, all my acts of worship, and my living and my dying are only for Allah, the Lord of the whole Universe.'

[*al-Anʿām* 6: 162]

All these verses clearly state that whatever has been placed at man's disposal for temporal use does not belong to him – including his own body. The real Owner and Ruler is God Almighty. It does not befit man to declare ownership rights over these things and use them as he wishes. His status is that of only a trustee and the extent of his power resides solely in the foundational principle that he must follow God's guidance fully and use all worldly things according to Divine instructions. Any attempt to exceed Divine limits or follow one's personal desires or follow the dictates of anyone other than the True Ruler amounts to waywardness and rebellion.

The First Precondition for Temporal Success

The Qur'ān lays down this prerequisite for man's success:

As for those who believe in falsehood and are engaged in infidelity with Allah, it is they who will be the losers.

[*al-ʿAnkabūt* 29: 52]

… whoever from amongst you turns away from his religion and dies in the state of unbelief their work will go to waste in this world and in the Next.

[*al-Baqarah* 2: 217]

The work of he who refuses to follow the Way of faith will go to waste, and he will be among the utter losers in the Hereafter.

[al-Mā'idah 5: 5]

From these verses we see that man's temporal success – in his status as God's vicegerent – depends on his fully accepting the ascendancy of the One Entity of which he is the subordinate. Whatsoever action he undertakes in the world must reflect the mindset of God's representative and trustee. Without this basic premise, whatever he partakes of the world can only be a mutinous act. It is a matter of very basic understanding that even if a rebel who is in unlawful occupation of an area acts in an admirable way, the lawful government would not consider such conduct with approbation. In the eyes of the lawful ruler, a rebel is and always will be a rebel, notwithstanding his good character and disposition or the excellent manner in which he may have managed the affairs of the area under his mutinous control.

Engaging in and dealing with a Temporal Life
The Qur'ān instructs:

O people! Eat of the lawful and pure things in the earth and follow not in the footsteps of Satan. For surely he is your open enemy; he only commands you to do evil and commit acts of indecency and to ascribe to Allah the things concerning which you have no knowledge.

[al-Baqarah 2: 168-169]

Believers! Do not hold as unlawful the good things which Allah has made lawful to you, and do not exceed the bounds of right. Allah does not love those who transgress the bounds of right. And partake of the lawful, good things which Allah has provided you as sustenance, and refrain from disobeying Allah in Whom you believe.

[al-Mā'idah 5: 87-88]

16

Say (O Muḥammad): 'Who has forbidden the adornment which Allah has brought forth for His creatures or the good things from among the means of sustenance?'

[*al-A ʿrāf* 7: 32]

He enjoins upon them what is good and forbids them what is evil. He makes the clean things lawful to them and prohibits all corrupt things and removes from them their burdens and the shackles that were upon them.

[*al-A ʿrāf* 7: 157]

It is no offence for you to seek the bounty of your Lord.

[*al-Baqarah* 2: 198]

As for monasticism, it is they who invented it; We did not prescribe it for them. They themselves invented it in pursuit of Allah's good pleasure.

[*al-Ḥadīd* 57: 27]

And certainly We have created for Hell many of the *jinn* and mankind; they have hearts with which they fail to understand; and they have eyes with which they fail to see; and they have ears with which they fail to hear. They are like cattle – indeed, even more astray. Such are utterly heedless.

[*al-A ʿrāf* 7: 179]

All these verses from the Qurʾān show that it is not proper for man to renounce a temporal life, for it is not something to abstain or run away from. The immense blessings and embellishments of worldly matters and businesses are lawful and cannot be self-proscribed or added to a forbidden list. This world has been made for human utilization. Therefore, it is man's duty to use and use well. However, during this process of consumption, he must make a distinction between good and bad usage, between manners appropriate and inappropriate, between the pure and the impure. For instance, the eyes have been given for vision, the ears for hearing, and the intellect for good judgement. If the individual were to refrain from using his mind or any part of his body, or were to use it improperly, then there would be no difference between him and a lower animal.

The Assets of Worldly Life

The Qur'ān's directives about leading life are as follows:

> Surely Allah's promise is true. So let the life of this world not beguile you, nor let the Deluder delude you about Allah.
>
> [*Luqmān* 31: 33]

> The wrong-doers kept pursuing the ease and comfort which had been conferred upon them, thus losing themselves in sinfulness.
>
> [*Hūd* 11: 116]

> (O Prophet), propound to them the parable of the present life: it is like the vegetation of the earth which flourished luxuriantly when it mingled with the water that We sent down from the sky, but after that the same vegetation turned into stubble which the winds blew about. Allah alone has the power over all things. Wealth and children are an adornment of the life of the world. But the deeds of lasting righteousness are the best in the sight of your Lord in reward, and far better a source of hope.
>
> [*al-Kahf* 18: 45-46]

> Believers, let your possessions and your offspring not make you negligent of Allah's remembrance. For whoever does that, they will be the losers.
>
> [*al-Munāfiqūn* 63: 9]

> It is not your riches nor your children that make you near-stationed to Us, except for him who has faith and acts righteously.
>
> [*Saba'* 34: 37]

Know well that the life of this world is merely sport and diversion and adornment and an object of your boasting with one another, and a rivalry in the multiplication of riches and children. Its likeness is that of rain: when it produces vegetation it delights the tillers. But then it withers and you see it turn yellow, and then it crumbles away.

[*al-Ḥadīd* 57: 20]

What, you build a monument on every hill merely for fun, and erect huge palaces as though you will live forever.

[*al-Shu'arā'* 26: 128-29]

Do you believe that you will be left here to live securely in the present state, amidst gardens and springs, and corn-fields and date-palms laden with juicy fruits? You hew dwellings in mountains and exult in that.

[*al-Shu'arā'* 26: 146-49]

Wherever you might be, death will overtake you even though you be in massive towers.

[*al-Nisā'* 4: 78]

Every being shall taste death, then it is to Us that you shall be sent back.

[*al-'Ankabūt* 29: 57]

Did you imagine that We created you without any purpose, and that you will not be brought back to Us?"

[*al-Mu'minūn* 23: 115]

Thus it is clear how the Qur'ān sees the world and states that it has been created for human use – and that it is to be used well. Now, we see the other side of the picture being presented. It is made abundantly clear that man has not been created to be used up and devoured by the world. Indeed, man is not supposed to lose himself in the world. Deceived by the lure of the world, human beings cannot fool themselves into believing that they are here to stay eternally. It must be remembered – and remembered very clearly – that all this material wealth and means of pomp and glory are temporary, fleeting pleasures. Everything must end in 'death' and like man himself all matter will be united with the 'dust'. In this impermanent universe, if anything is to outlive the material milieu it can only be good actions, beauty of heart and soul, and piety of thought and action.

Responsibility and Accountability for Actions
The Qur'ān alerts man thus:

> The Hour of Resurrection is coming. I have willed to keep the time of its coming hidden so that everyone may be recompensed in accordance with his effort.
>
> [*Ṭā Hā* 20: 15]

> Will you be recompensed for aught other than what you do?
>
> [*al-Naml* 27: 90]

> And that man shall have nothing but what he has striven for, and that (the result of) his striving shall soon be seen, and that he shall then be fully recompensed, and that the final end is with your Lord.
>
> [*al-Najm* 53: 39-42]

> Whoever lived in this world as blind shall live as blind in the Life to Come; rather, he will be even farther astray than if he were (just) blind.
>
> [*Banī Isrā'īl* 17: 72]

> Whatever good deeds you send forth for your own good, you will find them with Allah. Surely Allah sees all that you do.
>
> [*al-Baqarah* 2: 110]

And have fear of the Day when you shall return to Allah, and every human being shall be fully repaid for whatever (good or evil) he has done, and none shall be wronged.

[*al-Baqarah* 2: 281]

The Day is approaching when every soul shall find itself confronted with whatever good it has done and whatever evil it has wrought.

[*Āl 'Imrān* 3: 30]

The weighing on that Day will be the true weighing: O those whose scales are heavy will prosper, and those whose scales are light will be the losers, for they are the ones who have been iniquitous to Our signs.

[*al-A'rāf* 7: 8-9]

So, whoever does an atom's weight of good shall see it; and whoever does an atom's weight of evil shall see it.

[*al-Zilzāl* 99: 7-8]

Their Lord answered the prayer thus: 'I will not suffer the work of any of you, whether male or female, to go to waste'

[*Āl 'Imrān* 3: 195]

And spend of what Allah has granted you by way of sustenance before death should come to any of you and he should say: 'Lord, why did You not defer my return for a while so that I might give alms and be among the righteous?' But when a person's term comes to an end, Allah never grants any respite.

[*al-Munāfiqūn* 63: 10-11]

Would that you could see the guilty standing before their Lord with their heads downcast, (saying to Him): 'Our Lord, we have now seen and heard, so send us back (to the world) that we might act righteously. For now we have come to have firm faith.' '... So taste the chastisement on account of your forgetting the encounter of this Day. We, too, have forgotten you. Taste the eternal chastisement as a requital for your misdeeds.'

[al-Sajdah 32: 12 and 14]

Here, through all these verses of the Qur'ān, we are informed that the world is an 'Abode of Action'. It is a place for making effort and striving. The Ākhirah (literally, 'Final End' – metaphorically, the Life to Come) is the Place of Reward and Retribution. It is a house where the fruits of good and evil shall be received. Human beings are free to act in the world until the very last minute of every individual's passing away. After that time, no one shall ever have the chance of any action. Accordingly, in this period of life, human beings must act after fully realizing that every action of theirs, even the slightest movement, every good deed and every evil act shall have its consequence. People have to be fully convinced that only by virtue of the weight and consequence of their actions shall individuals be rewarded or punished in the life to come; that is, whatsoever any one receives shall be in return for his efforts and actions here. Neither will any good action be lost, nor any punishment be withheld for evil actions.

Individual Responsibility

In order to give further weight to the generic sense of responsibility, it has been underscored that every person is responsible for his own actions. No one shares the responsibility of another person. Nor is any one able to save another from the consequences of his actions.

Believers, take heed as regards your own selves. If you are rightly-guided, the error of he who strays will not harm you.

[al-Mā'idah 5: 105]

Everyone will bear the consequence of what he does, and no one shall bear the burden of another.

[al-An'ām 6: 164]

On the Day of Resurrection neither your blood-kindred nor your own offspring will avail you. (On that Day) He will separate you. Allah sees all that you do.

[*al-Mumtaḥinah* 60: 3]

Whenever you did good, it was to your own advantage; and whenever you committed evil, it was to your own disadvantage.

[*Banī Isrā'īl* 17: 7]

No one can bear another's burden. If a heavily laden one should call another to carry his load, none of it shall be carried by the other, even though he be a near of kin.

[*Fāṭir* 35: 18]

O people, fear (the wrath) of your Lord, and dread the Day when no father will stand for his child, nor any child stand for his father.

[*Luqmān* 31: 33]

He who disbelieves will suffer the consequence of it and he who acts righteously, they will pave the way for their own good.

[*al-Rūm* 30: 44]

All these verses place the burden of all good and bad actions fully upon each individual human being – acting in his own personal capacity. No hope is held out to the effect that one person will be able to pay any recompense or compensation for another's shortcomings and mistakes. No quarter is left for any expectation that someone will be able to save himself or herself from the justice due against his crimes by way of any connection with another person. No room is left for any apprehension that someone else's crimes may have an effect on a person's good character or that the will of anyone else, other than God, shall have any influence on the acceptability or rejection of our actions.

Just as no one can save the person who places his hand in a fire from being burned, or prevent a person who partakes of honey from tasting its sweetness, no one else can truly share in the pain of the person who has been burnt or really appreciates the taste of honey. Similarly, every individual has a distinct position in terms of the unpleasant consequences of evil actions and the good results of pious acts. Accordingly, in order to properly interact with the world, everyone must be aware of his own individual responsibility. he should live out life in a way that he considers himself or herself to be responsible for his own actions, notwithstanding any and all external influences. He has to consider that the burden of evil actions has to be bone individually, just as the rewards of good actions are also to be enjoyed personally.

From our elucidation of the Islamic view of temporal life that has been presented in the foregoing, all the constituent elements of this picture should now be clear. This is a composite concept. Now, momentarily leaving aside this analytical process, let us see how far the complete picture emerging from the various constituent concepts conforms to our innate nature. Moreover, we also need to see what the status of this worldview is when compared and contrasted with the views of other civilizations and intellectual traditions vis-à-vis temporal life. We will also see how the foundational worldview upon which any civilization is based moulds human thought and action.

The *Fiṭrī* (Primary and Instinctive) Concept of Life

Now, for a brief time, please empty your mind of all the various concepts that have been presented by different religions regarding the world and temporal life and take a look at the world around you with the eyes of a neutral observer. Contemplate on what your position in this whole setting is, for only then will you be able to see certain things clearly.

You should be able to appreciate that whatever powers you enjoy are all limited. All the senses, upon which all your knowledge is based, do not extend much further than your immediate environment. Your physical body upon which your actions are based has power over very few things in nature. All around you there are numerous things that are larger than your bodies and powers. Compared to these things, your existence appears very flimsy and inconsequential. Few, if any of the immense forces that are in play in this great factory are in your control. You find yourself helpless before these forces. In terms of physical dimensions, man is no more than any other average entity that is dominant over things smaller than itself and overawed by things greater than itself.

Yet, there is one force inside yourselves that elevates you above all these things. It is by virtue of this power that you are able to control all other animals and subdue their physical powers that exceed your own. It is because of this power that you are able to harness numerous resources in your environment and derive appropriate benefit from them. Utilizing this power you are able to discover ever-new treasures and then avail yourself of them in countless new ways. It is on account of this power that you are able to expand your means of accumulating knowledge through which you then gain access to objects that are otherwise beyond the reach of your physical capacities. In short, there is this one force by virtue of which all things in the temporal realm are placed at your disposal and because of which you gain mastery over them.

Moreover, these Divine forces that are otherwise not under your control, generally act in ways that are not detrimental to you, but are rather beneficial to your plans. Air, water, light, heat and numerous other physical forces upon which your life depends are available to serve your interests. All of these exist and operate under a system, the very purpose of which is to serve you. Thus, it could very well be said that these have been subdued for human use.

When you consider the human environment with a deeper, analytical observation, you are able to discern a powerful law, a powerful mechanism in operation. Caught within the confines of this great system are all forms of existence, from the lowest of the low to the most powerful. The survival of the whole universe is contingent upon a strict operation of this system. Yet, there is a great difference between human beings and all other temporal objects. None of these non-human entities possesses the least power to act against the great law (of nature). Human beings, on the other hand, not only have the power to oppose the great natural law but indeed, quite paradoxically, this law itself aids them in their contravention of its stipulations. Of course, every such contravention carries with it certain harmful effects. Never has it been nor will it ever be possible for human beings to escape the detrimental consequences of their contraventions of this natural law.

Within the operative confines of this irrevocable universal law, various expressions of distortion and corruption can be found. The whole universe is undergoing a constant process of creation and destruction. The very same laws under which an object is brought into existence serve as the reason for its decimation and death. No temporal object is safe from this ongoing process of change. Even the things which apparently seem to be safe from this process and manifest a semblance of permanence are subject to movement and transformation and are bound by the laws of creation and obliteration. No other entity in the universe possesses the powers of intellect and enlightenment, or at least we do not have knowledge of such faculties, and hence such entities are neither able to perceive this creation and destruction occurring within themselves nor are they able to feel the pleasure of birth or pain of death. Amongst the animal species, even if there is any experiential discernment of such processes, to the best of our knowledge, its extent is minimal. Human beings, on the other hand, are a creation gifted with intellect and enlightenment. They are able to discern changes taking place within and around themselves and also feel the pain and pleasure of the accompanying transformational processes. Moreover, at times, they are so overcome by the pleasant sensations generated through agreeable affairs that they tend to disregard and neglect the evil that exists all around them and similarly, at times, dreadful experiences lead to such pain that they only see malevolence throughout, forgetting the fact that there also exists much benevolence.

All the same, howsoever contradictory the feelings of pleasure and pain are that one may carry within oneself, and whatsoever may be one's worldview towards temporal life as a result of the influence of such feelings – either oriented towards expansion or regression – human beings are constrained to deal with the world. They are forced to practically interact with the world and put to use the instinctive forces placed within themselves. The desire to live and go on living has been implanted in the human make up. In order to carry out the dictates of this instinct, the great force of hunger has also been placed deep within their existence; this forces human beings to continuously undertake one productive activity or another. The law of nature dictates the utilization of human energies for the continuation of the species. In order to fulfil this imperative, nature has placed within the human body a force that simply refuses to go away and only departs when it has achieved its purpose: the libido.

Similarly implanted within man's instinctive make up are other forces that have been so placed as to achieve other objectives. All of these forces act to exact and extract their purposes through coercive means. It now remains for human wisdom to channel the dictates of these forces – through proper means or improper, by way of actions that please the soul or those that offend it. And, it does not end here; 'Nature' has also granted human beings the discretion of either acting in the service of these objectives or shunning cooperation with them and acting defiantly. Together with this broad statement of principle, there is another immutable natural law by virtue of which it is beneficial for human beings to act in consonance with natural laws (and not against them). If human beings were to either contravene natural law, or not follow it completely or appropriately, then this would only be detrimental to their own interests.

Conceptions of Temporal Life in other Religious Traditions

When a good-natured and broadminded person casts his eyes on the world, and then analyses his state, all the factors described above will surely come before his vision. However, various human groups have seen this collage from different angles. Often, it has so happened that a group has found only one angle or aspect of reality to be more obvious amongst the various options possible or available. And when that has happened, the holders of that (limited) vision have been known to go on and establish a worldview on the basis of that particular perception without even attempting to examine the various different views possible.

For instance, one group of human beings viewed the human state with its weakness and helplessness and contrasted this to the immense coercive forces of nature. It reached the conclusion that man was a very insignificant being. Naturally, this conclusion was based on the assumption that these beneficial and detrimental forces were autonomous and self-regulating – or at least semi-independent – and not subject to any universal law. This concept so dominated their minds that the alternate worldview wherein man has ascendance over the whole universe disappeared from their scope of possibilities. Thus that group lost sight of the positive aspects of their existence. It allowed the human position of high esteem and superiority to be overcome by this exaggerated, self-professed confession of frailty and feebleness. Various forms of idolatry, including tree-worship, star-worship and veneration of various natural objects and force, are an outcome of this worldview.

Another group viewed the world as a place full of evil and corruption; they concluded that the whole cosmos existed merely to subject human beings to pain and sorrow. According to this group, all the various relationships and interactions of the world existed only to entangle them in webs of difficulty and anguish. And what to say of the human milieu, when the whole cosmos was caught in the grip of misery and death? Spring only came about to be decimated by autumn. The tree of life bore fruit only to cause a momentary halt to the juggernaut of death. The beauty of creation was adorned time and again only because it pleased the god of destruction to play afoul with it, once again.

This worldview naturally led people to lose interest in the temporal world. They saw their deliverance only by way of shunning all their worldly desires, by leaving worldly life altogether and adopting self-denial and asceticism. In so doing, they believed they could undo the machinations of the unjust law of nature, which used human beings merely as an instrument for its self-propagation.

Yet another group saw this world as an abode that provided human beings with (unlimited) means of pleasure and gratification, albeit for a brief time. As sensations of pain and expressions of sorrow made life disagreeable, if men and women were able to deny these feelings then there would be nothing but pleasure on earth. Such people reached the conclusion that this temporal life was all that existed. Accordingly, all the happiness that had to be enjoyed was to be here and now. Nothing would remain after death, neither the earthly abode, nor its means of self-contentment. Thus was born hedonism or the philosophy of pure and unlimited pleasure.

Opposed to this was still another group that considered not only the pleasure and happiness of this world, but worldly life itself, to be a sin. They believed that all material corruptions of the world were a curse for the human soul, which had to be avoided like any other contamination. There was no aspect of good or piety in interacting with the world, participating in its business, or enjoying its pleasures. According to this philosophy, whosoever desired not to receive the blessings of earthly kingdoms ought to dissociate themselves from the world. As for those who wished to enjoy wealth, worldly power and pleasures, they could rest assured that there would be no share for them in the Kingdom of Heaven.

When this group realized that human beings were, by their very innate nature, constrained to interact with the world and to become involved in its various occupations, and also realized that howsoever gratifying the thought of entering the Kingdom of Heaven may be it was still not strong enough to enable them to confront instinctive imperatives, they found a way to bridge this dilemma. They invented a philosophy (of a universal saviour) wherein one man's atonement relieved all others in the remaining humanity of their personal responsibility with regard to free will and good or bad actions that emanated from it. Whosoever placed his faith upon that one revered person was assured eternal salvation, notwithstanding his own personal actions.

Another group, viewing the comprehensiveness of Natural Law assumed man to be a totally enslaved entity. This group considered the evidence presented by psychology, biology, and even jurisprudence, and reached the conclusion that man was certainly not a free creature. This group felt that human beings certainly did not possess a free personality but rather one that was bound by nature's laws. They could neither go against this Natural Law nor really contemplate it. In their view, it was neither possible for them to form any independent desires nor could they become powerful enough to carry out any autonomous action. Accordingly, human beings could not be held responsible for any of their actions.

Diametrically opposed to this philosophy was yet another group that considered men and women to not only possess a decisive personality but also believed that they were neither subject to any greater plan nor subordinate to any greater power than their own. Moreover, in terms of their actions, human beings were not answerable to anyone except their conscience and in a collective realm to the man-made laws of the land. They were the owners of the world and all things therein had been subjugated for their benefit. They had the power to use them at will. While there were certain self-imposed limits on both individual and group actions, these had come about to improve the human quality of life and to create a social order in a normative collective sense, the human being was all-powerful. To the proponents of this group (the self-labelled 'enlightened'), the very concept of being subordinate to any Higher Authority was totally nonsensical.

These are the various concepts held by different religions and philosophical schools of thought vis-à-vis the place of human beings in the universe. Upon some of these foundational human ideologies, civilizations have been raised. The fact that we observe differences amongst civilizations can be attributed to the underlying philosophy and concept of worldly life upon which the structure of each civilization has been raised. It is this worldview that has led to the particular developmental path adopted by each civilization. If we were to take a detailed look at the intricacies of each foundational worldview and how it had led to the development of very different and peculiar civilizations, it would be an interesting discussion. However, such a discussion is not fully relevant to this discourse that aims primarily to highlight the salient features of the Islamic civilization.

Here it only needs to be stated that all these various concepts about worldly life are, quite obviously, the outcome of looking at the temporal realm from specific viewpoints. There is not a single worldview amongst these that has been formed after undertaking a comprehensive cosmic review and making a proper determination about the status of human beings in the cosmos. It is for this reason that, sooner or later, when we change our viewpoint and observe the world from any other angle, every philosophy loses its value. And, finally, when we take another look at these worldviews after undertaking a comprehensive cosmic analysis, the flaws of these theories become very obvious.

The Special Significance of the Islamic View

By now it should be clear that amongst all the various worldviews about life in this world, only the Islamic view is one that conforms to the essence of nature and truth. It is only this view that maintains a balanced relationship between man and the material world. Here we observe that the world is neither something to be abandoned nor one to be abhorred. Conversely, on the other hand, the world is not something for which one should fall head over heels and become lost in its pleasures. The world is neither totally honourable nor totally corrupt. It is neither something to be totally refrained from, nor one in which to be fully engrossed. It is not completely impure and polluted nor all virtuous and untainted.

The relationship between man and this world is neither akin to one that exists between a king and his subjects nor is it one that can be likened to a prisoner's association with the place of his incarceration. Human beings are neither so insignificant that they should bow before every temporal power nor so powerful that they demand homage from all others. They are neither so helpless that their personal resolve amounts to nothing, nor so potent that only their (personal or group) outlook becomes all encompassing. Neither is man the domineering ruler of the temporal milieu nor a poor slave of millions of authoritative masters. The fact is that man's real status is one that is finely balanced between the various extremes.

Till this point, nature and our own intelligence are able to guide us. But Islam moves beyond these and provides an authoritative elucidation of the true status of human beings and their relationship with the world. It provides an answer to whether humans should consider the material world to be one that is overriding or one which is subservient.

Islam opens the eyes and minds of men and women by stating that while they are no ordinary creatures: they are none other than viceroys of the Lord of Universes. They are a creation for which all the forces of the world have been made acquiescent. They are the rulers of all and the slave of just one Power. Human beings enjoy a status of reverence over all other creatures. However, the right to this honour is available only and until they themselves are respectful and dutiful to the One Who has given them the status of trusteeship in the world and follow His commands. Human beings have been placed in the world to involve themselves in its affairs. Howsoever they act therein – rightly or wrongly – will lead to consequences which shall only become apparent in the Hereafter. Accordingly, throughout this temporal life, they should be mindful of their personal responsibility and carry with themselves the conscious awareness of their high status of trusteeship every moment. No man or woman may, at any point in time, be forgetful of the fact that he will have to account in full for everything that has been placed in his trust by the Lord of the Universes.

There can be little doubt that the foregoing concept is not present – or at least not in its full form – in the mind of every Muslim. Apart from a specific group of intellectuals, few if any have awareness of the finer points of this concept. Yet, because this concept is so central to the belief system upon which the Islamic civilization is based, Muslims, in spite of having lost a great measure of their true character and original glory, are still not fully bereft of it. Any Muslim who has been brought up in an Islamic cultural environment, howsoever sullied by external influences, continues to hold certain beliefs which include a sense of human self-esteem and an awareness of not submitting to any deity but God, of not being afraid of nor accepting anyone other than Allah as the one True Master, of considering himself or herself as God's trustee in the world, of regarding the world as a place of cause and the Hereafter as a place of effect, of considering success or failure in the Hereafter to be based upon personal actions and regarding temporal wealth and pleasures to be temporary and the consequences of actions as permanent. These beliefs are very deeply rooted in the Muslim psyche and any seasoned observer should be able to detect the effects of this belief system, no matter how faint and faded they may be, as these effects too are part of the Muslim heart and soul.

Any reader of Islamic history is definitely able to appreciate the fact that as long as the Muslim civilization maintained its true Islamic character, it also remained a purely practical civilization. For its followers, the temporal milieu was the proving field of the Hereafter. For as long as they lived in this world, all of them strived to plant the seeds and till the fields of the crop they desired to harvest in the life to come. Indeed, they attempted to plant as many seeds as possible so as to harvest as rich a yield as possible in the Hereafter. They interacted with the world with such a fine balance – a state exactly halfway between monasticism and hedonism – that even its remotest resemblance was not to be seen in any other civilization.

The ideal of establishing God's kingdom on earth inspired them to interact fully with the world around them, and yet the restraint of trusteeship and consciousness of personal responsibility prevented them from crossing the bounds of probity. Again, it was this same sense of balance that disallowed pride and vanity from setting up a permanent abode in their personalities. In order to run the affairs of state, they were inclined towards all those actions that were necessary for carrying out temporal affairs, but at the same time they were not disposed towards worldly enjoyment that led to a neglect of their duties. In short, they managed the affairs of the world in a manner that was very much amenable to a permanent residence therein and yet were still able to avoid worldly desires by treating the world as a wayside inn where they had put up merely for a short while.

Later, when Islamic influences waned and Muslims began to be influenced by other civilizations, true Islamic glory was naturally no longer to be seen in their characters. Thereupon, they behaved in ways that were contradictory to the Islamic ideal of temporal life. They drowned themselves in hedonistic amusements and pleasures, constructed grandiose palaces, indulged in music, painting, sculpture and other fine arts, and, on the whole, adopted a way of life that was replete with wastefulness and ostentation which were totally contrary to the Islamic way. In spite of all this, the Islamic concept of the ephemerality of worldly life that had been embedded in their hearts invariably left its mark in some manner or another and at some point in time or another. It was this influence that created within them a distinction when compared to other rulers. A Muslim king[2] built a magnificent palace on the banks of the River Jamuna within which he provided every manner of pleasure and amusement that could be imagined at the time. Yet, within the confines of the most enjoyable amusements, he had the following quatrain inscribed on the side farthest to the river – in the direction of the *qiblah*.

> O you whose feet are bound, and whose heart is sealed, Beware!
> O you whose eyes are sewn up and whose feet are stuck in the mud, Beware!
> You intend to go toward the West but you have turned your face toward the East;
> O you who have your back toward your destination, Beware!

That palace is certainly not without precedent. Even better royal residences can be found in other countries. Still, there is no example amongst any of the numerous nations of the world of the thought and inspiration represented by the verse and which warns the maker of this earthly paradise to be aware of his real, ultimate destination.

Islamic history is replete with instances in which rulers who, while otherwise reigning like Roman caesars and Persian emperors, displayed unique behaviour at that moment in time when they had vanquished their opponents: instead of proclaiming their greatness, they immediately fell in prostration, submitting in gratitude to God. On many an occasion when the most vicious of rulers, infamous for their murderous ways, attempted to go against the dictates of Islamic *Sharī'ah*, some God-fearing commoner openly raised his objection in a manner that indeed caused those kings to tremble with the fear of God. At many a time, the most wayward amongst the élite and the worst of powerful evildoers were cautioned by some very ordinary mortal; history is witness that all of a sudden the whole complexion of their lives changed. The hearts of people who were totally obsessed

---

[2] The reference here is to the great Mughal Emperor, Shah Jahan, and the building referred to is the Red Fort at Delhi – Ed.

with temporal wealth were suddenly struck with the impermanence of the world and overcome with the thought of rendering account in the Hereafter; they then distributed all they possessed and adopted a simple ideologically-driven lifestyle.

Briefly, in spite of all the non-Islamic influences that have made a place in the lives of Muslims, one can find, at every step, in some form or another, the radiance of Islamic idealism in the national ethos of Muslim groups. Time and again, one truly feels as if a bright light has suddenly been beamed from an unseen source into a very dark milieu.

2 The Ideal of Life

After determining the worldview of a civilization, the second question that occupies a central place in the analysis of its positive and negative aspects is, 'What ideal of life does that civilization present?' The importance of this question lies in the fact that the natural direction of a person's intentions and practical efforts is necessarily towards the one end and goal that he has declared to be his ideal of life. The formation of a mindset, right or wrong, good or bad, and the appropriateness or inappropriateness of a lifestyle is fully dependent upon the correctness or lack thereof of this goal. Contingent upon this ideal being right or wrong are the highs and the lows of thoughts and concepts, the superiority or the inferiority of ethics, and the loftiness or the diminutiveness of economic and social pursuits.

Contingent upon this goal being clear and well directed or blurred and misdirected is the basis of life's totality – and that includes the organization or distortion of a person's thoughts, constancy and inconsistency of the pattern of everyday life and the utilization of energies and capabilities in a focused or dispersed manner. Taken as a whole, the ideal is that criterion on the basis of which a person is able to choose his path from the many available paths of thought and action and then spending all of his mental and bodily energies as well as material and spiritual resources in that direction. Accordingly, when we wish to measure any civilization on the scale of excellence, an investigation into its 'Ideal of Life' is indispensable.

The Essential Characteristics of a True Collective Ideal[1]

However, prior to taking the first steps in the direction of research and discussion, we should clearly determine as to what we mean by this 'True Collective Ideal' or 'Ultimate Civilizational Ideal' (which as we go along will, for convenience sake, be simply rendered as 'ideal'). It is quite clear that when we use the word 'civilization' we do not mean the 'personal views of civilization' of the component people but the collective view and definition of that civilization. Accordingly, individual personal ideals cannot be the ideal of the civilization as a whole. On the contrary, it is fundamental that whatever is the ideal of a civilization also be the ideal of every one of its members, whether or not they are consciously aware of the same or not. Thus, the ideal of a civilization is that ideal which, consciously or unconsciously, has become the common collective aim of a large group of people and which has so overcome the 'individual ideals' of those people that by now individuals – in their personal capacities – also espouse the ideal that is held by the group.

There is one essential condition for this kind of collective ideal to be valid: that it should be in total consonance and agreement with the (separately held) individual ideals so that it is able to simultaneously be both the ideal of the individual singularly as well as that of the group collectively. The reason for this is that if the collective ideal were not in accord with the ideals of the individual members, then, it would be difficult for it to become the collective ideal because a concept that is not individually acceptable to the members of a group is not likely to become collectively acceptable. And if, by virtue of some strong external pressure, it does become the group's ideal, a subtle conflict between the group and individual ideals would then ensue until such time that the individuals reverted to their personal objectives whenever the collective philosophy was weakened. Thereupon the centripetal or communicative forces that maintained the collective

---

[1] Although the Urdu term *naṣb al-ʿayn* [literally 'direction in which the eye is pointed' or focus] can variously be translated as 'ideal', 'objective', or 'ultimate aim', the translator has decided in favour of 'ideal'.

structure dissipate in a process that not only nullifies the group's ideal, but also ensure that no sign of the civilization itself remains.

Therefore, the true civilizational ideal can only be one that is wholly and indisputably the natural aim of the whole group of people. A civilization's true merit lies in its ability to present a collective ideal that is or can also become the individual ideal of its members in an unaltered form.

From this viewpoint, two questions arise. Without answering them, we cannot move ahead with our analysis. These are, first, 'What is the natural (normative) personal ideal of human beings?' And, secondly, 'What are the ideals that the various civilizations of the world have put forward, and how far are these in agreement with that natural ideal?'

Man's Natural Ideal and Ultimate Aim

The question about man's natural ideal is actually a question about the purpose for which human beings naturally strive in this temporal world – the primary object of the desire of their inner selves. Researching this, if one were to individually ask a large number of people as to what they each wished to achieve in this world, many different answers would be forthcoming. It is possible that one does not find two people whose objectives and desires are exactly the same. However, upon deeper probing, one would learn that the outcomes which people have termed to be their objectives are not the end in themselves but only the means to reach such an end. By and large, that one end is prosperity and peace of mind. Every human being, irrespective of the intellectual status and social class to which he may belong, and in whichever walk of life he may be active, only has one ideal: the achievement of peace and tranquillity, happiness and deep-felt harmony. It would not be wrong to call this the natural ideal of every human being.

A Critical View of Two Popular Collective Ideals

If one were to view the collective sets of ideals presented by various civilizations in their minute entireties, there would be many differences between them, the coverage of which is neither aimed at here nor is possible. However, in terms of broad principles, we can divide civilizations into two types:

(i)   Civilizations that are not based upon any religious or spiritual concepts. These present an ideal of superiority to their followers. This ideal is a compound of several ingredients, the important among which are the following:

- A craving for political domination and hegemony
- A desire to exceed everyone in wealth and material well-being, irrespective of whether this comes through geographic conquest or control over commerce and industry.
- A yearning to surpass all and sundry in the manifestations of sociological progress, be it in the arts and sciences or architectural grandeur and civilizational excellence.

This group ideal is apparently not in contradiction with the individual ideal mentioned above. This is because, even after some reflection, it can be easily stated that if the collective ideal is established on these bases, then the respective individual ideals shall also be so established on similar orientations – and, indeed, with even greater vigour. The very fact that millions upon millions of individuals willingly allow their personal ideals to be amalgamated with the group ideal is sufficient proof of its false facade. However, with a deeper view, and also from practical experience, it can be shown that this collective ideal is extremely incompatible with the 'natural ideal' of individuals.

It should be evident that at any given point in time, several nations have this collective ideal of national superiority and domination and all of them strive to achieve it. The net result of this competition is strong conflict – political, economic and social – that ensues amongst them and severe disorder caused by the ongoing competitiveness and resistance. So much so, that in this milieu of anxiety and disarray it becomes virtually impossible for individuals to attain peace and tranquillity, prosperity and peace of mind.

It is this situation with which we see the Western world confronted today. However, if we were to assume that there could be a period in history in which only one nation strove for this [domineering] ideal, and that there was no other nation offering resistance, even then there is no possibility that such individual ideals will be successfully manifested in the wake of collective success. The reason for this is that it is a natural attribute of such a collective ideal that it not only generates rivalry between nations, but that it also brings about a competitive mentality amongst the vast numbers of individuals who comprise such nations. As a consequence, domination over fellow national compatriots – enabling them to exceed others in terms of wealth and power, status and luxury, and access to public office – become every individual's aim of life. They desire to capture others' means of sustenance and become sole masters of as many sources of wealth, benefit and profit as possible, leaving others only with loss and frustration, so that they become the people of authority and others become their followers and subordinates.

Firstly, there is no end at which the greed for material acquisitiveness of such people is satiated and, therefore, they always remain dissatisfied and troubled. Secondly, when competitiveness of this kind is internalized within the members of a nation, then every home and every workplace becomes a battlefield. Naturally, peace and harmony, happiness and prosperity vanish, notwithstanding the preponderance of wealth, power and material means.

Furthermore, it is but natural that progress defined purely by way of material attributes – one in which spirituality has no part – shall never satisfy human beings. This is because the exclusive attainment of corporeal pleasures is entirely an animal aim. If it be true that human beings are something more than their essential animal existence, then it must also be true that the mere achievement of those pleasures which only gratify their animal nature will not be sufficient for fully satisfying such a supra-animal creature.

(ii) Civilizations whose foundations have been established upon religious and spiritual principles.

Generally such civilizations have declared their collective ideal to be ultimate salvation. Undoubtedly, this ideal carries within it the spiritual element that provides people with tranquillity and peace of mind. It is also true that the achievement of salvation that can become a national ideal can just as well become the individual ideal of its members. However, upon undertaking a deeper critique, it appears that this ideal cannot become a true ideal. There are several reasons for this:

First, there is a certain selfishness that lies concealed within this 'salvation ideal', the essential nature of which empowers individualism at the cost of collective enfeeblement. The reason for this is simply the fact that if every individual could attain salvation by doing certain specified acts, totally on his own, there would remain nothing in the ideal that could give it a collective status, instead of an individual one, and which could encourage individuals to cooperate with the group for its establishment. This spirit of individualism is diametrically opposed to the ideal that a civilization holds dear by virtue of being a collective entity.

Secondly, the issue of salvation is very deeply linked with the process specified for attaining such deliverance. Thus, the fact of the salvation ideal being considered right or wrong is profoundly correlated with the suggested procedure for attaining salvation being considered right or wrong. For instance, salvation can neither become the individual ideal nor the collective ideal in religions that consider monasticism and renunciation of the temporal world to be the way to salvation. In order to separate the temporal from the spiritual while still maintaining a pathway for the salvation of 'worldly' individuals, the followers of such faiths have been forced to invent 'middle paths' like service to the servants of the faith and atonement. The result of this has been twofold: first, this ideal has ceased to remain, in its cohesive entirety, the common ideal of both the individuals as well as the group. Secondly, apart from a small number of faithful followers the ideal no longer holds the loftiness, significance, and magnetism for the remainder of the group that once could have kept them devoted to it. As a consequence, most temporally-oriented people have decided to follow the materialistic ideal outlined above.

On the other hand, religions that have declared salvation to be dependent upon the pleasure of certain idols and deities have failed to maintain the shared values of the ideal. Different groups turn to different deities[2] due to which the ideal loses its true unity, the maintenance of which and uniting of all followers within whose fold is the real work of civilization. Thus, whenever the followers of such religions wish to embark upon the path of temporal success – naturally by severing their links with the group – they feel the need for another ideal.

There is another category of religions whose message is not directed towards human beings in their generic nature as human beings, but is instead intended for a particular nation of a certain ethnicity or one living within certain geographic boundaries.[3] On this account, in the view of such religions, salvation is limited to that special ethnic group or nation. Such an ideal can undoubtedly serve as a successful collective ideal in the early stages of a civilization, but since it does not meet the standards of true intellect – the fundamental premise of restricting salvation to a certain race is something that any sane person will reject – the followers of such faiths themselves rebel against their ideal after moving only a few steps on the road to

---

[2] For instance, amongst the Hindus, one group has a preference for Shiva (the god of fertility) which they may revere over and above other deities, and similarly there are devotees of Ganesh (the elephant-saint) or Hanuman (the monkey-saint) for whom they hold complete festivals in their honour, thus displacing the group purpose – Translator.

[3] While the author does not make any specific reference to any particular faith or creed (and for a deliberate purpose), the examples of Jews and the followers of Shinto come to mind; some Hindus regard all people living within India as originally Hindu (from *Hind*, the Arabic word for India) – Translator.

progress. While exorcizing such an ideal from their minds, they adopt some other ideal.

Thirdly, howsoever pure the salvation ideal may be from a religious or spiritual viewpoint, it does not have any substance within it that could, from a temporal point of view, elevate a group as a nation, and energize it with a force that is essential for mobilizing it to achieve national progress. It is because of this that no progressive nation has ever made salvation its collective ideal. Even amongst those nations whose religions have presented salvation as an ideal, its status has been relegated to that of an individual ideal.

These are the reasons because of which both material and spiritual ideals do not equate with the true measure of success. Let us now see as to what the Islamic civilization has declared to be its ideal and what those qualities are that make it a correct ideal.

The Ideal of Islamic Civilization and its Characteristics

At the very start of this discussion, it should be evident that the whole issue of an ideal is deeply linked with the subject of a worldview or *Weltanschauung*. Whatever view we maintain about the temporal world – and whatever view we have about our role in that temporal world and the place of the corporeal world in our lives – naturally generates an ideal for life. Accordingly, we begin to spend all our energies towards the establishment of that ideal. If we consider the world to be a pasture, and our view of life defines it as a time period granted us for eating, drinking and being merry, then this animalistic concept will necessarily inculcate within our beings a primeval and corporeal ideal. We will then spend all our lives in efforts to obtain the materials that impart sensual pleasure.

On the contrary, if we consider ourselves to be natural wrongdoers and instinctive sinners, and our view about this world is that of a place of torment in which we have been thrown for suffering the punishment of our inborn delinquency, then, naturally this concept produces in us a desire for release from this affliction, and upon this basis we consider salvation to be our ideal.

However, if our concept about the temporal world is beyond that of either a pasture or a torture chamber, and, as human beings, we consider ourselves to be above and superior to both animals and criminals, we will certainly look for an ideal that is loftier than the mere pursuit of physical pleasures or the attainment of salvation. Our insightfulness, then, does not stop at any inferior and lowly standpoint.

Keeping this principle before us, when we see that Islam has declared man to be God's viceroy and His representative on earth, then the intellect necessarily reaches the one ideal that can and should naturally arise from this worldview. By virtue of being a viceroy what else can the ideal of the subordinate representative be other than attaining the approval and pleasure of the power that he represents and that he be considered a good, loyal, and conscientious employee. If a person is a truly straightforward and well-intentioned individual, can he make his ideal anything else except service to the superior and attainment of his pleasure? Would such a person fulfil his duty only because of a longing for an increase in his payment, an incentive for promotion or reward, or a desire for enhancement in rank or status? It would be altogether a different matter that upon being pleased, this superior grants him all these, or holds out the promise of granting all these in return for superior performance. Moreover, there would be no harm in bearing the self-knowledge that if the person were to carry out his duties in the best manner possible and please the superior then the said rewards would be his. On the other hand, if he were to make the rewards his goal, and perform his duties only because of the expectation of gain, would any wise person call such a servant dutiful?

Based upon this illustration, we may reflect on the subject of God and His viceroy. If man is considered to be God's viceroy on earth, can the ideal of his life be anything but the seeking of His approval and pleasure? This is the ideal that the intellect and innate disposition create out of the said worldview. Without any omission, this is precisely the ideal that Islam has presented to humankind. By following the statements of the Qur'ān given below we can see that the whole endeavour is directed towards placing this one ideal in the hearts and minds of people and towards internalizing it by employing different forms of address. Simultaneously, there is also a forceful negation of all other viewpoints. The Qur'ān states:

> Say: 'Surely my Prayer, all my acts of worship, and my living and my dying are only for Allah, the Lord of the whole Universe. He has no associate. Thus have I been bidden, and I am the foremost of those who submit themselves (to Allah).'
>
> [al-An'ām 6: 162-163]

> Surely Allah has purchased of the believers their lives and their belongings and in return has promised that they shall have Paradise. They fight in the Way of Allah, and slay and are slain. ... Rejoice, then, in the bargain you have made with Him. That indeed is the mighty triumph.
>
> [al-Tawbah 9: 111]

In *Sūrah al-Baqarah*, while distinguishing the obedient person from the disobedient, the former is described as:

> Among men there is a kind who dedicates his life seeking to please Allah; Allah is Immensely Kind to such devoted servants.
>
> [al-Baqarah 2: 207]

In *Sūrah al-Fatḥ* Muslims have been described as a people whose friendship and enmity, whose devotions and prostrations, are all for Allah:

> Muḥammad is Allah's Messenger, and those who are with him are firm with the unbelievers but compassionate with one another. You see them occupied in bowing and prostrating and in seeking Allah's bounty and good pleasure.
>
> [al-Fatḥ 48: 29]

In *Sūrah Muḥammad*, the reason for the loss of the unbelievers' deeds is described by pointing out the fact that they do not do anything for God. Instead, they act out of a motivation for achieving other objectives, and thus do not earn God's pleasure:

> That is because they have followed a way that angered Allah, and have been averse to His good pleasure. So He reduced all their works to nought.
>
> [*Muḥammad* 47: 28]

In *Sūrah al-Ḥajj*, such worship of God that is actually undertaken for worldly benefit is declared to be totally useless which will entail only misery:

> And among people is he who worships Allah on the borderline; if any good befalls him, he is satisfied; but if a trial afflicts him, he utterly turns away. He will incur the loss of this world and the Hereafter. That indeed is a clear loss.
>
> [*al-Ḥajj* 22: 11]

In *Sūrah al-Baqarah*, it is stated that charity given for public display, and wealth whose mention is constantly reiterated after being given away, is malevolent. The parable with which it is described is that of a rocky surface that is covered with a very thin layer of soil, and which after being planted with seeds is washed away by a torrent. On the other hand, charity that is given with a positive personal affirmation and purely for God's pleasure is likened to a garden, which while receiving a fair rainfall yields superior fruit, but is nonetheless sufficiently productive even with a small drizzle and does not require a heavy downpour. (cf. *Surah al-Baqarah* 2: 264-65)

This theme – of doing good acts exclusively for God's pleasure and not associating any other purpose with it – is described in various contexts at different points:

> Whatever wealth you spend in charity is to your own benefit for you spend merely to please Allah.
>
> [*al-Baqarah* 2: 272]

(Those) who are steadfast in seeking the good pleasure of their Lord; who establish Prayer and spend both secretly and openly out of the wealth We have provided for them, and who ward off evil with good. Theirs shall be the ultimate abode.

[*al-Raʿd* 13: 22]

The God-fearing who spends his wealth to purify himself; not as payment for any favours that he received, but only to seek the good pleasure of his Lord Most High. He will surely be well-pleased (with him).

[*al-Layl* 92: 18-21]

So give his due to the near of kin, and to the needy, and to the wayfarer. That is better for those who desire to please Allah. It is they who will prosper.

[*al-Rūm* 30: 38]

As for the *Zakāh* that you give, seeking with it Allah's good pleasure, that is multiplied manifold.

[*al-Rūm* 30: 39]

Those who, for the love of Him, feed the needy, and the orphan, and the captive, (saying): 'We feed you only for Allah's sake; we do not seek of you any recompense or thanks, we fear from our Lord a Day that shall be long and distressful.' So Allah shall guard them against the woe of that Day, and will procure them freshness and joy.

[*al-Dahr* 76: 8-11]

It also belongs to the poor emigrants who have been driven out of their homes and their possessions, those who seek Allah's favour and good pleasure and help Allah and His Messenger. Such are the truthful ones.

[*al-Ḥashr* 59: 8]

Allah indeed loves those who fight in His Way as though they are a solid wall cemented with molten lead.

[*al-Ṣaff* 61: 4]

Those who have faith fight in the Way of Allah, while those who disbelieve fight in the way of *Ṭāghūt* (Satan).

[*al-Nisā'* 4: 76]

All this teaching has been rendered into one sentence by 'the one who was unsurpassed in pithy eloquence' – the Prophet Muḥammad (peace be on him). In fact he stated the one basic principle that encompasses all charitable acts and acts of worship. The words of the *ḥadīth* (tradition) are:

> *Allah only accepts those deeds that are purely for Him and for the sole purpose of earning His Pleasure.*

[al-Nasā'ī]

From this discussion, it is clear that, putting aside all intents and purposes of this world and the Hereafter, Islam makes just one thing the ideal of life, the ultimate goal of all human endeavours, and the fundamental principle of all intentions and desires: namely, the attainment of Allah's Will and His Pleasure. Now we need to see as to what are the characteristics of this ideal that make it the best of all ideals:

1. *The Harmonization of Physical and Intellectual Aims*
The Islamic view of the cosmos – which is much more than merely being a viewpoint and underscores belief and certainty – is that the Ruler of this limitless expanse of existence is One God. All that exists is subservient to Him, follows His orders, and is in prostration before Him [al-Nasā'ī].

> To Him belong all who are in the heavens and all who are on the earth. All are in obedience to Him.

[*al-Rūm* 30: 26]

48

All the mechanics and statics of this workshop of existence are subject to His command and Will:

Judgement lies with Allah alone.

[*al-An'ām* 6: 57]

The central point of all things in this universe and all other universes is His Being:

To Allah shall all matters be ultimately referred.

[*al-Baqarah* 2: 210]

This very act is called Islam: the bowing of one's head in submission and of obeying orders. Every speck of the cosmos, by its very nature, follows Islam (that is, submits to the Will of God), whether voluntarily or involuntarily:

All that is in the heavens and the earth is in submission to Him – willingly or unwillingly.

[*Āl 'Imrān* 3: 83]

Like the rest of the cosmos, man too is bound to this immutable universal law that knows no exceptions. His nature and temperament are also obedient and dedicated to God and to follow His *dīn* (religion):

(O Prophet and his followers), turn your face single-mindedly to the true Faith and adhere to the true nature on which Allah has created human beings. The mould fashioned by Allah cannot be altered. That is the True, Straight Faith.

[*al-Rūm* 30: 30]

According to this view, the natural ideal of everything that exists in the cosmos, including mankind, is the possessor of truth – God. He is the ultimate of causes and the ultimate desire and destination. The natural direction of every being is focused towards that centre.

Now, for man – the intellectual entity – all that remains to be done is that he not only attains his natural ideal and knowledge, but that, after intellectually and philosophically internalizing these, he also focuses all his intentions and actions towards that direction. In this way, his intellectual ideal will become harmonized with the natural ideal that he and all other beings possess. At that point, all the forces of this material world and every part of the 'system of existence' shall aid him in reaching that ideal. By virtue of his intellectual status, he shall become the leader of this grand assembly.

However, if man forfeits this ideal and makes some other entity his intellectual ideal, then its illustration would be like that of a rider who while travelling with a group moving in a westerly direction, with his own steed also galloping in that direction, is actually facing the back end of his horse. With his heart still tied up in the east, the cataleptic rider is oblivious to the direction of both his group and his own steed. Pulling at the reins and digging in his heels into the poor horse's sides, he is trying to make the animal move backwards. Even if he succeeds in restraining the horse from moving forwards or even, perhaps, moving it backwards, the direction of the larger group and the animal's own natural inclination forces it to once again take off on the same western course.

In short, this traveller is forced, in spite of his intention and determination, to travel in the same direction as that of the group – but not as a successful and satisfied passenger. Instead, he is an unsuccessful and dismayed individual who has failed to remain at the place of his desire. The destination he has actually reached is neither one of his own choosing, nor one for which he has made any preparations.

2. The Centripetal Force of the Islamic System

As stated above, the very centre and core of the Islamic system is the personage of God. The whole system orbits around that Centre. Whatever lies within this system, whether it falls within the grouping of faith and intention or that of worship and devotion, or whether it is related to matters temporal, its direction is focused, in each and every case, towards that central entity. In this system every object is held in place – fully and immutably – by the invisible mesh of its centripetal forces. The very words *dīn* (obedience) and *Islām* (submission) with which this religious system is referred to appropriately reflect their nature and reality. The very meaning of *dīn* and *Islām* is that the adherents submit and bow their heads before God and become followers of His commands:

> And whose way of life could be better than that of he who submits his whole being to Allah, and does good.
>
> [*al-Nisā'* 4: 125]

> Whoever surrenders himself to Allah and lives righteously grasps the most firm handle. The ultimate decision of all matters rests with Allah.
>
> [*Luqmān* 31: 22]

Beyond this, the essence of Islam can be judged from the act of the Prophet Abraham and his son submitting before the will of God. The son, uttering the words, 'O my father, do that which you are commanded' [*al-Ṣāffāt* 37:102] places himself at the mercy of the knife and his father who is ready to slaughter his son merely for the pleasure of God. The actions of both these individuals are represented by the word 'Islam':

> When both surrendered (to Allah's command) and Abraham flung the son down on his forehead
>
> [*al-Ṣāffāt* 37: 103]

It is for this reason that whatever Islam contains is solely dedicated to God. If the daily ritual prayer, *ṣalāh*, were not God-directed, it would become a meaningless exercise comprising a cycle of standing, sitting and prostration. If fasting were not solely for God, it would merely become self-enforced hunger. *Zakāh* and other alms given for God are a cause of good and expenditure in the way of Allah, otherwise they would only constitute wasteful expenditure. War and *jihād* undertaken purely for Allah are the best of worship, otherwise they are merely the cause of anarchy and the bloodletting of innocents. Similar are all the other acts that have been prescribed by Islam: if these are performed for the pleasure of God, they are good and deserving of reward, otherwise they are useless and of no consequence. As for acts proscribed by Islam, if abstinence from them is for Divine pleasure then it is beneficial, otherwise the same would be totally fruitless.

This total devotion a focal point that is seen in the Islamic system is a product of its ultimate ideal. It is this centripetal force that has energized all components of the Islamic system and has led to the development of a centralist tendency in them, by virtue of which this system has become as complete and as well built as the solar system is stated to be on the basis of our knowledge of physical structures. Had this ideal not existed, Islam too would not have been able to demonstrate its sublime and orderly structure.

3. *The Harmony between Thought and Action*
Just as its ideal has generated a centrality, a focus, a discipline and an order in the Islamic system, in the same way it has imparted a 'total focus' to man's reflections and thoughts, intentions and plans, and beliefs and actions. Together with this focus, it has also shown man such a lofty objective beyond which there is no other grand, towering or higher viewpoint and objective.

The person who has before him only the satisfaction of his natural desires or attainment of his base corporeal purposes – or even purely spiritual objectives – shall never be able to achieve this unity of thought and action. This is because the processes of intellectual evolution and theoretical or practical discovery cause new desires and new inclinations to develop at every stage, and he continues to declare ever-new objects to aspire towords aspirations. It is not at all possible that having once reached a higher level of knowledge and intellect, man continues to be unwavering about those physical inclinations or bodily and spiritual demands which were the focus of his attention and motivator of his actions at the previous, lower stage. If that were to be the case, man's whole life would be spent in moving from one purpose to another, and never would he be able to develop within his mind a 'core idea' that could, in turn, lead to the creation of a total focus for which he could spend all his intellectual and physical energies. This advantage is only to be found in the Islamic ideal that enables it to become man's sole and 'ultimate aim' at every intellectual level. Even after reaching the highest of high statures, there is no need to revise it. This is because God's personage is above and higher than any intellectual or practical plane that we can imagine and yet its relationship with every entity, from the lowest of the low to the highest of the high, is the same. If there is any difference [in relating to the reality of God] then it is only in terms of our intellectual stature and wisdom.

4. *The Reintegration of a Purely Human Collective*

Just as the Islamic ideal can become the ideal of an individual, it can also become the ideal of a group, a nation, and indeed, of all humankind. The reason for this is because the ideal is totally bereft of the element of personal and collective selfishness which has a natural tendency to divide humanity firstly into ethnic groups and nations, and then into individuals, and secondly to create amongst them sentiments of envy and resentment as well as competition and resistance.

On the contrary, this ideal directs man towards the Being Who has an equal relationship with all humankind, and in fact the whole cosmos. After turning towards this Entity, there comes about unity in human thought and purpose that, instead of competition and resistance, there develops amongst people a spirit of cooperation, unanimity and brotherliness. With worldly materialistic objectives, no two people can ever be true partners in any of them, notwithstanding the quality of cooperative spirit with which these are pursued. Even for people linked in very close relationships, like those of siblings, or paternal relationships like those between a father and son or a mother and daughter, it becomes difficult to avoid tussles, and sometimes even hostility and enmity, when they are joined in a materialistic purpose. We all are aware of such cases of the disintegrating blood and biological ties. We have witnessed, and continue to witness numerous occurrences in which the closest of relatives have ruined the lives, property and honour of each other for worldly objectives. All such actions are the consequences of the worldliness and selfishness that are the most important elements of temporal aims and objectives. Conversely, the great truth is the ultimate source towards which millions upon millions can run simultaneously without any mutual tussle, competition or conflict, and indeed in such a way that no one even steps on the toes of another.

In fact this journey is one in which every traveller sincerely helps fellow travellers, gives preference to others' comfort over his own pleasure and happily endures a greater degree of toiling and suffering as compared to others. Instead of travelling in luxurious comfort, he considers it much better to be of service to others, carrying the burden of his comrades, and reaching the destination gasping and trembling, so as to attain the maximum pleasure of his Master.

The core concept which is required for the formation of a global nation and a reunification of an international human grouping, through the removal of all differences based upon race and colour, language and geography, is borne within this ideal in its greatest measure. There can be no better ideal for such a worldwide civilization, because, on the one hand, this ideal does not do away with the individualism of the persons concerned, and yet on the other, it fully integrates them into a pure human collectivity by eliminating the centrifugal tendencies of individualism.

5. *The Attainment of All Human Desires through Obedience*
One of the most important attributes of this ideal is that all human objectives which can possibly exist, whether in our individual or collective life, are attained to a degree of certainty by following this ideal, without it specifically ever being designated our objective. The Qur'ān has enumerated, one by one, all those objectives that are necessarily obtained along with the attainment of God's pleasure.

In temporal life, the one feature that we desire most is peace and tranquillity, bodily comfort and peace of mind. The Qur'ān states that these shall automatically come to us if we turn towards God and become seekers of His pleasure:

(None has any special claim upon reward from Allah.) Whoever submits himself completely to the obedience of

Allah and does good will find his reward with his Lord. No
fear shall come upon them, nor shall they grieve.

[*al-Baqarah* 2: 112]

Surely in Allah's remembrance do hearts find rest.

[*al-Ra'd* 13: 28]

The other aspect of life that human beings desire in this world is
economic prosperity – a life free from distress and lack of resources.
The Qur'ān states that by placing one's belief in God and by adopting
piety with a view to precluding His wrath, this objective is also
achieved in a beautiful way:

Had the people of those towns believed and been God-
fearing, We would certainly have opened up to them
blessings from the heavens and the earth.

[*al-A'rāf* 7: 96]

Whosoever acts righteously – whether a man or a woman –
and embraces belief, We will surely grant him a good life;
and will surely grant such persons their reward according
to the best of their deeds.

[*al-Naḥl* 16: 97]

All those who accept Allah and His Messenger and the
believers as their allies should remember that the party of
Allah will be triumphant.

[*al-Mā'idah* 5: 56]

Surely We wrote in the Psalms, after the exhortation, that
the earth shall be inherited by My righteous servants.

[*al-Anbiyā'* 21: 105]

Allah has promised those of you who believe and do righteous deeds that He will surely bestow power on them in the
land even as He bestowed power on those that preceded

them, and that He will firmly establish their religion which He has been pleased to choose for them, and He will re-place with security the state of fear that they are in.

[*al-Nūr* 24: 55]

Similarly, human beings also desire salvation in the life of the Hereafter. In this respect, the Qur'ān states that this can only result through the attainment of God's pleasure:

O serene soul! Return to your Lord well-pleased (with your blissful destination), well-pleasing (to your Lord). So enter among My (righteous) servants, and enter My Paradise.

[*al-Fajr* 89: 27-30]

Thus we see that Islam does not even turn its attention towards those things that others have declared to be their objective and purpose. Instead, it makes the attainment of that one supreme value its central aim by which all these other desired features are also automatically achieved (i.e. those things that other systems have designated as their aims). In Muslim eyes, things and phenomena which others have made their ideals are not worth considering even for a moment. Before the Muslims is an ideal that is loftier than all these things and everything else. They know that when they are able to reach that highest ideal, everything else that lies below it automatically becomes theirs, just as those who reach the highest floor of a building find all the other floors below their feet.

6. *The Best Motivation for the Virtuous and Pious*

Another characteristic of this ideal is that it is the only pure and honourable way in which man can follow the high standard of virtue and piety that Islam has set. It is also by virtue of this ideal that people can abide by the code of conduct that presents a set of actions which are to be put into effect and a set of actions that are to be eliminated from society.

There is no shortage of people in this world who say that morals should be followed because it is good and that immorality should be avoided only because it is bad. However, the people who make such statements do not know the real meaning of their words. Acting virtuously only for the sake of being virtuous would mean that the good is good and capable of becoming a human ideal, irrespective of any benefit or reward that might accrue from this action. Similarly, the act of shunning evil only because of its being bad would mean that notwithstanding any detriment or damage that may accrue from a certain act, evil action is bad in its own right, as if there is something in its very make up that could be the cause of its abstention. In truth, however, no such pure virtue exists in the world that can be totally divorced from all contextual benefits and rewards accruing to the person concerned. Neither is there any existence of an absolute evil that is devoid of any beneficial effects that may impact upon the actor. In fact, it would be more accurate to state that the very concept of good and evil has been created in the human mind by way of experiencing profit and loss, advantage and disadvantage. Man calls 'good' any such thing from which he stands to gain some real benefit, even if it has certain detrimental aspects within itself. So is the definition of 'bad' and the word is used to refer to an act that is likely to lead to a cumulative loss notwithstanding any advantages that it may fetch.

If any act is totally separated from all aspects of gain and loss, and that deed simply becomes an action bereft of its consequences, we would not be able to label it as 'good' or 'bad.' Undoubtedly, there is a possibility that once 'good' has been perfected and has reached the highest intellectual plane human beings may be able to totally eliminate the concept of gain and loss from their minds. They may then be able to act virtuously purely on the intrinsic values of the act, and refrain from 'evil' only on account of its being bad. However, first, this concept ignores the sources of good and evil and not a pointer towards their origins. Secondly, this state is merely the attainment of the loftiest summit of philosophers' conceptual consciousness that has eluded even the wisest of the wise. Given this difficult state, how could ordinary human beings adopt unmixed good and refrain from a pure evil as their ideal?

It is clear from the foregoing discussion that the concept of good and evil cannot be separated from the concept of profit and loss.

'Good' cannot be the object of human desire, in its own capacity, until there is some benefit at its core and 'evil' by itself cannot be considered avoidable until it has within itself some negative features. Now, if we wish to raise *taqwā* and virtue from a low status of selfishness to the higher stature of selflessness and sincerity (untainted with any hidden agenda), and declare it to be the basis of a code of moral conduct that is valid for the commoners and the privileged alike, the best manner for this is to establish a standard of gain and loss that is above all material and selfish considerations. Such a standard would be one on the basis of which a good act, in spite of being associated with material and selfish detriments, would appear to be full of benefits and an evil act, in spite of its possessing numerous advantages, would appear to be totally harmful.

This is the way that Islam has adopted. The attainment of Divine pleasure or the lack of such attainment has been declared to be a criterion that is totally devoid of all material and selfish corruption. Acting in accordance with this decisive standard, a pious human being continues to believe that he has made a gain even after having sacrificed his life and wealth, family and honour in order to attain Divine pleasure. And an impious person, who after having risked God's wrath and gained all manner of temporal wealth and selfish gains continues to be apprehensive about having made a loss. It is this attitude that leads a person to disregard worldly gains and losses and adopt piety with full sincerity and purity of intention.

Up to this point, two aspects of the Islamic view on piety have been explained. One, the state that Islam has declared to be its ideal has been presented. Moreover, the reasons why it considers it to be the best ideal have also been presented. Now we need to turn to the third aspect of this issue: the part played by this ideal in making the Islamic civilization a distinct civilization and the special characteristic it imparted to this civilization.

7. Determination of the Ideal and Its Impact on distinguishing between Various Methods

Earlier, a reference was made to the fact that just as it is essential to determine the ideal or objective – 'the end' – in all areas of one's life, so it is essential to determine the method of achieving that ideal – 'the means'. The selection of the means to be adopted cannot be based upon anything other than the appropriateness of the objective. If a person does not have before him any predetermined purpose other than spiritual quest and drifts from one path to another, we would call him a fool or a vagabond. Moreover, even if he did have before him a certain purpose, but was not inclined to follow any particular course towards achieving that end and was willing to take any path that he considered to be the means to his objective, we would call him thoughtless. This is because, logically speaking, a person who attempts to travel on ten different avenues just to arrive at one destination would never be able to reach his objective. Similarly, we would not consider a person as wise who while declaring a certain destination as his objective adopts a route that runs in an opposite direction – like the bedouin who takes the path towards Turkey while desiring to reach the Ka'bah. It is essential for a person's practical success (as opposed to a theoretical one) that he determines and settles upon the one objective that he would like to achieve and then directs all efforts towards attaining this. And if there are many ways to achieve or reach a particular objective, then it is incumbent upon him or her to choose the one means that is best in his opinion and leave all the other options.

This process of picking and choosing between options is fundamental to the intellect and a very logical requirement for progress in any field. A rational conclusion that flows from the determination of an objective is that a person adopts the one way that is best suited for reaching a given objective and abandons all other possible routes. Whenever a sagacious person undertakes a journey, he adopts that one route which is best suited for reaching the destination amongst all the various possible routes. Apart from this one chosen path, he does not even take into consideration the numerous possibilities that may be encountered on the way. An intelligent student takes up the one particular specialization amongst the many that are available which is likely to be most helpful in achieving his academic objective and does not like to waste time and intellect in pursuing other irrelevant areas which may be important in their own right. A wise and pragmatic trader chooses the one area of business activity that he considers the best means to achieve his goals. He deems it foolish to place his investments in all manners of activities and divide his energies in a number of unfocused areas. The only discussion that a critic can undertake with regard to this process of adopting or rejecting any particular option is whether or not the particular means that was adopted was the best one or not. No criticism is possible against the very basis of picking and choosing one from amongst the many available options.

Just as this fundamental principle of choosing between options holds true for a particular action in life, it is also valid in an all-encompassing way for one's whole life. People who have no ideal of life, that is, those who merely while away their time, are free to adopt whatever means of living that they may choose. For this purpose, a choice between good and bad, right and wrong, high and low is meaningless. Such people can fulfil their desires and requirements in whatever way that pleases them. Even if external constraints force them to adopt a certain way of life, these cannot be helpful in bringing their lives within the bounds of any discipline or principled limits because of the absence of internalization of any source or any motivation of such an ideal. On the other hand, if any such individual maintains a certain aim in life, or in other words, there exists in his mind a human or intellectual aim higher than the animal or physical aim, then he will necessarily distinguish between the various ways of living. Moreover, if such an individual is indeed a judicious person it will be necessary for him to adopt the one manner of living amongst the many available that is best suited to achieve his aims. Exercising the total freedom that only an aimless person believes to be his right is in no way suitable for a person who has determined an aim in life.

Let us now extend this principle further by considering a group in place of separate individuals. In this way, we are sure that the principle is just as valid for a group as it is for an individual. As long as a human group is in the very early stages of communal life, it does not have before itself any higher aim of life beyond the physical and animal. In its day-to-day routine, such a group exists in a state of freedom similar to the aimless individual. However, when by way of intellectual evolution and civic refinement the group reaches a higher civilizational status, that civilization establishes for the group a certain intellectual aim. As a consequence it becomes inevitable for the group to develop a system of beliefs and concepts, customs and manners, and social and economic protocols appropriate to the aim through which the followers of the civilization are to be bound to its systemic discipline. No longer can such individuals be allowed the freedom to adopt a belief or pattern of behaviour that is alien to the system while still remaining within its folds.

Protecting its canon with vigour and strength is an essential feature of civilization's nature. Any civilization that loses its grip in this regard and that displays weakness or laziness in its disciplinary dynamism will never be able to survive intact. This is because the continued existence of a civilization is dependent upon its participants adhering to the system of belief and action that it has developed. When a civilization's own followers cease to abide by its code and when external influences come to dominate their intellects and actions that civilization effectively ceases to exist. Accordingly, a civilization can rightfully demand of its followers their adherence to the system that it has developed and to distinguish it from other external systems. All that the critic can debate is whether that particular civilization's ideals are right or wrong, whether the means adopted to achieve the ideals are appropriate or not and whether adherence to the given system is possible under all conditions or not. However, what cannot be debated is a civilization's right to demand of its followers their compliance and conformity to the system that it has instituted as long as they remain its voluntary adherents.

Moreover, when it has been principally established that the specific means designated to manage the intellectual and practical aspects of a group's life are determined by the group's ideals and that differing ideals necessarily lead to differing means and manifestations, it must also be accepted, as a corollary, that the civilizations which differ in their ideals necessarily differ in their system of belief and action. While it is possible that certain ingredients of these differing civilizational systems resemble each other, or where one system may have adopted certain minor aspects from another, the fact remains that no conclusion of total concurrence can be drawn from constitutional resemblance. Nor can it be established that a borrowing of some parts amounts to borrowing the whole concept.

From this principle, two further corollaries can be derived: one, that in order to analyse or judge a particular civilizational system that maintains a certain ideal, a different civilizational system which upholds a dissimilar ideal cannot be taken as the criterion. In other words, criticism based upon the line of argument 'If this system conforms to that system, then it is good, otherwise not' is not acceptable.

Secondly, it is not possible to keep a civilization intact while replacing its system of belief and action. Nor is it possible to amalgamate the core ingredients of one civilization with or into the core of another competing civilization. One who believes such assimilation to be either possible or acceptable is unaware of the fundamental principle of formulation of civilizational systems and is incapable of understanding the temperament of civilizations.

8. *The Role of the Ideal in the Development of Islamic Civilization*
In the light of the above arguments, one is able to recognize the role that the ideal plays in making the Islamic civilization an altogether separate and distinct civilization. The fact that the ideal of life established by Islam is fundamentally different from the ideals of other religions and civilizations has been stated in detail. It has also been proved that dissimilarity in ideals leads to fundamental divergence in the belief and action systems of civilizations. Accordingly, as a logical conclusion, the ideals of Islam have made its attendant social system such a specifically identifiable civilization that it is fundamentally different from other civilizations and is one whose belief and action systems maintain a fundamental disagreement from other such systems.

While it is possible that certain elements of the Islamic civilization may also be found in other civilizations, it is certain that these elements cannot be found in the Islamic system in precisely the same manner as they are in other systems. After being incorporated into any system a part loses its individual identity and acquires the character of the assimilating whole. Moreover, when the outlook of one whole is different from the character of another whole, then it necessarily follows that every part of one given whole shall also be different in character and nature from the corresponding parts of the other whole, irrespective of any apparent similarity that certain elements of the given whole may have with some elements of the other whole.

As has been stated earlier, Islam has declared man to be the vice-gerent of God on earth and has established as the ideal of his life, the seeking of the pleasure of that One Entity Whose subordinate and representative he is and shall always remain. Since this ideal is central to human life, it is essential that all our actions be directed towards that ideal. All the energies of the body and the spirit should be spent on the path leading to this ideal. All ideas, concepts and actions as well as inactions should be ruled by this ideal. Our lives and death, sleeping and awakening, eating and drinking, daily transactions and relationships, friendships and enmities, economic and social activities – in short, every aspect of this temporal life – should be for that one ideal.

This ideal should become so internalized and integrated in a person that it may become the very spirit by virtue of which he remains alive and active. It should be clear that a person who upholds such an ideal of life, and who continues to exist for that ideal, cannot spend his life in the manner of a person who has no ideal, or one whose ideal is different from the Islamic ideal. This ideal, by its very nature, transforms a person into a person who only exists for the purpose of achieving its ideal of life.

Thus, after having established the ideal, Islam selects one special way of life amongst the many possible options available, and obliges Muslims not to waste their cherished time or precious energies by following any other way. Based upon the nature and character of its ideal, Islam creates a distinctive system of belief and action and demands of human beings that under no condition should they cross the bounds of this system. It declares this system to be one of total obedience and names it as '*dīn*' – a word that means wholesale surrender; it states:

> The true religion with Allah is Islam.
>
> [*Āl ʿImrān* 3: 19]

It is on the basis of this *dīn* that Islam draws a line of distinction between its followers and non-followers. The people who, while acting in compliance with this special ideal, follow the system of the *dīn* are referred to as Muslims (the submitters) and *mu'mins* (the faithful). Those who do not agree with this ideal and thus do not follow the system of the *dīn* are termed *kāfirs* (the rejecters).[4] Doing away with all criteria of distinction – whether based on race, national origin, language, statehood or other similar differences – it creates just one distinction amongst the offspring of Adam. This is the distinction between the two states of *kufr* (disbelief) and *īmān* (belief). Whosoever follows this system, whether he is in the East or the West, is Islam's very own. Anyone who does not follow its system is an alien, irrespective of whether he resides under the very walls of the Ka'bah and whether his flesh and bones have been completely nourished on dates from Makkah and the water of Zamzam.

Just as Islam has created the distinction of *kufr* (disbelief) and *īmān* (belief) on the basis of differences in belief and action, it has also created a division between the *ḥarām* and *ḥalāl* (the permissible and the forbidden), the legitimate and the illegitimate, and the *makrūh* (distasteful) and the *mustaḥabb* (desirable). Those actions and ways that are helpful in the achievement of the ideal and proper discharge of the duties of vicegerency are, by virtue of their rank, classified as *mustaḥabb* or *ḥalāl*. Similarly, actions that obstruct or prevent the attainment of the ideal are, by virtue of their status, *makrūh* or *ḥarām* (disapproved or forbidden). The *mu'min*[5] who respects this line of

---

[4] Even in the choice and use of the word *kāfir*, great eloquence has been employed. In Arabic, the basic meaning of '*ka-fa-ra*' is to hide; hence the night-time is also called *kāfir*, as is the farmer who sows the seed by hiding it within the soil. In the case of certain fruits, the outer covering which hides the 'real fruit' is called *kafūr*. Metaphorically, the act of hiding God's bounties and not expressing gratitude for them is also called *kafara*, while the person who acts in such a manner is called *kāfir*. Islam has declared this term to be the opposite of *īmān*. From this emerges the fact that people who decline the opportunity to accept Islam actually cover up their own natures and instincts.

[5] Generally translated as 'believer', a better equivalent of '*mu'min*' would be 'acceptor' – Translator.

distinction is the true *muttaqī* (pious or God-conscious individual) and the one who does not observe the distinction is a *fāsiq* (one who goes beyond the boundaries set by God). Amongst the members of 'Allah's party,[6] any distinction between the low and the high is not on the basis of wealth, genealogy or descent, social status, or colour of the skin but only on the basis of their *taqwā* (God-consciousness or piety). As the Qur'ān states:

> Verily the noblest of you in the sight of Allah is the most God-fearing of you.[7]
>
> [*al-Ḥujurāt* 49: 13]

Similarly with regard to concepts and thought-processes, manners and characteristics, economic and social actions, culture and living styles, politics and governance, or, in short, all walks of human life, the path taken by the Islamic civilization becomes distinct from the

---

[6] The term Allah's party here is very much used in the literal sense of those who are close to God and is not intended to convey any specific political or social usage – Translator.

[7] In the verses above, the Muslims are provided with the necessary directives to keep their community immune from evil and corruption. But now through the present verse mankind is being warned about the major erroneous notion that has always led to the spread of evil around the world; namely, the notion of prejudice based on race, colour, language, homeland and nationality. Addressing all human beings, the Qur'ān emphasises three basic points: (1) that all human beings have the same origin, that all of us have arisen originally from the same father and mother. Thus, all ethnic and racial entities that exist today are branches of the same family, their ultimate parents having been the same. (2) That it was natural for mankind to become divided, despite their common origin, into diverse national and tribal entities. While this diversity is quite natural, it does not provide any justification for some people to claim any inherent superiority over others; to consider some on these grounds as high and others as low, some as noble and others as ignoble. Considerations of colour, race or nationality do not warrant people of any particular colour, race or nationality to regard themselves as superior to others. God created such diversities to foster greater cooperation and to enable these different entities to become mutually introduced. (3) There is only one basis for regarding one as better than the other and that is on account of their moral excellence – Translator.

one taken by other civilizations. This is because the Islamic worldview differs from the worldviews of other civilizations. The purpose of life that Islam upholds is distinct from the one determined by other civilizations. Accordingly, acting in consonance with its ideology, the way in which Islam deals with the world and all that exists therein, and the manner that it adopts in this life for the attainment of its ideal, is also fundamentally distinct from the ways adopted by other civilizations.

The numerous thoughts and concepts, the many temperamental inclinations and various ways of living one's life which other civilizations not only consider permissible, but are occasionally even civilizational imperatives, are declared by Islam to be forbidden or *ḥarām*. This is because, while such features are in precise harmony with the *weltanschauung* – the outlook of life – of those civilizations and are helpful in attaining their ideals, these have no connection with the Islamic outlook of life and are an obstruction in the attainment of its ideal. For instance, the fine and performing arts are in many civilizations the very essence of civilization and people who hold high stature or expertise in these fields attain the status of national heroes. However, Islam considers some of these to be forbidden (*ḥarām*), others *makrūh* (disapproved) and some to be permissible to an extent. Under Islamic law, the nourishment of artistic refinements and indulgence in man-made ornamentation is only allowed to the extent where man can continue to maintain the remembrance of God, act to seek His pleasure, and be able to discharge his duties as God's vicegerent.

Wherever and whenever artistic inclinations overcome the sense of duty (as God's vicegerent), when the single-mindedness of seeking pleasure makes human beings beauty or art-centred rather than God-centred, when fondness for the arts leads to a penchant for sensuous indulgence, when bodily emotions under the influence of these arts gain such power that the intellectual hold of reason weakens and the heart becomes deaf to the voice of conscience, when attention is no longer paid to the call of duty nor is obedience considered necessary, it is right at that point that Islam creates a *cordon sanitaire* of disapproval and prohibition. The reason for this is simple: Islam does not aspire to produce classical musicians, grand masters of painting, sculpture or letters, and film actors.[8] Rather, it seeks such role models to emerge as Abū Bakr Ṣiddīq, ʿUmar Fārūq, ʿAlī ibn Abī Ṭālib, Ḥusain ibn ʿAlī, Abū Dharr Ghifārī and Rābiʿah Baṣriyyah.

Same holds true for other aspects of social life and culture. The Islamic stance on gender relations, the ties between the rich and the poor, between the ruler and the ruled and various classes is, in principle, different from that of all the classical and modern civilizations. To take the latter as the norm and to judge the Islamic system against these is a basically flawed exercise. Only those with superficial knowledge, unaware of the truth, carry out such an exercise.

---

[8] The author mentions names like Tansen (a seventeenth century Indian classical musician at the court of Mughal emperor Akbar), Mānī and Behzād (Persian painters/artists), Charlie Chaplain and Mary Pickford (early twentieth century film actors) who being dated are no longer familiar to modern English readers; these have been made into categories that are more representative of the author's thought – Translator.

3 Foundational Philosophy and Beliefs

The Reality and Importance of Belief (*Īmān*)

After having covered the ideology and aims of life, the third question that arises is: 'What is the basis or foundation upon which Islam builds human character?'

Character and Its Rational Foundation

The source of all human actions is the mind. There are two states of the mind with regard to it being the source of actions. The first is that there are no particular concepts deeply embedded in it. Instead, various scattered thoughts pass through it and whichever amongst these are strong become the stimuli for actions that are undertaken by the possessor of this mind.

The second state is one in which the mind no longer remains the abode of such stray thoughts, and instead a few distinctive concepts become so deeply rooted in it that the bearer's practical life permanently comes under their influence. Instead of taking unfocused actions, this mind becomes the centre of organized and disciplined acts. The first state may be likened to a public road that is open for use by all and is not a restricted thoroughfare. The other state is like a mould that gives rise to parts of a specific design and distinct appearance.

When the human mind is in the first state we say that it does not have a character. The bearer of such a mind could be Satan – or could be an angel.[1] There is unpredictability in his temperament. It cannot

---

[1] Although in the Christian tradition Satan is often referred to as 'the fallen angel', Islamic tradition – based upon the Qur'ān – explicitly holds that Satan is a member of another category of creation, the *jinn*. Indeed, in the Qur'ānic narrative it was the angels who prostrated themselves before Adam, whom God had made His vicegerent, while Satan refused to do so. Thus, the term 'angel' stands diametrically opposed to 'Satan' – the two being metonyms for obedience and rebellion – Translator.

be said with certainty as to what kind of actions such an individual may carry out at any given time. On the contrary, when a person comes into the second state we say that he has a character and that there is a discipline and a certain order in his practical life. It can now be predicted with confidence as to what actions such an individual would carry out under certain given conditions.

The First Prerequisite for Organizing Behaviour

Thus, we know that a human being's actions leading towards the adoption of a dependable system for ordering and organizing his practical life is contingent upon the development of a permanent character. That character, in turn, is dependent upon this individual's mind ridding itself of a state of mental discord brought about by a fullness of scattered thoughts. Instead, there comes about a state in which a few selected ideas come to dwell in the mind, and with such influence, firmness and strength that these do not allow any other ideas to enter and upset the bearer's mental world. The more deeply embedded these ideas are, the stronger will be the individual's character and the more organized, disciplined and dependable his practical life will be. On the contrary, the greater the weakness that exists in a person's mental state and the greater the propensity to giving way to opposing ideas, the more likely it is that such an individual's character will be proportionately weaker and that his life will be disorganized and undependable.

The Meaning of Belief (*Īmān*)

In the terminology of the Qur'ān, this mental foundation of human character is called *īmān*. The root of *īmān* is from the root '*a – m – n*'. The true meaning of this root is 'the state of the self in which it becomes satisfied and free of fear.' Also derived from the same root is the word *amānah* (trust, security), the opposite of which is *khiyānah* (doubt, insecurity); thus *amānah* is the state in which there is no fear of *khiyānah*. An *amīn* (trustee) is so called because others are confident about his trustworthiness and are certain that he will not betray their confidence. An obedient she-camel is called *amūn* or one from which there is no danger of unruly behaviour or trouble. The gateway

69

of actions derived from this root is *īmān* (usually rendered as 'belief') which essentially means something being so embedded in the self – on the basis of truthfulness and absolute certainty – that no fear of anything else taking its place remains. A weakness of *īmān* means that the self is still not fully convinced about a particular idea or issue and that the heart has not yet achieved the state of full satisfaction. In such a state, extraneous ideas will enter that person's mind and consequently weaken his character. From this follows a process of disintegration in the person's life. The strength of one's *īmān* is reflected in its own image. A strong *īmān* means that the character has been established on absolutely firm foundations and that it is now certain that all actions will spring from the ideal that is embedded in the heart and from which the conceptual mould of character has been shaped.

The Status of Belief (*Īmān*) in the Establishment of Civilization
If different people believe in varying sets of beliefs and philosophies, and their characters come to be established on differing and contradictory bases, then no collective structure can emerge. This state can be likened to a field littered with numerous stones. Undoubtedly, each of these stones is strong in its own character, yet there is no connection between them. On the contrary, if one common thinking were to become settled in the hearts of many people as *īmān*, their shared affiliation to that belief system would make a strong group or a nation out of them. This could be likened to a situation in which those scattered stones were to be cemented together to form a strong wall. A cooperative process would have to come about as a result of which the pace of development becomes increasingly expeditious. The one single kind of *īmān* would create harmony amongst their characters and uniformity in their actions. From this would arise a special culture and a singularly glorious civilization would manifest itself. A new nation would rise with a new character and a new mindset; a new process for building its citadel with a fresh design.

Thus the status of a foundational ideology in the development of a civilization is clear. This central thought is the collective ideal that permeates itself within the followers of that civilization and becomes an all-encompassing *īmān*.

The Two Types of Belief (*Īmān*)

Now we need to analyse various civilizations of the world vis-à-vis the states of their *īmān* or belief systems. Although the term *īmān* is, in its essence, an Islamic religious term, nonetheless when used to refer to a foundational ideal, as in the present discussion, there can be said to be two types of *īmān*.

The first one is that *īmān* which has a religious character. The religious type of *īmān* can become the foundation of only that civilization which itself is based upon a religious creed. This is because *īmān* controls both the spiritual and temporal spheres. However, in case of a civilization that is not based upon a religious faith, the temporal *īmān* breaks away from the spiritual *īmān* and in this way the latter no longer has any effect upon individual or national lives.

1. *Religious Belief* (Dīnī)

Religious *īmān* generally exists with respect to such matters that build human character on spiritual and moral foundations. The instances of such belief include one or many deities that have been accepted on the basis of certain special traits, scriptures whose revealed nature has been accepted, or leaders whose guidance and way of life has come to form the basis of faith and action.

Leaving aside the spiritual viewpoint, even from a purely temporal viewpoint, the success of this type of *īmān* is contingent upon two things: the issues that have to be ascertained and of which religion demands acceptance should, from an intellectual viewpoint, be amenable to verification. Secondly, these should be matters on the basis of which human character may be properly raised. In other words, these matters should build the character in such a way that its spirituality establishes a first-rate moral system and that together with moral purity and cleanliness also prepares man for temporal successes.

The first of the above conditions is essential because if the belief system were to be merely a collection of mythological assumptions, or if there were to be more mythology and less truth in the system, the human mind would forever be hostage to ignorance. As soon as human beings take steps towards the higher stages of intellectual development, the spell of false superstitions begins to break down, the foundations of the belief system start to shake, and at the same time the whole system of spirituality and morality on which the structure of individual and national character so far stood also begins to disintegrate. We can illustrate this by way of beliefs that various polytheistic religions present with regard to their gods and goddesses, deities, and religious or saintly leaders. The qualities with which these figures have been associated, the actions that have been attributed to them, and the supernatural stories invented about them are such that good sense refuses to verify or believe in them. Often it so happens that a nation that places belief in such mythological matters fails to progress and gain dominance in the temporal realm. False beliefs affect their mindset in such a negative manner that their best energies are exhausted. Neither is there loftiness in their aspiration nor a sharpness of ambition; there is no breadth of vision, no illumination in the mind nor courage in the heart. Finally, these are attributes that become the cause of perpetual disgrace and enslavement.

On the contrary, those nations that have had their paths of progress opened to them in some other way find that the more they progress in terms of intellect and knowledge, the greater is their level of progressive disbelief in their deities and spiritual figures. First, attempts are made to prop up these false beliefs merely for the vested interest of protecting the collective system. In time, however, slowly and steadily, the rebellion of their hearts and minds against these traditional beliefs becomes so strong that these no longer have any control over the collective consciousness or national and group mindsets. Only a limited, residual group is left to govern their beliefs for them either in a real or a professional manner. As for the rest of the nation, their spirits and consciousness come to be ruled by another belief system which we refer to as temporal *īmān*.

The need for the second condition should be very obvious. A belief system that cannot prepare human beings for worldly success will naturally have its influence restricted to only the spiritual and moral spheres of people's lives, and not reach its material aspects of life. In terms of practical results too, this would not be without a duality of outcomes. A nation that believes in such a dichotomous system will either not progress at all, or otherwise if it does progress then it will soon free itself of the control of its belief system. The religious *īmān* will make way for the temporal *īmān* and when the nation's preoccupation with the efforts and actions geared towards material indulgence increases, both morality and spirituality will also be outside the influence of religious *īmān*.

I do not wish to consciously negate any religion, and hence will not comment on the belief systems of various religions. However, if one studies religions deeply, it is clear how these belief systems have stopped their followers from progressing in worldly life and how they have not kept pace with intellectual developments and growth in knowledge. It would also become clear from such studies how some nations held fast to their religious beliefs when passing through periods of decline, only to abandon these in periods of progress.

On the contrary, Muslims were the strongest in terms of their *īmān* when they also led the field of progress in worldly affairs. Their *īmān* grew weak only when they began to lag behind in the temporal race for intellectual and material progress and other nations overcame them. Today, Muslims are in a state of extreme material degradation and at the same time they also suffer from the acute malady of weak *īmān*. About a thousand years ago when the Muslims were enjoying a state of rapid progress, they were, at the same time, strongly rooted in their religious *īmān*. Conversely, when the Christians of Europe or the Buddhists of Japan were strong adherents of their faiths, they were in a state of decay; and when they progressed materially, they lost their respective beliefs. This, then, is the vital difference in the belief systems of Islam and those of other religions that can be discerned by every person of intellect and vision without much deliberation.

2. *Temporal Belief* (Dunyawī)

Let us now look at those systems that encompass beliefs that I would like to include in 'temporal *īmān*'. There is no religious element here, nor any deity or religious leadership, no revealed scripture nor any guidance that could raise human character on spiritual or moral foundations. The concerns and issues included herein are purely temporal and deal with the physical world.

The most important entity within this category is 'nation' – a deified construct that the residents of a particular geographical region first invent and then revere with great solemnity and devotion. All 'nationalists' declare their belief in the notion that the nation is the title-holder of their lives and properties and that protecting and serving this nation is their duty, so much so that contributing all their possessions and energies, even laying down their lives, in the service of this nation is a mark of distinction. They believe that it is the duty of every individual to raise the flag of his nation. Not only this, but these people also believe that only their nation is the one rightful entity which is the true owner and inheritor of the earth. They believe that all the nations of the world exist to serve them.

The second deity of this belief system is 'national law' – a corpus which these individuals themselves create and then worship. This deification accounts for their collective discipline and organization.

The third object of their worship is the 'self' – their very own 'selves'. It is this material bodily existence that they nurture; the fulfilment of its needs and desires is their constant preoccupation.

The fourth deity of this belief system is 'knowledge and wisdom' in which they affirm faith, in the light of which they walk, and guided by which they embark upon the path of progress.

This belief system is certainly beneficial for worldly life to some extent. However, notwithstanding the status of these individual objects of worship from viewpoint of truth and soundness, even from a purely worldly point of view, we can say that their benefit is neither real nor permanent. The main shortcoming of the system is that there is no spiritual or moral element in it. Thus, as soon as the linkage with religion is severed, the gateway to moral problems gets wide open. It is not the duty or role of law to create a moral sphere within the hearts of individuals or to establish a standard of moral conduct. Nor does it have sufficient coercive power to be able to protect morals in individual or collective lives as its impact and area of operation is limited.

The laws that human beings make for themselves have proved to be especially powerless in the respect of inculcating moral uprightness as it is within the power of people to adhere to or abandon these. As people's desire for freedom of action increases, old moral restrictions increasingly appear constrictive and unbearable. When this feeling of being held back by one or more moral restriction becomes common, the power of public opinion forces the law to relax its grip and in this way all moral restrictions are gradually forced open. This leads to widespread moral decadence. Such moral decay is one fact whose fatal effects can neither be checked by an abundance of wealth nor by the power of governments, neither by the force of material resources nor the stratagems of knowledge and wisdom. This is a rot that starts from inside and soon reduces even the strongest of edifices, along with all its paraphernalia, to naught.

Moreover, the detriments of this deification of nationalism and individualism are so well known that they need little elucidation. In order to gain an understanding of these negative aspects, one no longer needs a vision or even a debate. Having come down from a theoretical arena, these are now part of our daily impressions and observations. We see and are aware that it is because of these detriments that a very significant civilization has now reached the very precipice of death and destruction, the inevitability of which is now keeping the world in a state of anxiety.

Some Foundational Principles

From the above discussion some essential principles can be derived. It is important to internalize these principles – in the proper order – before proceeding to the discourses that are to follow.

(i)   A disciplining and organizing of human action is contingent upon the development of a permanent and ascertainable character. Without an undeviating character, man's practical life remains chaotic and uncertain.

(ii) Character is based upon those concepts that have been so forcefully internalized in the mind and have gained such control that all human energies now operate under their influence. The Islamic term for this internal force of conviction is *īmān* and the full range of concepts that come to be so internalized is referred to as the 'belief system.'

(iii) The good or bad, right or wrong, strong or feeble configuration of character is fully dependent upon the health of this belief system and the extent of its internalization. If the individual features of the belief system are correct, naturally the character will also be right. If the *īmān* is strong, so will be the character. Accordingly, for human life to be brought within the fold of discipline, it is imperative that the character be founded upon sound and strong *īmān*.

(iv) Just as *īmān* is essentially required for the life actions of an individual to be lifted out of chaos and into a rule-based order, so it is essential that in order to remove a number of individuals from a state of disorder and strife and create a unified, organized group out of them that their hearts be imbued with *īmān*.

(v) When a large number of people influenced by *īmān* are able to form a common national character, then by way of the influence of this character there comes about a homogeneity in their actions. As a result of this, a very special and distinct civilization comes into existence. In this way, the elements of a belief system that shape and strengthen the national character have an immense role in the establishment of every civilization.

(vi) A nation whose belief system comprises spiritual elements comes to have a common religion and civilization, while a nation whose belief system is made up of temporal elements has its civilization divorced from its religion. In this latter instance, religion no longer has any significant influence on the individual or collective lives of its members.

(vii) The process of a civilization gaining independence from its religious foundations ultimately leads to moral decay and destruction.

(viii) The fact of a civilization remaining under the influence of its religion is necessarily dependent upon that religion's belief system comprising elements that are also able to provide support to the intellectual evolution of its members from the lowest to the highest levels at once and which are able to shape human character in such a way that it is simultaneously supremely spiritual as well as supremely temporal. In fact, the temporality of such character should be its spirituality and *vice versa*.

(ix) The *īmān* of a nation whose religion and civilization are one is not solely a religious *īmān*, but is very much a temporal *īmān*. Any wavering in this *īmān* is devastating both for religion and civilization, for its temporality as well as spirituality.

These are the fundamental principles with respect to which the Islamic standpoint towards *īmān* or belief must be critically examined. After seeing the true status of *īmān*, its primary importance in personal character as well as its core status in collective civilization, the aspects towards which Islam invites our belief will also be considered. We shall analyse the extent to which this belief system conforms to the standard of intellectual criticism, and shall also examine the status of *īmān* in this system and the influence that it has on the personal dispositions of its followers as well as the collective character of human groups.

The Belief System (*Īmāniyāt*) of Islam

The Qur'ān elucidates the belief system of Islam in such detail that there remains no occasion for dispute. However, people who have not understood the features of the Qur'ān or those who have failed to follow its themes correctly, will certainly have some misconceptions. Thus, it is one manner of Qur'ānic stylistics that while at places it states all the elements of the belief system collectively, at other points, depending upon the context, it only presents some or just one of the elements with greater emphasis. From this, some people have come to misunderstand that the belief system of Islam can be easily analysed, that it is sufficient to pronounce belief in any one or a few of the elements, and that one may still achieve salvation while negating and dismissing some of these elements. This in spite of the clear Qur'ānic pronouncement that it is essential to accept all the various aspects that it has presented as part of its belief system. These elements cannot be separated from one another as they collectively form an indissoluble whole that has to be accepted *in toto* as a single indivisible unit.

The negation or rejection of any one of these elements falsifies the acceptance of all others. At one place the Qur'ān states:

> Those who say 'Allah is our Lord' and then remain steadfast, upon them descend angels.
>
> [*Fuṣṣilat* 41: 30]

This verse only states the requirement of pronouncing belief in Allah upon which basis the success of this life as well as the Hereafter is proclaimed.

At another point, together with the mention of Allah, belief in the Day of Judgement is also stated:

> Those who believe in Allah and the Last Day, and do righteous deeds – their reward is surely secure with their Lord.
>
> [*al-Baqarah* 2: 62]

The same theme is repeated in *Sūrahs Āl ʿImrān* [3: 114]; *al-Māʾidah* [5: 59] and *al-Raʿd* [13: 29].

In a third instance, there is the invitation to affirm belief in Allah and the Prophets:

> So believe in Allah and in His Messengers; and if you believe and become Godfearing, yours will be a great reward.
>
> [*Āl ʿImrān* 3: 179]

The same theme is repeated in *Sūrah al-Ḥadīd* [57: 28]

At yet another place, a believer is said to be the person who affirms belief in Allah and the Prophet Muḥammad (peace be upon him):

> The true believers are only those who sincerely believe in Allah and in His Messenger.
>
> [*al-Nūr* 24: 62]

This message is also repeated in *Sūrahs Muḥammad* [47:33]; *al-Jinn* [72: 23] and *al-Fatḥ* [48: 17].

At another place, four elements of the belief system, namely Allah, the Books of Allah, the Qur'ān and the Last Day are mentioned:

> The believers, they believe in what has been revealed to you and what was revealed before you. ... firmly believe in Allah and in the Last Day.
>
> [*al-Nisā'* 4: 162]

At yet another point, rejection of Allah, the angels, the Prophets and the Qur'ān is equated with *kufr* and *fisq* (unbelief and wickedness):[2]

> Whoever is an enemy to Allah, His Angels and His Messengers and to Gabriel and Michael will surely find Allah an enemy to such unbelievers." We surely sent down to you clear verses that elucidate the Truth, (verses) which only the transgressors reject as false.
>
> [*al-Baqarah* 2: 98-99]

In the verse 285 of same chapter (*Sūrah al-Baqarah*) the people who believe in Allah, the angels, the Divine books including the Qur'ān, and the Messengers of Allah have been called the 'believers' (*mu'minūn* – sing. *mu'min*):

> The Messenger believes, and so do the believers, in the guidance sent down upon him from his Lord: each of them believes in Allah, and in His angels, and in His Books, and in His Messengers.
>
> [*al-Baqarah* 2: 285]

At still another point, all the five basic elements of the Islamic 'belief system' are listed – Belief in God, the Last Day, the angels, the Divine scriptures and the Prophets:

---

[2] For further elucidation of these and other Islamic and Qur'ānic terms please see the glossary in Dr. Zafar Ishaq Ansari's translation of *Tafhīm al-Qur'ān*, entitled *Towards Understanding the Qur'ān* published by the Islamic Foundation, Leicester, UK. (Translator)

True righteousness consists in believing in Allah and the Last Day, the angels, the Book and the Prophets ... Such are the truthful ones; such are the God-fearing.

[al-Baqarah 2: 177]

In a verse of *Sūrah al-Nisā'* emphasis is laid on professing belief in the Prophet Muḥammad (peace be upon him), and the Qur'ān in addition to the above five elements. Those who refuse to do so are called *kāfir* (rejecters) and misguided:

Believers! Believe in Allah and His Messenger and in the Book He has revealed to His Messenger, and in the Book He revealed before. And whoever disbelieves in Allah, in His angels, in His Books, in His Messengers and in the Last Day, has indeed strayed far away

[al-Nisā' 4: 136]

At one point emphasis is only placed on belief in the Last Day:

Those who consider it a lie that they will have to meet Allah are indeed the losers.

[al-An'ām 6: 31]

The same theme is reiterated at several other places in the Qur'ān such as *al-A'rāf* [7: 147], *Yūnus* [10: 7-8], *al-Furqān* [25: 11], *al-Naml* [27: 4-5] and *al-Ṣāffāt* [37: 16-25].

At another place, rejection of the Last Day as well as rejection of the Divine scriptures is said to be the cause of a grave punishment:

For indeed they did not look forward to any reckoning, and roundly denied Our Signs as false.

[al-Naba' 78: 27-28]

At a third point, the Qur'ān is included in the 'Belief System' along with the Last Day and Divine Books:

who believe in what has been revealed to you and what was revealed before you, and have firm faith in the Hereafter. Such are on true guidance from their Lord; such are the truly successful.

[al-Baqarah 2: 4-5]

At a fourth point, it is stated that rejection of the Last Day, the Divine Books and the Prophets leads to the loss of all other actions. Such a person is destined for Hell and none of his actions have any worth, see *Sūrah al-Kahf* [18: 105-106]:

At numerous places in the Qur'ān, mention is made of professing belief in Divine Scriptures, and specific reference is made in this regard to the Torah, New Testament, Psalms and the Books of Ibrāhīm. However, at countless other points, it is also made amply clear that merely accepting these Books is not sufficient. Together with belief in these Divine Books, it is also essential to accept the Qur'ān. If a person believes in all the Divine Books, but rejects the Qur'ān (as not being a revealed text), he is a *kāfir* (a disbeliever) in exactly the same way as a person who rejects and does not profess belief in all the Divine books, see *Sūrah*s *al-Baqarah* [2: 89, 99, 121, 136]; *al-Nisā'* [4: 47]; *al-Mā'idah* [5: 10, 68]; *al-Ra'd* [13: 36]; *al-'Ankabūt* [29: 48] and *al-Zumar* 39: 32].

This is not, however, all, because a person must profess belief in the complete text of all the books. A person who accepts part of the text of a revealed book but at the same time rejects one or more parts of it is also a *kāfir* (see for example *Sūrah al-Baqarah* 2: 85)

Similarly, it is clearly stated that a believer must acknowledge belief in all the prophets, specifically those who are mentioned by name and generally all of them whose names might not be mentioned. However, if a person professes belief in all the prophets but rejects the Prophethood of Muḥammad (peace be upon him), he is certainly a *kāfir*. This essential requirement is clarified at numerous points in the Qur'ān. Together with an acceptance of all other messengers of Allah, belief in the Prophethood of Muḥammad (peace be upon him), has been made an essential condition of *īmān* (See for example *Sūrah*s *al-Baqarah* 2: 121; *al-Nisā'* 4: 47; *al-Mā'idah* 5: 12, 86; *al-An'ām* 6: 124;

al-Aʿrāf 7: 158; *al-Anfāl* 8: 20; *al-Muʾminūn* 23: 69; *al-Shūrā* 42: 48; *Muḥammad* 47: 2; and *al-Ṭalāq* 65: 11).

Many of the above verses are those in which the followers of the Prophets Moses and Jesus have been invited to profess *īmān* in the Prophet Muḥammad (peace be upon him). They have been told that guidance will not be forthcoming to them until they believe in the Qur'ān and the Prophet Muḥammad (peace be upon him). From the foregoing elucidations, we come to know that the belief system of Islam comprises the following five elements:[3]

> (i)   God or Allah
> (ii) Angels
> (iii) Revealed Books or Scriptures including the Qur'ān
> (iv) Messengers of Allah including the Prophet Muḥammad (peace be upon him).
> (v)   Last Day (of Judgement)

This is, of course, a summary. Later in this book, the detailed beliefs in each of these elements and the advantages of including them in the belief system will be discussed. We shall also read about the mutual relationships between these elements because of which any one or more of them cannot be separated from this list and because of which rejection of any one must necessarily be treated as rejection of all.

Intellectual Criticism

All of these elements of the belief system belong to the category of 'matters of the unseen'. Thus, according to our scheme these belong to the class of religious or spiritual belief systems. However, their distinction lies in the fact that Islam has not only established its

---

[3] Although mention of a sixth element, belief in *qadar* or the fact that all good and evil comes from Allah, occurs in *Ḥadīth*, this is essentially a part of belief in Allah and is mentioned in this way in the Qur'ān. The reason it is mentioned separately in *Ḥadīth* is that while this element is rather concealed and implicit its importance needs to be underscored. Accordingly, it is mentioned separately for better mental impact and retention.

spiritual system upon their foundation, but has also raised its moral, political and cultural systems upon them. By bringing the temporal and spiritual realms together, Islam has created a system in which all the many departments of life function at the same time. All the power that this system requires for its existence and sustained operation is derived from these five elements. This belief system is a fountainhead from which the supply of such spiritual power is incessant. We now need to see the intellectual status of these elements of the Islamic belief system which have been put to such immense a purpose. We need to examine whether these elements are capable of serving as a basis of and providing a driving force for such a comprehensive and constantly developing system, and if so to what extent?

All the same, before taking steps towards further researching this question, we have to bear in mind, and very deeply so, that Islam aims at creating a civilization that is truly a human civilization, that is a civilization which is not related to any particular country or race, or one which is characterized by its association with any particular skin colour or a nation that uses a particular language, but instead is one that aims at the welfare of the entire human race. This civilization should be one under which a collective system can be established that will cultivate and give rise to all that is a cause of good for every man and woman – in his essential capacity as a human being – and obliterate all that is a cause of evil and malevolence. Such a pure human civilization cannot be established on the basis of a belief system that is only associated with the physical and natural realm. The reason for this is that the material and the tangible belong to one or the other of two categories. These belong either to a group of objects that is equally related to all human beings, for example, the sun, moon, earth, air and light, or can be placed in a group that is not equally related to all human beings, for example, a nation, a race, a colour, or language.

The things in the first group do not have the capability of forming the basis of a belief system because professing belief in their mere existence is meaningless and believing in them as having deliberate power in bringing about human welfare is academically and intellectually flawed. Moreover, professing belief in them does not result in any benefit accruing in any aspect of human life, be it spiritual, moral or work-related. As for the elements in the second category, these cannot become the bases for a collective human civilization because they are the criteria of division and separation and not the sources of unity. Thus, it is absolutely indispensable that a universal civilization be founded upon a belief system whose elements are beyond the material and tangible.

However, it is not enough for these bases to be simply outside the realm of the material and the tangible. Together with this, it is essential that they be endowed with certain other characteristics. Thus, it is important that these elements:

(i)   not comprise of the fabulous and the mythological but should instead be matters that can be rationally verified;

(ii) not be matters beyond our experience but should instead be things which have a deep association with our lives;

(iii) and be endowed with a powerful rational force that may be drawn upon by the resultant civilizational system in its drive to win over human beings, both in terms of their intellect and actions.

When we take a look at the fundamentals of the Islamic belief system in this light, we see that these fully satisfy all the three elements. First, there is no intellectual defect in the concept of God, angels, revelation, Prophethood, and the Last Day that is presented by Islam. There is nothing in it which may be factually impossible, neither is there anything in this conceptual scheme that may be rejected on rational grounds. While it is certainly true that our intellects cannot fully comprehend this scheme nor fathom its full depth, the fact remains that this was also true (at one point in time or another) of all the abstract thoughts and entities that have so far been verified by our thinkers and scientists.

Whichever field one looks into, we see that the confirmations of hypotheses regarding matter and energy, gravitational attraction and distraction, life in its microscopic and chemical details were not drawn up on the basis of our having fully observed and understood them, but on the basis of certain indications and causes which could not have been explained otherwise. The theories that we have drawn up about the hidden intricacies of various natural systems are based upon the external manifestations that confirm the existence of matters and forces which we cannot directly observe, and demand our acceptance of the same.

Thus, it is not essential for the confirmation of the abstractions, upon which Islam calls us to believe, that our intellect fully understands those realities or is able to completely circumscribe them. Instead, it is sufficient for our intellect to comprehend that the conceptual framework presented by Islam with regard to the cosmos and man is not contrary or contradictory to the rational faculty. The probability of this guiding framework being right is overwhelming and, thus, it demands the existence of all those five elements that Islam presents as part of its belief system. It is Islam's view that:

(i)   the cosmos has been established by an All-Powerful Being Who continues to operate its systems;

(ii)   subordinate to this one All-Powerful Being are innumerable other beings who assist in managing this vast cosmos according to that All-Powerful Being's commands;

(iii) the Creator has placed within human beings a predisposition both for good and bad. Wisdom and lack thereof, knowledge and ignorance combine within these beings who can then either follow the path of good or the path of evil. Men and women follow whichever of these two contradictory forces and mutually opposed inclinations dominate them;

(iv)   in order to assist the forces of good in this struggle between good and evil and to guide man on the straight path[4], the Creator Himself selects from within the human race one most suited person, imparts him with the appropriate knowledge, and then assigns him the task of guiding his fellow beings, and

---

[4] The Qur'ānic term for the way in which the pious and those who have been blessed by God live their lives – Translator.

(v) human beings are not irresponsible or helpless creatures. They are answerable before their Creator for all their deliberate actions. One day, all will have to render a very complete account, to the last detail, and will have to face the consequences of their actions, good or bad.

This paradigm is itself demanding of the existence of all five elements of the Islamic belief system, being God, angels, revelation, Prophethood and the Last Day of Judgement. There is nothing in this view that is not rationally possible. On the contrary, the more we contemplate this view, the greater is our inclination towards seeking verification of the system.

Whether or not we are able to understand the reality of God, we have no option but to accept His existence. This is one such imperative without which the grand mystery of the cosmos can never be revealed.

We cannot determine the manner of the existence of angels, but there can be no doubt in the fact of their existence. All people of knowledge and wisdom have accepted their existence in one way or another, even though they do not call these by the name the Qur'ān uses.

The coming of the Last Day and the total destruction of the physical realm is not only intellectually probable but rather is certain.

The actuality of man being answerable to God for his actions – and suffering the consequences thereof – cannot be proved by any absolute and final argument. However, the intellect is at least forced to accept that inasmuch as the various theories and views that exist with regard to human death and the state after death are concerned, the best concept, which is also result-oriented and the closest to possibility, is the one presented by Islam.

As for the issues of revelation and prophethood, it is obvious that no scientific proof for these can be presented. However, by examining the significance of the books that have been presented as having been Divinely revealed and considering the lives of those who have been called God's prophets, we can reach the conclusion that no other texts nor people in leadership positions have had as deep and wide-ranging an impact or as long lasting and positive influence on humanity as these. It suffices to say that there is certainly something extraordinary in these books and individuals that is not found in works by ordinary authors and leaders.

From the above it is clear that nothing in Islam's belief system is contrary to intellect. Indeed, rationalism does not possess anything that may call into question Islam's beliefs. There is nothing in them that human beings may be forced to repudiate upon reaching a certain stage of academic and intellectual evolution. On the contrary, the intellect actually dictates their certainty. As far as Islamic belief (*īmān*) and its validation are concerned, the intellect is not concerned with these, intuition and conscience are. Indeed, the corroboration of all the abstractions and all the intangibles that we accept as being true is based upon our transcendental experiences. If we do not wish to accept any ethereal or intangible fact, or if our heart is unconvinced of the same, no rational proof can force the acknowledgment of its veracity upon us. For instance, none of the many proofs that have been advanced in favour of the existence of ether is able to conclusively establish the same without leaving some room for doubt. Based upon these arguments, some people of wisdom come to believe in it, while other wise people decline to do so on account of what in their views is insufficient proof.

Thus, the matter of belief and its validation is dependent upon a satisfaction of the conscience and transcendental evidence. All the same, the intellect is involved in this process with regard to arguments whose confirmation is contrary to rational thought and with regard to which a struggle ensues between the transcendental and the intellectual. As a result, *īmān* becomes weak. As far as validation of arguments that do not go against intellectual reasoning, or those that are actually strengthened by way of such an intellectual process, is concerned, their 'approval rating' by the conscience is actually enhanced and this, in turn, energizes *īmān*.

Secondly, most of the sub-elements amongst these intangible arguments are only of academic significance, i.e. these have no relationship with our everyday lives. These include, for instance, ether, matter, nature and its laws, cause and effect, and similar other academic imperatives or hypotheses. Whether we believe in them or not makes no difference to our day-to-day affairs. However, matters beyond human perception towards which Islam invites our belief do not belong to this category. Their status is not one of mere academic interest for they rather have a deep relationship with the ethical and practical aspects of our lives. Affirmation of these truths has been declared to be the basic principle of Islam on account of the fact that these are not just academic truths; rather, a correct understanding and total belief in these truths forcefully impacts upon our instincts and emotions, individual actions and collective affairs. A detailed discussion of this theme will follow later.

Thirdly, the power that is required by the civilizational system of Islam in order to establish and strengthen itself in widely spread human communities (who are themselves at varying levels of intellectual and academic capacities with respect to even the most peripheral development and hidden aspects of their lives) can only be derived from the belief system whose corroboration Islam demands. This is the demand of a firm conviction that an All-Hearing and an All-Seeing dominant God, full of Wrath and full of Mercy, rules over us, that His countless troops[5] exist everywhere, that the Messenger has been sent by Him, that all the commandments given by Him have not been put together or invented by Muslims, that we shall certainly have to see the good or bad consequences of our submission or insurrection, and that this God possesses an All-Powerful and All-Embracing power which cannot be obtained by any other source. While material forces can only constrain the physical, the influences of education or training can only reach the upper echelons of human society, and rulers can only govern to the extent their agents can reach, this is a power that conquers hearts, minds and souls.

This is a power that takes into its control all and sundry – the commoners as well as the elite, the ignorant and the learned, the wise and the thoughtless. It operates in the remotest corners of

---

[5] A symbolic reference to the angels – Translator.

wildernesses and stalks the darkest shadows of the night where there is no one to see the sin being committed, let alone stop such evil from taking place. The absolute certainty of God's Ever-Presence and All-Seeing capability, the firm belief in the truthfulness of the Messenger's teachings, the conviction in accountability of Judgement achieve the wonders that no policeman and no judge nor even a scholar's sermon can achieve. The manner in which this belief has brought together the many different and conflicting human elements spread over a vast earth, made them into nations, developed a high degree of unanimity in their thoughts, actions and manners, spread a civilization amongst them notwithstanding varying temperaments and circumstances, and breathed a spirit of dedication for the achievement of a supreme purpose cannot be found anywhere else even after the most diligent search efforts.

Whatever has been established so far is that within the terminology of Islam, belief or *īmān* means professing belief in Allah, his angels, Books, Messengers and the Last Day. All these five belief elements make up a whole that defies a dissectional analysis. So integrated is this whole that rejection of any part necessarily means refutation of the whole. Furthermore, through intellectual criticism, it has also been proved that only these elements can form the belief system of the civilization that Islam intends to establish and which essentially requires these beliefs. In short, there is nothing in these elements which cannot keep pace with intellectual and scholastic progress.

Now we need to pay attention to the third question and that is, 'What is the status of *īmān* or belief in Islam' and why is this status what it is? In order to be able to understand this issue, people have made many mistakes and indeed some famous people of scholarship and authority have also stumbled in this regard. Accordingly, it is important to explain this aspect in detail.

The Importance of Belief (*Īmān*) in Islam

If one were asked what the basic principle of the invitation of the Qur'ān is, the question could be answered in one word – and that word is *īmān*. The very purpose for the Qur'ān's revelation and the mission of the Prophet (peace be upon him), is an invitation towards *īmān*. Referring to the person who brought its message, the Qur'ān clearly states, that he is the campaigner of *īmān*:

> Our Lord! We indeed heard a crier calling to the faith, saying: 'Believe in your Lord.'
>
> [*Āl 'Imrān* 3: 193]

With regard to its own mission, the Qur'ān announces:

> It is a guidance for the pious, for those who believe in the existence of that which is beyond the reach of perception.
>
> [*al-Baqarah* 2: 2-3]

By way of sermonizing, persuasion, promises of reward and warnings of wrath, debate and reasoning, stories and anecdotes the Qur'ān invites people towards its message. Its first demand on human beings is that they accept *īmān*. It then takes steps towards purification of the soul, moral reformation, and the formulation of civic regulations. For the Qur'ān, *īmān* alone is truth, sincerity, knowledge, guidance and light. As for the absence of *īmān* – this is *kufr* (rejection) – it declares this state to be ignorance, *ẓulm* (or injustice), corruption, falsehood, misguidedness and darkness.

The Qur'ān, by drawing a very clear dividing line, places all the human beings of the world into two groups. The first group comprises those who have accepted *īmān* and the second one is the group of repudiators – the people of *kufr*. It considers the first group to be the upholder of Truth, endowed with knowledge and light, and one for which the doorway of guidance, self-discipline, and *taqwā* (God-consciousness) has opened. This group is destined to achieve *falāḥ* (success or deliverance). For the Qur'ān, the other group is that of the *kuffār* (disbelievers) and one that is unjust, ignorant and caught in darkness. The corridors of guidance are closed for this latter group, it has no share in bounties of self-restraint and *taqwā* and an assessment of failure has already been taken for this group. The Qur'ān describes the two groups by way of an illustration in which one comprises the blind and the deaf while the other the sighted and the hearing:

> The example of the two parties is that one is blind and deaf, and the other capable of seeing and hearing. Can the two be equal?
>
> [*Hūd* 11: 24]

The Qur'ān states that the way of *īmān* is the 'straight path':

> Surely you are directing people to the Straight Path.
>
> [*al-Shūrā* 42: 52]

It goes on to say that it is important to abandon all roads other than the straight path:

> This is My Way – that which is Straight; follow it, then, and do not follow other paths.
>
> [*al-An'ām* 6: 153]

Without any ambiguity the Qur'ān clearly states that those who believe in Allah, His Prophet and His Book (i.e. the Qur'ān itself) possess a bright lamp with the help of which they can progress on the straight path. In the presence of this guiding light, there is no possibility of anyone going astray. That holder of His light will be able to distinguish the right path from all the crooked routes and reach the destination of success in good stead.

As for those who do not possess the guiding beacon of *īmān*, they have no light. For them it is difficult to find the Right Path from the many crooked ways. They will walk in pitch darkness like a visually challenged person[6] and will proceed only by trial and error. It is possible that, by chance, they may tread a step or two on the straight

---

[6] This is now standard usage for people who cannot see; the traditional term 'blind' is now increasingly seen as deprecating; another term is 'unsighted' – Translator.

path, but this is no certain manner for proceeding on the right track. It is more than likely that such people will fall into a ditch here or get caught up in a thorny bush there; in short, they will go astray from the right path.

Regarding the first group, those who believe and proceed on the straight path, the Qur'ān has this to say:

> So those who believe in him and assist him, and succour him and follow the Light which has been sent down with him, it is they who shall prosper.
>
> [al-A'rāf 7: 157]

> Believers, have fear of Allah and believe in His Messenger, and He will grant you a twofold portion of His Mercy, and will appoint for you a light whereby you shall walk; and He will forgive you.
>
> [al-Ḥadīd 57: 28]

Regarding the second group who reject the *īmān*:

> Those who invoke others instead of Allah, associating them with Him in His Divinity, only follow conjectures and are merely guessing.
>
> [Yūnus 10: 66]

> They only follow their conjecture and conjecture can never take the place of the Truth.
>
> [al-Najm 53: 28]

> Who is in greater error than he who follows his lusts without any guidance from Allah? Allah does not guide those given to wrong-doing.
>
> [al-Qaṣaṣ 28: 50]

> He to whom Allah assigns no light, he will have no light.
>
> [al-Nūr 24: 40]

An elucidation of this comprehensive thesis is found in the second *sūrah* of the Qur'ān *al-Baqarah*. From this, it becomes absolutely clear that the distinction between belief and its rejection (*īmān* and *kufr*) leads to a great divergence between these two groups of humankind:

> There is no compulsion in religion. The Right Way stands clearly distinguished from the wrong. Hence he who rejects the evil ones and believes in Allah has indeed taken hold of the firm, unbreakable handle. And Allah (Whom he has held for support) is All-Hearing, All-Knowing. Allah is the Guardian of those who believe, He brings them out of every darkness into light. And those who disbelieve, their guardians are the evil ones; they bring them out of light into all kinds of darkness. These are destined for the Fire, and there shall they abide.
>
> [*al-Baqarah* 2: 256-57]

The Precedence of Belief (*Īmān*) over Action

The same fundamental difference that exists between belief and disbelief, also creates a distinction between the qualities of human actions. According to the Qur'ān a righteous and self-disciplined person can only be one who has professed *īmān*. Without *īmān*, no action can be labelled as good or based upon *taqwā*, no matter how virtuous that action may be in the eyes of humanity. The Qur'ān states:

> But he who brought the Truth, and those who confirmed it as true, such are the ones who shall be guarded against the chastisement.
>
> [*al-Zumar* 39: 33]

> This is the Book of Allah, there is no doubt in it; it is a guidance for the pious, for those who believe in the existence of that which is beyond the reach of perception, who establish Prayer and spend out of what We have provided them, who

believe in what has been revealed to you and what was
revealed before you, and have firm faith in the Hereafter.

[*al-Baqarah* 2: 2-4]

Thus, in the view of the Qur'ān, *īmān* is the very basis of *taqwā* and
the essence of self-moderation. The virtuous deeds of a person who
professes *īmān* grow, flower and fructify just as the trees of an orchard
that are planted in good soil and enjoy an agreeable climate. On the
contrary, a person who acts without *īmān* (even virtuously) is like the
person who plants an orchard in an unfertile, rocky soil located in an
area that has poor climatic conditions.[7]

It is for this reason that at every instance, the Qur'ān gives precedence to *īmān* over action. At no point is mere good action without
īmān declared to be a means of success and salvation.[8] In fact, if one
were to study the Qur'ān with some concentration, one would see
that whatever moral instructions and legal commandments have been
presented are solely addressed to those who have come to profess *īmān*.
All of these verses either begin with the words, 'O you who believe…'
or have it clarified in some way in the context that the communication
is only directed towards the *mu'minūn* (possessors of *īmān*). As for the
disbelievers, they have not been invited to carry out virtuous deeds,
but only to profess *īmān*. It has been stated in no uncertain terms that
the actions of those who do not possess *īmān* are of no value or worth,
nor do they possess any weight; they are without any consequence and
destined to be wasted:

But for those who deny the Truth, their deeds are like a
mirage in the desert, which the thirsty supposes to be water
until he comes to it only to find that it was nothing; he
found instead that Allah was with Him and He paid his
account in full. Allah is swift in settling the account.

[*al-Nūr* 24: 39]

---

[7] This thematic illustration is presented in the Qur'ān in almost exactly the
same way, see al-Qur'ān 2:265.

[8] For instance, see al-Qur'ān 2:25, 2:82, 2:277, 4:173, 5:9, 11:23, 16:97, 20:75,
and 20:112.

Say, (O Muḥammad): 'Shall We tell you who will be the greatest losers in respect of their works? It will be those whose effort went astray in the life of the world and who believe nevertheless that they are doing good. Those are the ones who refused to believe in the revelations of their Lord and that they are bound to meet Him. Hence, all their deeds have come to naught, and We shall assign no weight to them on the Day of Resurrection. Hell is their recompense for disbelieving and their taking My revelations and My Messengers as objects of jest.'

[al-Kahf 18: 103-106]

The same thesis is stated in many other verses including *Sūrahs al-Mā'idah* [5: 5]; *al-Anʿām* [6: 88]; *al-Aʿrāf* [7: 147]; *al-Tawbah* [9: 17]; *Hūd* [11: 16]; *al-Aḥzāb* [33: 19]; *al-Zumar* [39: 65] and *Muḥammad* [47: 1].

In Chapter 9 (*Sūrah al-Tawbah*) it is clearly spelled out that the apparently virtuous actions of a disbeliever can never equal those of a believer:

Do you consider providing water to the pilgrims and tending the Sacred Mosque equal in worth to believing in Allah and the Last Day and striving in the cause of Allah. The two are not equal with Allah. Allah does not direct the wrong-doing folk to the Right Way. The higher rank with Allah is for those who believed and migrated and strove in His cause with their belongings and their persons. It is they who are triumphant.

[al-Tawbah 9: 19-20]

Summary

From the foregoing thesis and the Qur'ānic verses that have been presented in its support, a few issues are proved beyond any reasonable doubt. These are:

(i)   *Īmān* is the very foundation of the Islamic system. The whole superstructure of the system has been built upon this groundwork. The sole distinction between Islam and *kufr* (disbelief) is based upon *īmān* or the absence thereof.

(ii) The first demand that Islam makes of human beings is that they profess *īmān*. Those who submit to this demand enter the circle of Islam; all of Islam's moral instructions and legal commandments are for these people. Those who reject this demand lie outside the bounds of Islam; neither any moral instruction nor legal commandment of Islam concern such people.

(iii) Islam considers *īmān* to be the basis of action. Only those actions have any significance, merit or weight as are based on *īmān*. Wherever this source and starting point is missing, all actions are false and without substance.

An Objection

Some people do not understand and appreciate the crucial importance of *īmān*. They say that the acceptance or rejection of a few intellectual concepts is not significant enough to be made the basis of dividing humanity into two groups. These people consider courteousness and good character to be the true criterion of differentiation. Based upon this standard, they uphold the distinction between good and bad, right and wrong. According to them, any person who demonstrates good manners and possesses an unblemished personal character must be called righteous and included in the group of God-conscious people, irrespective of whether or not they accept the concepts that Islam declares to be its belief system. As for people who are devoid of these traits of civility and humanism, for them the faith-based distinction is without significance. Such people must be called sinful, no matter what set of beliefs they profess. As for the hypothesis that the worth and weight of actions is dependent upon *īmān* and that no action may be righteous without *īmān*, this is merely a point of view. Without intellectual proof, it cannot be accepted that the moral blessings and good deeds of people who merely happen to possess a different set of beliefs regarding God, a Prophet, a book or the Last Day from that of Islam are put to waste.

If Islam considers a set of beliefs to be correct, it holds the right to propagate these. It can call people towards its belief system and ask them to profess *īmān*. However, the question remains as to how far is it correct to apply the constraints of faith upon issues of morality and action or making superior behaviour and better character traits dependent upon *īmān*?

Apparently this objection carries such weight that acting under its influence, some Muslims have also agreed to make an amendment in this Islamic principle. However, after understanding the real significance of *īmān* and its relationship with ethical character, this objection falls away by itself.

Examination of the Objection

First of all, it must be clearly understood that all distinctions relating to goodness or wickedness amongst members of humanity are based upon two distinct sources. The first relates to the natal character, the highs and lows of which are not in anyone's control. The other relates to what one has earned or striven for; this aspect is dependent upon either a proper or an improper use of the faculties of intellect and thought, volition and intent. With regard to their impact on human life, both these factors are so mutually intertwined that we can neither distinguish these sources nor their outcomes. However, from a theoretical perspective we do know that these two sources of good and bad thoughts and actions exist separately in the playing out of human life. The upright and virtuous aspects that are based upon one's instinct cannot be considered to hold any weight in the scales of justice because of its (controlled) origin. Only those good or bad aspects or deeds can be considered to be of significance that have been the result of one's free striving and unrestrained volitional endeavour.[9]

---

[9] This is precisely what is stated in the Qur'ān, verse 2:286: 'Allah does not lay a responsibility on anyone beyond his capacity.' Thus God does not hold any living being accountable for anything (thought or action) that is beyond its capability.

Whatever efforts are made towards the education, persuasion, guidance and acculturation of individuals are not related to the first factor, i.e. instinct. This is because it is not possible for human beings to interchange the good with the bad or *vice versa* in this respect: how can anyone change his basal instinct? In fact, these are all related to the second category of achieving goals by way of effort and exertion. In this regard, benevolent education and training lead towards virtue and malevolent education and training lead towards vice.

By virtue of this principle, what can be the correct manner of conduct for a person who directs the forces of his endeavour towards good and strives to progress on that path? Naturally, that he communicates the correct knowledge and designs a system of training in the light of that knowledge that has the capability to shape human morals and character in a better mould, in so far as these are related to free exertion (and not base instinct). In this respect, the predominance of knowledge over training is a foregone fact and no wise person can deny this relationship. This is because knowledge alone is the basis of action. Without the right knowledge, it is simply not possible for any action to be right.

Now let us take knowledge. One category of knowledge is that which is related to various aspects of our lives. This is the knowledge we gain in institutions of learning and which comprises countless fields of study in the sciences and humanities. The other branch of knowledge is 'Absolute Knowledge' – which, in the terminology of the Qur'ān, is called 'the Knowledge'.[10] This category is not related to our

---

That individual alone shall reap the benefits or damages of what he has earned and he shall be solely responsible for it. As for base instinct, this has been granted to each individual by Allah according to His Power: *Āl 'Imrān* 3: 6, 'It is He Who fashions you in the wombs as He wills.' As for how much measure one's instinct has in one's character and what part 'free will' plays therein, the Qur'ān states, 'Nothing in the earth and in the heavens is hidden from Allah.' (*Āl 'Imrān* 3: 5)

[10] This difference may be illustrated by the example of the International Islamic University in Malaysia where students are required to attend complementary studies in the two faculties of the University: namely, the Faculty of Revealed Sciences and the Faculty of Human Sciences – Translator.

day-to-day affairs but with ourselves. It ponders over questions such as the following:

- Who are we?
- What is our status in the world in which we live?
- Who has created this world and us?
- What is our relationship with the Creator of this world and ourselves?
- What is the right way to conduct our lives?
- What are guidance and the straight path and how may we find these?
- What is the destination of our life' journies?

Of the two kinds of knowledge, this second category holds pride of place as the foundation. All our minor fields of study are branches of this knowledge. The loftiness or sordidness of all our thoughts and actions is contingent upon the correctness or otherwise of this knowledge. Thus, whatever system is designed for the intellectual training and cultural development of human beings has to be based upon that absolute or foundational knowledge. If that foundational knowledge is right, the training and development system will also be right. If there is a defect in the knowledge base then whatever training and development system is put in place (on the basis of that knowledge) will be defective and also break down.

Whatever beliefs about God, angels, heavenly books, prophets and the Last Day that have been presented in the Qur'ān relate to this 'Absolute Knowledge'. The reason that the demand for professing belief in these elements has been made with such force is that Islam's system of acculturation and training is based upon this knowledge. For Islam, only that system of harnessing and developing human volition which is established on the basis of a true 'Absolute Knowledge' is right. Systems that have been set up without such an 'Absolute Knowledge' base or those whose foundations have not been laid on correct knowledge are fundamentally flawed. Based upon these systems, human volitional forces have been misdirected on to numerous wrong paths. Howsoever right these efforts may appear, the fact remains that whatever human energies that have been or are being spent upon these wrong paths have been and continue to be erroneously utilized. Their direction is not towards the right destination. These efforts cannot reach the point of success. It is for this reason that these energies are destined to be wasted and that human beings shall derive no benefit from them. It is for this reason that Islam declares its path – and only its path – to be the 'Straight Path' and demands that all other avenues, which have been adopted either on account of the absence of the 'Knowledge' or due to wrong knowledge, be abandoned:

> This is My Way – that which is straight; follow it, then, and do not follow other paths lest they scatter you from His path.
>
> [al-Anʿām 6: 153]

> The work of he who refuses to follow the way of faith will go to waste, and he will be among the utter losers in the Hereafter.
>
> [al-Māʾidah 5: 5]

Quite obviously, only those belief elements that have been presented by Islam are considered by it to be expressly and exclusively the right knowledge, the very truth, the right guidance and the true light. And being so considered, it necessarily follows that all the belief elements that stand opposed to those presented by Islam are expressly considered as ignorance, falsehood, damnation and darkness. If Islam had not made the demand to abandon these false beliefs with the extreme intensity that it has and if it had given the followers of false beliefs a status equal to those professing the true *īmān*, it would have acknowledged that its belief elements are not the very truth, and that it itself does not have an absolute belief in their being truth, guidance, and light. In that case, its act of presenting these belief elements, constructing a whole system of training and development upon their foundation, and then inviting people to join its system would all have been meaningless. This is because, if it had accepted that certain other forms of knowledge that stood opposed to its self-declared 'Absolute

Knowledge' could also be true, or that there was no harm even in the absence of any such 'Absolute Knowledge', there would no longer have been any meaning in presenting that 'Absolute Knowledge' in the first place and then calling people to profess *īmān* on its basis.

Similarly, if it had accepted that human beings could achieve *falāḥ* (success, prosperity) on the basis of some other knowledge opposed to its own 'Absolute Knowledge', or without recourse to any absolute knowledge and the system of training and development based upon it, then there would also have been no weight in inviting people to submit to the Islamic system.

Moreover, if the foregoing discussion on the 'reality and Importance of Islam' is still fresh in your mind, then you will be able to appreciate why Islam lays such strong emphasis on *īmān*. Those who live in the world of abstract ideas are free to build their castles upon sand, water or even in thin air, but Islam is a religion full of wisdom. It cannot raise the ramparts of human training and civilizational development upon false foundations. Accordingly, before everything else, it creates strong foundations within the depths of human soul and its intellectual faculty – the heart and the head. It then constructs a building that simply cannot be demolished.

First of all, it prompts man to internalize the fact that ruling over him is a God who holds dominion in both this temporal world as well as the Hereafter. No one can escape His sovereignty. No aspect of our lives is hidden from Him. It is He who sent down a Prophet for human guidance and through that Prophet's agency, the Book[11] and *Sharīʿah* ('the Path') by submitting to which human beings may gain the pleasure of that True Sovereign. Conversely, if one acts against Him, no matter how well covered such transgression may be, He will surely apprehend the violator and not let him off without due punishment.

After deeply etching this impression upon human hearts, it then undertakes to impart education of a noble morality. It states the rules of establishing good and eradicating evil. It is with the help of the power that results from this deep consciousness of *īmān* that Islam

---

[11] The Qurʾān repeatedly refers to itself as 'the Book' – Translator.

goes on to see its education followed and its laws adhered to. The deeper that this consciousness is etched, the fuller is the adherence, the stronger the submission, and the more powerful the system of human training and civilizational development. On the contrary, if this impression is faint, or totally absent or even worse there are some other impressions that are etched upon the heart, then the process of moral education constitutes little else but merely a writing on water. The rules of establishing good and eradicating evil would then be without any enforceability or value. The whole system of training and development would be a sand castle built by children, whose existence is a fleeting phenomenon. It may very well be good looking, or have towering ramparts, but stability would not be the one thing it possesses. The Qur'ān illustrates this with an example:

> Do you not see how Allah has given the example of a good word? It is like a good tree, whose root is firmly fixed, and whose branches reach the sky, ever yielding its fruit in every season with the leave of its Lord. Allah gives examples for mankind that they may take heed. And the example of an evil word is that of an evil tree, uprooted from the surface of the earth, wholly unable to endure. Thus, through a firm word, Allah grants firmness to the believers both in this world and in the Hereafter. As for the wrong-doers, Allah lets them go astray. Allah does whatever He wills.
>
> [*Ibrāhīm* 14: 24-27]

So far, we have taken a broad overview of the five fundamental belief elements of Islam. Now it needs to be seen as to what detailed codes and tenets have been presented by Islam with regard to each of these five elements. We will consider what the need is for and the thought behind each of these. We will also seek to answer the following questions: "What is the impact of each belief element upon the human intellectual faculty?", and, "How a virtuous and extremely stable character grows after these elements are embedded in the mind?"

4 Belief (*Īmān*) in Allah

The Importance of Belief (*Īmān*) in Allah

The first and most fundamental feature in Islam's total belief and its practically applicable systems is belief in Allah. All Islam's other beliefs are merely subsidiary branches of this single foremost factor. Indeed, all the other ethical stipulations and civilizational laws contained within Islam draw their force from this centre. The origin of whatever exists is the Personage of Allah. A belief in angels exists because they are God's angels. A belief in heavenly books exists because God has revealed them. Belief in the Messengers is on account of their having been sent by God. Belief in the Last Day is because that will be God's Day of Justice. Duties exist because God has laid them down and rights are present because they are based on God's commandments. Acting upon the good and enjoining its establishment (*amr bi'l-maʿrūf*) and abstaining from the bad and persuading others to do so (*nahy ʿani'l-munkar*) is essential because all these commissions and omissions have been laid down by God. In fact, all that there is in Islam, be it belief or action, exists only on the basis of *īmān* in Allah. If one were to remove from view or ignore this one central fact, neither angels nor the Last Day would be of any consequence; the Messengers would no longer deserve a following nor would the books that they brought with them be of value; there would be no meaning in the scheme of rights and duties nor would the stipulated acts of commission and omission remain endowed with the authoritative force they enjoy. As soon as this centre is displaced, this whole system becomes chaotic and, indeed, Islam ceases to exist.

The Comprehensive Structure of Belief (*Īmān*) in Allah

This belief serves as the very pivot of a grand system of thought and action. Its central force is not only confined to the extent of the statement 'Allah exists' but contains within itself a complete and precise conception of Allah's attributes (to the extent that it is possible for any human being to embrace such a concept). From this comprehension of Allah's attributes, we are able to derive an understanding of the power that comes to completely dominate all human powers of thought and action.

The mere acceptance of the existence of God cannot be termed a distinctive feature of Islam. Other religious and national groups have also, in one way or another, accepted the existence of God. However, the one feature that distinguishes Islam from all other religions is this true and comprehensive knowledge about God's attributes and its subsequent deployment as the very basis of belief or *īmān*. No other religion has employed a fundamental belief in this way towards the grand pursuit of purification of the inner spirit, reformation of morals, organization of actions, proliferation of good and eradication of evil and the establishment of an upright culture.

The condensed form of belief in Allah constitutes the first part of the statement of the *Shahādah*, *lā ilāha illallāh* (There is no deity but Allah). The formal physical recitation of this statement followed by its conscious attestation by the 'heart' is the first and most essential condition of entry into Islam. This is an open declaration by the tongue and its subsequent confirmation by the intellect that there is and can be no deity except the one that is called Allah. In other words, this is the act of disassociating all that exists in the cosmos from any semblance of Divinity and declaring that all attributes of this status are restricted to this One Entity. Furthermore, it is an act of positively associating all those emotions, conceptions, beliefs, ritual prayers, and acts of submission related to Divinity with this Entity. We see that there are three constituent elements of this compact statement:

(i)   a concept of Divinity;
(ii) a disassociation of all things from that concept (of the one Supreme Being),
(iii) an exclusive affirmation of that concept for Allah.

Whatever has been stated in the Qur'ān with regard to the personage and attributes of Allah is essentially a detail of these three elements.

First, the Qur'ān has presented such a complete and correct concept of Divinity that we do not find this in any other book or religion of the world. Undoubtedly, this concept exists, in some form or other, in all the nations and communities of the world, but the fact is that in every instance it is either incorrect or incomplete. In some instances it merely signifies an entity that came first ['the First Principle'] – in a sort of a formal manner – while in others it means the 'Origin' of things. In still other references, it is the synonym of power and force, or merely something to be feared and dreaded. Some consider it to be the source of all love, while for others its means merely a resource for the fulfilment of desires. In some traditions this concept is analysable and subject to dissection, while in others it has been corrupted by corporeality, subjected to artistic depiction or anthropomorphic representation and even debased with reproductive attributes or paternal associations. Some consider the Divine to be resident in the skies while for others it has come down to earth in some human disguise.

The only book that has remedied and perfected all false and flawed concepts of Divinity is the Qur'ān. This book has sanctified and glorified the concept of Divinity. It states that a truly Divine entity can only be One that is free of all want and one which is eternal, One that has always been and shall always remain, One Who holds absolute authority, One Whose knowledge is supreme and surpasses that of all others, One Whose mercy is most widespread, Whose power dominates all, Whose wisdom knows no flaw, Whose justice does not even have a speck of inequity, One Who gives life and provides resources for its sustenance, One Who is the possessor of all positive and negative forces of benefit and loss, of Whose benevolence and guardianship all are necessitous, One unto Whom all creations return, One Who shall take an account of all, and One Who alone has the authority to reward or punish. These attributes of Divinity are neither subject to scrutiny nor dissection. Moreover, it is also impossible for there to be at any one time many deities endowed with these attributes or any parts thereof. These attributes are neither restricted in time or space in so far as that one deity possesses a certain attribute at one time and is devoid of it at some other, nor are these transferable that they are found in one deity today and in another tomorrow.

After presenting this comprehensive and correct conception of Divinity, the Qur'ān, with its extremely strong way of expression, goes on to prove that the complete definition of a deified entity (given above) does not belong to any of the numerous entities or forces in the cosmos. All things that exist are found wanting of external sustenance, have themselves been conquered, and are in the process of chaotic decay. Far from being capable of powers of providing profit or inflicting loss, these are incapable of even removing any injury from their own bodies. The sources of their own actions and their consequences do not lie within their own selves. Instead they derive their wherewithal of existence, power of action, and authority for determining any outcome from elsewhere. Thus, there is nothing in the cosmos which even carries the least notion of any Divinity and that deserves any part of our devotion.

After this denunciation, the Qur'ān establishes exclusive deification for that One Entity Who is named Allah and demands of human beings that they profess exclusive belief or *īmān* in Him, bow before Him, revere Him, love Him, fear Him, expect from Him, entreat and request only Him, put all trust in Him at all times and in all states, and always bear in mind that unto Him all have to return to give an account to Him, and that all good or bad consequences depend upon His decisions.

The Moral Advantages of Belief (*Īmān*) in Allah

The belief in Allah that implants itself deeply into man's heart – together with this detailed concept of Divine attributes – carries within itself such extraordinary benefits that cannot be had from any other belief.

1. *Breadth of Vision*

The first feature of belief or *īmān* in Allah is that it broadens the scope and horizons of human perception to match the extensiveness of Allah's unlimited Kingdom. As long as human beings continue to view the world through the lens of their own existence, their vision will remain constrained in a narrow circle wherein their concept of their own nature, knowledge and desires are limited. Within this confined sphere, individuals and groups will continue to look for providers of their needs, fear those who are more powerful than themselves and be pressurized by them, and boast their authority over those who are weaker than themselves. Within this circle all their friendships and enmities, loves and hates, venerations and vilifications remain confined, because for all of these they have no standard but their own basal selves.

However, after professing belief in the One God, human vision breaks away from its immediate environment and transcends to spread far and wide over the entire cosmos. Now it views the cosmos not with reference to its possessors' own selves but by way of the possessors' relationship with God. Now, possessed of this new breadth of vision, human beings are able to establish an altogether different relationship with every entity in this extensive milieu. They no longer see anyone or anything capable of fulfilling their wants, no possessor of force, nor any dispenser of benefit or loss. They no longer consider anyone worth adulation or denigration, nor capable of generating fear or hope. Now their friendships or enmities, loves or hates, are no longer for their individual selves but only for God. They see that the God in which they profess belief, individually and collectively, does not belong to one person nor is He the Creator and Sustainer of just his family or his nation, but He is rather the Creator of all the worlds and heavens and the Sustainer of all the universes. They are able to see that the realm of this deity is not just restricted to their own country but rather that this Deity is the Owner of the firmament and the heaven and the Sustainer of the East and the West; they now see that they are not alone in worshipping that God but that all things on the earth and in the skies and heavens above are bent forward in supplication to Him:

All that is in the heavens and the earth is in submission to Him – willingly or unwillingly

[Āl ʿImrān 3: 83]

The seven heavens, the earth, and all that is within them give glory to Him.

[*Banī Isrā'īl* 17: 44]

When the cosmos is seen in this manner, it no longer appears to be alien or something that is not a part of us; everything appears our 'own'. Now, our compassion, love, and the desire to serve are no longer subject to any orbit bounded by the reference points of our existence.

Thus those who believe in Allah can never be narrow-minded. For the breadth of their vision, even words like cosmopolitan or global are limiting; it can only be called universalistic or cosmic.

2. *Self-respect*
This belief in Allah raises human beings from a lowly and disgraceful position to one of the highest stature with regard to self-respect. Until that point in time when they had not 'seen' and become aware of God, they bowed in supplication before everything in the world that appeared powerful, magnificent or respectful or seemed capable of causing gain or loss – and were fearful about its powers. Holding out their hands before these objects, they associated expectations with it. But then, upon becoming cognizant of God, they realized that all those before whom they had previously pleaded were themselves dependent and needy:

Those whom they call upon are themselves seeking the means of access to their Lord.

[*Banī Isrā'īl* 17: 57]

The one's before whom they had previously supplicated were only created beings like themselves:

Those whom you invoke other than Allah are creatures like you.

[*al-A'rāf* 7: 194]

Those whom you invoke other than Allah, they can neither help themselves nor you.

[al-Aʿrāf 7: 197]

That all power belongs to Allah alone.

[al-Baqarah 2: 165]

Judgement lies with Allah alone.

[al-Anʿām 6: 57]

And that none apart from Allah is your protector or helper?

[al-Baqarah 2: 107]

Help can only come from Allah, the All-Mighty, the All-Wise.

[Āl ʿImrān 3: 126]

Surely Allah is the Bestower of all provision, the Lord of all Power, the Strong.

[al-Dhāriyāt 51: 58]

His are the keys of the heavens and the earth.

[al-Shūrā 42: 12]

It is not given to any soul to die except with the leave of Allah.

[Āl ʿImrān 3: 145]

For in truth it is Allah alone who grants life and deals death.

[Āl ʿImrān 3: 156]

If Allah afflicts you with any hardship, none other than He can remove it; and if He wills any good for you, none can avert His Bounty.

[Yūnus 10: 107]

After having acquired this knowledge, human beings become free of fear and free of the need to adhere to worldly forces. Their heads refuse to bow before anyone but God and their hands decline to spread open before anyone but God. In their hearts there is reverence for none other than God. Apart from God, they associate no hopes and expectations with anyone.

3. *Humility and Fear of God*
This humility is not that false modesty that results from an appreciation of outward power, wealth or high merit. This self-respect is not that sense of worth that arises in a malevolent person as a consequence of pride and arrogance. Instead, this is the outcome of having understood one's relationship with God and all other temporal entities in the most appropriate way. Accordingly, people who believe in God combine self-respect with humility and self-esteem with submissiveness in a close-knit relationship. The believer knows that he is totally helpless before God. As the Qur'ān states:

And He alone holds sway over His servants.
[*al-An'ām* 6: 61]

O company of *jinn* and men, if you have the power to go beyond the bounds of the heavens and the earth, go beyond them! Yet you will be unable to go beyond them for that requires infinite power.
[*al-Raḥmān* 55: 33]

For Allah is All-Sufficient, whereas it is you who are in need of Him.
[*Muḥammad* 47: 38]

All that is in the heavens and the earth belongs to Allah.
[*al-Baqarah* 2: 284]

Every bounty that you enjoy is from Allah.
[*al-Naḥl* 16: 53]

The true servants of the Merciful One are those who walk
on the earth gently and when the foolish ones address
them, they simply say: 'Peace to you.'

[al-Furqān 25: 63]

4. The Elimination of False Expectations

One of the benefits of a proper understanding of the relationship
between the Creator and the created is the end of all erroneous
expectations and false dependencies that result from an absence of
true discernment. While many clearly understand that there is no way
towards salvation and deliverance other than through correct belief
and good actions, there are some who are without this knowledge and
believe that there are many mini-gods associated with God's work:

They worship, beside Allah, those who can neither harm
nor profit them, saying: 'These are our intercessors with
Allah.'

[Yūnus 10: 18]

Others believe that God has a son and that the son had assured
salvation for all by his Atonement:

The Jews and the Christians say: 'We are Allah's children
and His beloved ones.'

[al-Mā'idah 5: 18]

Beliefs like the one that can be summarized as 'Whatever we do,
we shall not be punished' – and similar other false hopes – always
keep people in the clutches of sin. On account of such erroneous
expectations they become oblivious to the need for purification of
their selves and improvement of their actions. But there is no chance
of any wrong expectations in the belief in God that the Qur'ān teaches.
For, it states that no nation has any special relationship with God:

You are the same as other human being He has created.

[al-Mā'idah 5: 18]

Verily the noblest of you in the sight of Allah is the most
God-fearing of you.

[*al-Ḥujurāt* 49: 13]

And say: 'All praise be to Allah Who has neither taken to
Himself a son, nor has He any partner in His kingdom, nor
does He need anyone, out of weakness, to protect Him.'

[*Banī Isrā'īl* 17: 111]

Nay, whatever is in the heavens and the earth belongs to
Him; to Him are all in obeisance.

[*al-Baqarah* 2: 116]

Who is there who might intercede with Him save with His
leave?

[*al-Baqarah* 2: 255]

And when Allah decides to make a people suffer punishment,
no one can avert it. Nor can any be of help to such a people
against Allah.

[*al-Ra'd* 13: 11]

5. Optimism and Peace of Mind

Together with the above advantages, belief in Allah creates an
optimism in human beings that is not overcome with dejection and
despair, no matter what the condition. For the believer, *īmān* is an
everlasting storehouse of hope from which he continues to receive
an unbroken supply of heart-rejuvenating energy and soul-enriching
satisfaction. Even when the individual has been turned away from all
worldly portals, has had all material and causal links severed, has seen
the parting of all means and resources, the one strongest support –
Divine support – never abandons him. It is on that basis that the
believer is always brimming with abundant hope. This is because the
God in which he has reposed his belief states:

(O Muḥammad), when My servants ask you about Me, tell them I am quite near; I hear and answer the call of the caller whenever he calls Me.

[*al-Baqarah* 2: 186]

'That is in recompense for your own deeds.' Allah does no wrong to His servants.

[*Āl ʿImrān* 3: 182]

As for My Mercy, it encompasses everything.

[*al-Aʿrāf* 7: 156]

My sons! Go and try to find out about Joseph and his brother and do not despair of Allah's mercy. Verily only the unbelievers despair of Allah's mercy.

[*Yūsuf* 12: 87]

He who does either evil or wrongs himself, and then asks for Allah's forgiveness, will find Allah All-Forgiving, All-Compassionate.

[*al-Nisāʾ* 4: 110]

Tell them, (O Prophet): 'My servants who have committed excesses against themselves, do not despair of Allah's Mercy. Surely Allah forgives all sins. He is Most Forgiving, Most Merciful.'

[*al-Zumar* 39: 53]

Those who say 'Allah is our Lord' and then remain steadfast, upon them descend angels (and say): 'Do not fear nor grieve, and receive good tidings of Paradise which you were promised.'

[*Fuṣṣilat* 41: 30]

Surely in Allah's remembrance do hearts find rest.

[*al-Raʿd* 13: 28]

6. Ṣabr *(Fortitude) and Trust in God*

This optimism then progresses to reach the higher planes of persever-
ance and fortitude (*ṣabr*), steadfastness and trust in Allah. Once there,
the believer's heart becomes as strong and solid as an indestructible
rock. All the difficulties, enmities, pains, wrongs, and counter forces
combined cannot budge the believer from a principled position. This
power cannot be had from any source or through any means except
by way of belief in Allah. This is because, they who do not believe in
Allah place their trust in those material resources or mythical causes
which are devoid of any intrinsic power. Living on the supposed support of these props is like holding on to the strands of a spider's web.
Thus, God says:

> The case of those who took others than Allah as their pro-
> tectors is that of a spider who builds a house; but the frailest
> of all houses is the spider's house; if they only knew.
>
> [*al-ʿAnkabūt* 29: 41]

> Powerless is the supplicant; and powerless is he to whom
> he supplicates.
>
> [*al-Ḥajj* 22: 73]

> Hence he who rejects the evil ones and believes in Allah has
> indeed taken hold of the firm, unbreakable handle.
>
> [*al-Baqarah* 2: 256]

> If Allah helps you, none shall prevail over you.
>
> [*Āl ʿImrān* 3: 160]

> Say: 'All is from Allah.'
>
> [*al-Nisāʾ* 4: 78]

> Say: 'Nothing will befall us except what Allah has decreed
> for us; He is our Protector.' Let the believers, then, put all
> their trust in Allah.
>
> [*al-Tawbah* 9: 51]

The manner in which the Prophets of Allah battled with Divinely-gifted powers and against the most terrible odds, faced immense tribulations, single-handedly took on powerful nations and the greatest of empires, stood up with a zeal to triumph over the world without any temporal means, and did not waver from their mission in spite of raging storms of opposition was only possible because of the power of fortitude (*ṣabr*) and an unflinching trust in God. One only needs to look at the Prophet Ibrāhīm: he took on the most despotic ruler of his times in a debate and fearlessly jumped into a fire with which he was being tried. And finally, he left his homeland without any material possessions by proclaiming:

'Lo, I am going to my Lord; He will guide me.'

[*al-Ṣāffāt* 37: 99]

The Prophet Hūd challenges the overwhelming force of the ʿĀd:

So conspire against me, all of you, and give me no respite. I have put my trust in Allah, Who is my Lord and your Lord. There is no moving creature but that He holds it by its forelock. Surely, My Lord is on the Straight Path.

[*Hūd* 11: 55-56]

The Prophet Moses battled the immense forces of the Pharaoh, armed only with his trust in God. When Pharaoh threatened him with death, he answered, 'I have obtained the protection of Him Who is my Sustainer as well as yours, in the fight against haughty individuals.'

Moses said: 'I have taken refuge with my Lord and your Lord from everyone who waxes arrogant and does not believe in the Day of Reckoning.'

[*al-Muʾmin* 40: 27]

Upon Moses's departure from Egypt, Pharaoh pursued his people with all his might. Overcome by anxiety, his cowardly nation said, the enemy has overtaken us: 'We are indeed caught' [*al-Shuʿarāʾ*

115

26: 61]; but with the most peaceful of composure Moses said, 'Certainly not, God is with me and he would lead me on the path of safety' [al-Shuʿarāʾ 26: 62].

And finally, look at the example of the Prophet Muḥammad (peace and blessings be upon him). On the occasion of the *hijrah* (the migration from Makkah to Madīnah), he was camped inside a cave. With him there was just one Companion. Bloodthirsty infidels arrived at the very opening of the cave, but even then he was not the least bit perturbed and said to his Companion:

'Do not grieve. Allah is with us.'

[al-Tawbah 9: 40]

How else can this invincible power, this iron-willed determination and rock-hard steadfastness be obtained, but from belief in Allah?

7. *Bravery*
Another similar attribute that is generated in extraordinary measure through belief in Allah is courage and boldness. There are two things that make human beings cowardly: one is the love that individuals have for their own lives, family and relatives, and material possessions. The other is fear which itself is the outcome of a false belief that the power to harm and kill somehow intrinsically exists in those objects that are merely used as agents of destruction. Belief in Allah expunges both these elements from believers' hearts. In its place, believers' minds and bodies are infused with the belief that Allah has the greatest right to be loved:

But those who (truly) believe, they love Allah more than all else.

[al-Baqarah 2: 165]

Once a person has clearly understood that material possessions and loved ones are merely temporal ornaments whose loss is a certainty, at one point in time or another, the realization that a permanent everlasting good can and shall only be granted by God is not far away:

Wealth and children are an adornment of the life of the world. But the deeds of lasting righteousness are the best in the sight of your Lord in reward, and far better a source of hope.

[al-Kahf 18: 46]

This temporal life is fleeting and will soon come to an end, no matter what efforts we undertake to preserve it; death will certainly overtake us, one day:

Tell them: The death from which you flee will certainly overtake you.

[al-Jumu'ah 62: 8]

Wherever you might be, death will overtake you even though you be in massive towers.

[al-Nisā' 4: 78]

Then why should we not sacrifice this life for an eternal life of happiness that will only be had upon return to Allah?

Think not of those slain in the Way of Allah as dead. Indeed they are living, and with their Lord they have their sustenance, rejoicing in what Allah has bestowed upon them out of His bounty.

[Āl 'Imrān 3: 169-70]

Why should we not sacrifice some fleeting pleasures and temporary benefits for gaining the pleasure of Allah Who is the real owner of our lives and our possessions, and the One Who is going to provide us with a better life and permanent benefits?

Surely Allah has purchased of the believers their lives and their belongings and in return has promised that they shall have Paradise. They fight in the Way of Allah, and slay and are slain.

[al-Tawbah 9: 111]

As for fear, the believer has been instructed that the real power to harm, hurt or kill does not reside with a human being or an animal, some (figures of) wood or stone, and swords or canons, but rather that the same only exists with God.

Even if all the forces of the world were to come together to cause harm to someone, the individual would not so much as even lose a hair if God did not so command it:

> They could not cause harm to anyone except by the leave of Allah.
>
> [al-Baqarah 2: 102]

> It is not given to any soul to die except with the leave of Allah, and at an appointed time.
>
> [Āl 'Imrān 3: 145]

> Say: 'Even if you had been in your houses, those for whom slaying had been appointed would have gone forth to the places where they were to be slain.'
>
> [Āl 'Imrān 3: 154]

> It was Satan who urged you to have fear of his allies. But do not fear them; fear Me, if you truly believe.
>
> [Āl 'Imrān 3: 175]

> Although Allah has greater right that you fear Him.
>
> [al-Aḥzāb 33: 37]

> But when fighting was enjoined upon them some of them feared men as one should fear Allah, or even more.
>
> [al-Nisā' 4: 77]

The true Muslims are those who if confront the superior strength of their enemies instead of becoming fearful become more courageous. This is because they exclusively rely on Allah and do not rely on worldly powers.

When people said to them: 'Behold, a host has gathered around you and you should fear them,' it only increased their faith and they answered: 'Allah is Sufficient for us; and what an excellent Guardian He is!'

[Āl 'Imrān 3: 173]

8. *Contentment*

This belief in Allah removes from the human heart all traces of greed and lust, envy and jealousy which otherwise constantly spur an individual to adopt various immoral and illegal means for seeking gain and which lead to conflict and discord in humanity. *Īmān*, on the other hand, leads to contentment and the believer no longer competes with others in materialistic terms. The believer does not struggle in the vales of injustice and animosity, but always seeks the blessings of his Sustainer in honourable ways. The believing man or woman is contented with whatever, little or great, that comes his way, and considers this to be God's bounty. The believer has been taught that social prioritization – the process whereby individuals and groups are placed above and below each other – lies firmly in Allah's jurisdiction. He grants whatever to whom He Wills:

Say: 'Surely bounty is in the Hand of Allah; He gives it to whom He wills. Allah is All-Embracing, All-Knowing. He singles out for His Mercy whomever He wills.'

[Āl 'Imrān 3: 73-74]

The bestowal of means of sustenance is in God's hands and He bestows whatever portion to whomsoever He desires:

Allah grants the provision of whomsoever He wills abundantly and grants others in strict measure.

[al-Ra'd 13: 26]

The dominion too is in Allah's hands and He grants kingdoms and positions of governance to whomsoever He deems fit:

The earth is Allah's, He bestows it on those of His servants
He chooses.

[al-Aʿrāf 7: 128]

All material wealth and means of social status are the prerogative
of Allah; He allows power to whom He desires and debases whom He
wills:

Say: 'O Allah, Lord of all dominion! You bestow dominion
on whomever You please, and take away dominion from
whomever You please, and You exalt whom You please, and
abase whom You please. In Your Hand is all good. Surely
You are All-Powerful.'

[Āl ʿImrān 3: 26]

This temporal system which is based upon various measures of
esteem and wealth, power and prominence, beauty and merit, is
one in which some are at heightened levels and others at lower ones.
This system has been established by God Who Himself best knows
His Own plans. Any attempt to change the Divine scheme is neither
appropriate for human beings to undertake, nor is success possible in
such an effort:

Allah has favoured some of you with more worldly provi-
sions than others.

[al-Naḥl 16: 71]

Do not covet what Allah has conferred more abundantly
on some of you than others.

[al-Nisāʾ 4: 32]

9. *The Improvement of Morals and Organizing Behaviour*
The greatest benefit that accrues to a culture by way of belief in
Allah is the birth of a sense of responsibility both in individuals and
larger human groupings. Souls are purified and moderation becomes
ingrained in actions. Mutual interactions are put on the right track. An

attitude of lawfulness and desire to abide by the law develops. A spirit of submission to (lawful) command, tolerance and orderliness takes hold. Spurred on by a tremendous internal force, individuals reform themselves from within to gear up for making a righteous and well-organized society. In fact, this is a miracle that emanates from belief in Allah, and is exclusively reserved for it. No other controlling force in the world nor a programme of instruction, training or sermonizing can accomplish such a widespread and deep-rooted moral reform or behavioural organization. Temporal forces do not have access to the soul, and even their power over the body is tenuous, not being assured at all times and in all locales. The influence of instruction, training and sermonizing is also limited to the intellect and formal thought, and that too to a certain extent. As for the basal instincts of the carnal soul (*al-nafs al-ammārah*), these not only remain uninfluenced, but on the contrary also make every effort to dominate the intellect.

However, *īmān* is the one factor that makes is way deep into hearts and souls, taking along its reforming and organizing forces, and having reached there, it arouses and sustains, at all times and all places, a powerful conscience that continues to guide human beings on the Straight Path of God-consciousness (*taqwā*) and submission. Even with the most mischievous and wayward of souls, *īmān* does not depart without leaving behind some impact of its disapproval and warning.

This immense advantage is only obtained through that faith in God's knowledge and will that is an essential ingredient of *īmān*. At numerous places in the Qur'ān, man is cautioned about the fact that God's knowledge dominates over everything else and that nothing remains hidden from Him:

> The East and the West belong to Allah. To whichever direction you turn, you will be turning to Allah. Allah is All-Embracing, All-Knowing.
>
> [*al-Baqarah* 2: 115]

> Allah will bring you all together wherever you might be, for nothing is beyond His power.
>
> [*al-Baqarah* 2: 148]

Nothing in the earth and in the heavens is hidden from Allah.

[*Āl 'Imrān* 3: 5]

He has the keys to the realm of the Unseen which none knows but He. And He knows what is on the land and in the sea; there is not a leaf which falls that He does not know about and there is not a grain in the darkness of the earth or anything green or dry which has not been recorded in a Clear Book.

[*al-An'ām* 6: 59]

Surely We have created man, and We know the promptings of his heart, and We are nearer to him than even his jugular vein.

[*Qāf* 50:16]

Never is there any whispering among three but He is their fourth; nor among five but He is their sixth; nor fewer nor more but He is with them wherever they may be.

[*al-Mujādalah* 58: 7]

They can hide (their deeds) from humans, but they cannot hide (them) from Allah for He is with them even when they hold nightly counsels that are unpleasing to Allah. Allah encompasses all their doings.

[*al-Nisā'* 4: 108]

Are they unaware that Allah knows all that they hide and all that they disclose?

[*al-Baqarah* 2: 77]

Moreover, there are two scribes, one each sitting on the right and the left, recording everything. He utters not a word, but there is a vigilant watcher at hand.

[*Qāf* 50: 17-18]

It is all the same for Him whether any of you says a thing secretly, or says it loudly, and whether one hides oneself in the darkness of night, or struts about in broad daylight. There are guardians over everyone, both before him and behind him, who guard him by Allah's command.

[*al-Ra'd* 13: 10-11]

In addition human beings have been very clearly communicated to bear in mind that surely they have to appear before God one day:

Know well that one Day you shall face Him.

[*al-Baqarah* 2: 223]

Know well that to Him you all shall be mustered.

[*al-Baqarah* 2: 203]

Surely Allah takes good count of everything.

[*al-Nisā'* 4: 86]

Stern indeed is your Lord's punishment.

[*al-Burūj* 85: 12]

This belief in God, which has been made to reach and then settle into the hearts of people in countless ways, is indeed the one authoritative force that stands behind the whole law of Islam and makes its implementation possible. The enforcement of whatever bounds of the permissible and the forbidden that Islam has established and all the various rules that it has decreed with regard to moral behaviour, civic life and human transaction is neither dependent upon armed force nor on tutoring and sermonizing. Instead, such legal enforcement derives its force of implementation from the belief that the Promulgator of these legal bounds is that Plenipotentiary Ruler Whose sovereignty and knowledge dominates over all and sundry.

The offender who breaks God's decrees neither has the power to hide his crime, nor to escape accountability for it. Thus, after stipulating the various laws, the Qur'ān, time and time again, gives the warning:

> These are the bounds of Allah (established by Him); do not cross them.
>
> [*al-Baqarah* 2: 229]

> Know fully well, whatever you do, God is watching.
>
> [*al-Baqarah* 2: 233]

5 Belief (*Īmān*) in the Angels

The Purpose of Belief in Angels

Muslims' belief in the angels is actually a continuation of and an essential appendix to their belief in Allah. Its purpose is not just to affirm the existence of the angels, but rather to understand their correct position in the system of existence so that belief in Allah is established on *tawḥīd* (absolute monotheism) and that worship of Allah is totally cleansed of any *shirk* (polytheism) and doubt.

As has been indicated earlier, a general concept of angels has existed in all religions and all human communities in one form or another. Based upon this general concept, various religions have developed different belief structures. For some, angels are forces of nature that operate the various functional operations of the cosmos. For others, they are deities, each one of whom is the head of a branch of the cosmic organization, for instance one is responsible for the control and operation of winds, another for rains, one for controlling light and another incharge of heat and fire. In the belief of still others they are beings who serve as God's assistants and helpers. Some consider them to be the lords of various types of creations, while in the opinion of others they are the corpus of intellect. In the opinion of some, angels are a manifestations of the highest intellect Divine conceptual construct, while some even consider them to be God's children. Then there are those who have accepted them as having a material and corporeal existence while others count them amongst the intangible and the abstract. Some have united them in existence with the planets and the stars while others have come up with similarly strange concepts about them. On the whole, the belief that the angels are in some way co-sharers of God's Divinity has been quite prevalent amongst both leaders and followers of various faiths. Accordingly, they have been represented as idols, temples have been raised for them, their images have been worshipped, supplications have been made to them, they have been considered providers of human needs, redressers of grievances, and intercessors. In this way, much *shirk* (polytheism) has been created and continues to exist in the world.

The Reality of Angels in this System of Existence

The Qur'ān has, on the one hand, established a comprehensive paradigm of *tawḥīd* (monotheism), complete with God's existence, attributes and actions, and on the other hand it has presented a correct concept of the angels, so as to permanently close the door through which *shirk* (polytheism) enters. It does not hold any discussion on the nature of angels because such a discussion is superfluous and has no meaning in itself. Neither is there any advantage for human beings in such a deliberation nor would they in any case have the capacity to understand it. Instead, the real issue that required elucidation was with regard to the true status of angels in the scheme of existence. This the Qur'ān has clearly expounded. It states that the angels are not God's offspring, nor His helpers or associates but only His creations and workers yoked to His service:

> They say: 'The Most Compassionate Lord has taken to Himself a son.' Glory be to Him! Those whom they so designate are only His honoured servants. They do not outstrip Him in speech and only act as He commands. He knows whatever is before them and whatsoever is remote from them and they do not intercede except for him, intercession on whose behalf pleases Him, and they stand constantly in awe of Him. [*al-Anbiyā'* 21: 26-28]

According to the Qur'ān, the angels' status is only that of agents who carry out specific orders (*mudabbirāt al-amr*) with regard to affairs that have been entrusted to them by Allah. Let alone any association in Divinity, they do not dare exceed their orders by the least degree. Their assignment is to merely worship and submit. Not even for a moment do they neglect their duty. At all times, they are busy in extolling the perfection of their Creator and paying respect to their Sustainer:

The thunder celebrates His praise and holiness, and the
angels, too, celebrate His praise for awe of Him?

[al-Raʿd 13: 13]

All living creatures and all angels in the heavens and on the
earth are in prostration before Allah; and never do they
behave in arrogant defiance. They hold their Lord, Who is
above them, in fear, and do as they are bidden.

[al-Naḥl 16: 49-50]

To Him belongs whosoever dwells in the heavens and on
earth. Those (angels) that are with Him neither disdain
to serve Him out of pride, nor do they weary of it. They
glorify Him night and day, without flagging.

[al-Anbiyāʾ 21: 19-20]

A Fire held in the charge of fierce and stern angels who
never disobey what He has commanded them, and always
do what they are bidden.

[al-Taḥrīm 66: 6]

This concept, presented by the Qurʾān, leaves no possibility for
shirk. The reason for this is that all those things in which there could
have been the least doubt of Divinity have been proved to be creations
themselves. After this, who else but Allah could be the recipient of
our prayers, submissions, our pleas for help, our confidence and our
trust?

The Additional Status of Human Beings and Angels

This is not all! Beyond this, the Qurʾān also stipulates the additional
status of human beings and angels so that humans can clearly
understand their own place in the Divine scheme vis-à-vis the angels.
Wherever in the Qurʾān, the creation of Adam is mentioned, this issue
is also clarified: When Allah bestowed the status of vicegerency upon
Adam, He ordered the angels to bow in submission to the father of
man. Except for *Iblīs* (the Satan) all the angels complied with this

order in *Sūrahs al-Baqarah* [2: 34]; *al-Aʿrāf* [7: 11]; *Banī Isrāʾīl* [17: 61]; *al-Kahf* [18: 50]; *Ṭā Hā* [20: 16] and *Ṣād* [38: 72].

When the angels laid claim to their superiority on the basis of their virtues of constantly extolling their praises of the Lord and paying their homage to Him, God disallowed this by way of a test in which it was proved that Adam had been granted greater knowledge. When *Iblīs* (the Satan), basing his claim of superiority on the substance of his creation (fire as opposed to clay), refused to accept the pre-eminence of Adam and to bow in submission before him, he was forever banished as a renegade. This status, on the one hand, develops in man a sense of self-respect, and, on the other hand, concentrates all devotional sentiments and fidelity that a strong adherent naturally offers onto a central core of Divine commitment. From these Qurʾānic references we see that, with the sole exception of God, there is nothing superior to man in the whole realm of existence. Although the angels are, in Qurʾānic terminology, 'the respected devotees', and are above all other things in existence, they too have bowed in submission to man. Who else but God can be man's Deity, his Helper, the Provider Who answers his desires and the object of submission to Whom he bows in respect? In this way, when belief in the angels is established on the basis of correct knowledge, it purifies belief in Allah and makes it wholesome.

The Second Purpose of Belief in Angels

The second role of the angels that has been described in the Qurʾān is that God sends His communications and commandments to His Messengers through them. It is through the agency of the angels that God ensures that His message reaches the Prophets free from any and every admixing, doubt and external interference. In the first instance, these angels are themselves beings who are good-natured and obedient, God fearing and submitting to His commands without the least disagreement, free from any evil inclination and personal vested interest. Accordingly, they do not add to or subtract from any message sent through them, and, in fact, they cannot do so. Secondly, they are so powerful that no Satanic force is able to cause the least interference in their tasks of guarding and relaying messages. This theme is stated at many places in the Qurʾān:

It is contained in scrolls highly honoured, most exalted and purified, borne by the hands of scribes, noble and purified.

[ʿAbasa 80: 13-16]

Verily this is the word of a noble message-bearer; one mighty and held in honour with the Lord of the Throne; there he is obeyed and held trustworthy.

[al-Takwīr 81: 19-21]

Other than to a Messenger whom He chooses (for the bestowal of any part of the knowledge of the Unseen), where after He appoints guards who go before him and behind him, so that He may know that they have delivered the messages of their Lord. He encompasses in His knowledge their surroundings and keeps a count of all things."

[al-Jinn 72: 27-28]

Tell them: 'It is the spirit of holiness that has brought it down, by stages, from your Lord so that it might bring firmness to those who believe.'

[al-Naḥl 16: 102]

Indeed this is a revelation from the Lord of the Universe; which the truthful spirit has carried down.

[al-Shuʿarāʾ 26: 192-3]

That this indeed is a noble Qurʾān, inscribed in a well-guarded Book, which none but the pure may touch; a revelation from the Lord of the Universe.

[al-Wāqiʿah 56: 77-80]

From this we see that belief in the angels is important not only with respect to belief in Allah but also for the various other components of the Islamic belief system i.e. belief in the Divine Books and belief in the prophets. Professing belief in the angels means that we are expressing confidence in the means of communication through which the message of God reaches His messengers. Our belief in the message and the prophets who present that message cannot be complete until we are fully convinced about the infallibility of the medium that works to provide the link between God and His prophets.

The Third Purpose of Belief in Angels

Apart from the above, a third role of the angels also finds mention in the Qur'ān: whereby the angels are the functionaries of God's kingdom. The workers through whom God ensures the complete organizational operation of the cosmos are the angels. In other words, the role of the angels in God's kingdom is akin to members of the state services (civil and military) in temporal states. It is through them that God unleashes His wrath upon some and showers His blessings upon others, seize the souls (i.e. causes people to die) and gives life to others, causes rain to come down at places and ensures a drought at others. The angels are busy in making a complete record of the actions, words and even thoughts of every human being. Indeed, they have their eyes on our every movement.

As long as human beings continue to function within the confines of time and space granted them by God, these workers continue to cooperate with him – governed under God's commands as they are – and enable him to accomplish their tasks, in spite of being aware of all their good and bad aspects. However, as soon as this window of opportunity closes, these same workers seize and detain those individuals who until a moment ago were busy carrying out the tasks of God's Vicegerency. The same air on the basis of which they were alive a minute ago, now rages in to destroy their settlements, the same water over which they were riding proudly now becomes their grave, the earth on which they lived as peacefully as if in a mother's lap, makes them a part of itself by a momentary tremor. All it requires is one command, subsequent to which the Vicegerent's closest aides place him in custody. At numerous places, this scenario is sketched in great detail in the Qur'ān.

Thus, belief in the angels is an essential constituent of the Muslims' belief in Allah. This means that together with the 'Ruler of the Cosmos' human beings also acknowledge the presence of His workers and agents. Without this belief, they can neither understand their own position in the scheme of Divine order. Nor can they carry out their stipulated tasks after having been so equipped with a full knowledge of that understanding.

6 Belief (*Īmān*) in the Messengers and Prophets[1]

The Reality of Prophethood

After *tawḥīd*, the second fundamental creed of Islam is *risālah* or prophethood. Just as *tawḥīd* points towards the true way in faith, prophethood is the true pointer in the direction of submission. The literal meaning of the Arabic term *risālah* is the act of carrying a message – or messengership. Thus, any person who carries the message of one person to another is a 'messenger' in literal terms. However, in Islamic terminology a *rasūl* or messenger is a person who, by God's command, takes God's message to His followers and guides them onto the right path. It is for this reason that the Qur'ān has also used the term *hādī* (a guide or instructor) for a prophet by way of referring to a person who guides people on the true course.

---

[1] The English translation of *risālah* and *rasūl* are rather problematic. The close equivalents are messenger, prophet and apostle, all of which are used variously by authors and translators for God's human messengers who came to guide humanity. Although in wide use for Prophet Muḥammad the term 'apostle' appeared to be a strictly Christian term for the original companions of Christ or a Christian ambassador to a country in all the dictionaries consulted. Many translations translate *rasūl* (from the Arabic root *ra-sa-la*, 'to convey, send or communicate' as the 'messenger' – and quite correctly so in my opinion. However the use of 'messengerhood' is neither found in any dictionary nor seems to click as being good coinage. While the term 'prophet' is commonly used for God's spiritual guides and representatives and the term 'prophethood' is also standard usage, the terms do not explicitly give a sense of a 'messenger' (but tend more towards conveying the sense of one who gives a prophecy). However, most dictionaries do include the meaning of conveyance of a message under the entry for 'prophet'. Therefore I have chosen this term for the various Urdu usages of *paighambar*, *rasūl*, and *piyambar* – Translator.

God has appointed a 'guide' within man's own soul.[2] Through Divinely-mediated intuition, this 'guide' shows human beings the straight path of thought and action by distinguishing for them the good thoughts from the bad and right actions from the wrong.

And by the soul and by Him Who perfectly proportioned it, and imbued it with (the consciousness of) its evil and its piety: he who purifies it will prosper. and he who suppresses it will be ruined.

[*al-Shams* 91: 7-10]

However, because the 'guidance' of this internal 'guide' is not very obvious, and also because many internal intellectual as well as external forces are operating with a view to drawing human beings towards bad deeds, therefore the guidance of this instinctive guide alone is not sufficient for enabling them to ascertain the straight path of truth from the numerous crooked pathways. Accordingly, God has supplemented this gap through external mediation by sending His messengers so that they are able to assist the hidden internal 'guide' by way of strengthening it with the light of knowledge and cognitive skills. It is this light and cognition that provide clarity to the vague, natural inspirations of the 'internal guide' through the clear verses (of the Qur'ān). This mediation is essentially required because the internal light of goodness often grows dim in the midst of ignorance and the hordes of misguiding forces.

This high stature of guiding humanity is the foundation of prophethood. People conferred with this status of eminence also have had extraordinary knowledge and vision bestowed upon them by God. It was through these faculties that they came to learn the truth about issues on which ordinary people were in disagreement; their search for truth was not on the basis of conjecture or approximation but

---

[2] Obviously this 'guide' is not a physical entity and the closest physical concept to which it may be compared is an internal gyroscope; in Freudian terminology this is the super-ego – Translator.

Divinely inspired knowledge of certainty. It was with this vision that they were able to clearly distinguish the straight path of truth from all the many crooked ways.

The Difference Between Prophets and Ordinary Leaders

The need for an external guide has been accepted by man in all ages and locales. Never has it been claimed that man's internal 'guide' – his intrinsic or instinctive sense of right and wrong – is alone sufficient for his guidance. Throughout history, eminent ancestors, elders of the family, clan and nation, teachers, scholars, religious and political leaders, collective reformers and other similar people whose superior wisdom could be depended upon, always had the mantle of leadership bestowed upon them by their followers who adhered to their teachings.

However, the one factor that distinguishes prophets from ordinary people in leadership positions is 'knowledge'. Ordinary leaders do not have true knowledge; instead they form opinions on the basis of assumptions and estimations, as they have no other source of inspiration. Furthermore, elements of their own personal desires also influence their opinions. Thus, whatever creeds or laws such temporal leaders develop are necessarily a mixture of the good and the bad, the right and the wrong. The whole truth is not to be found in the ways and means put forward by them. The Qur'ān warns us against this:

> They are merely following their conjectures and their carnal desires.
>
> [al-Najm 53: 23]

> Although they have no knowledge regarding that. They only follow their conjecture and conjecture can never take the place of the Truth.
>
> [al-Najm 53: 28]

> But the wrong-doers follow their desires without any knowledge.
>
> [al-Rūm 30: 29]

And among people are those that wrangle about Allah without knowledge, without any true guidance, and without any scripture to enlighten them. They wrangle arrogantly, intent on leading people astray from the Way of Allah.

[*al-Ḥajj* 22: 8-9]

And who is in greater error than he who follows his lusts without any guidance from Allah?

[*al-Qaṣaṣ* 28: 50]

As opposed to this state of affairs in the field of human leadership, prophets have knowledge imparted to them by God. Their guidance is not based upon speculation or personal proclivity. Instead, thanks to the light of knowledge bestowed upon them by God, they are able to very clearly see the straight path. It is towards this path that they guided people (and continue to guide through their teachings). Therefore, wherever the Qur'ān mentions the fact of people being raised to the eminent status of prophethood, it also states the fact of their being granted knowledge. For instance, the Qur'ān has the Prophet Ibrāhīm declare his own prophethood in the following words:

Father, a knowledge that has not reached you has come to me. So follow me that I may guide you to a Straight Way.

[*Maryam* 19: 43]

The bestowal of Prophethood on the Prophet Lūṭ (Lot) is mentioned in the following way:

We bestowed upon Lot sound judgement and knowledge.

[*al-Anbiyā'* 21: 74]

With respect to the Prophet Moses, it is stated:

When Moses reached the age of full youth and grew to maturity, We bestowed upon him wisdom and knowledge.

[*al-Qaṣaṣ* 28: 14]

Similarly, the prophethood of Prophets David and Solomon is declared as:

And We had granted each of them judgement and knowledge.

[*al-Anbiyā'* 21: 79]

Should you follow their desires disregarding the knowledge which has come to you, you shall have no protector or helper against Allah.

[*al-Baqarah* 2: 120]

After this explanation about the high office of prophethood and its distinct status vis-à-vis ordinary leaders, we now turn our attention towards those issues of principle that have been presented by the Qur'ān with reference to prophethood.

The Mutual Relationship between Belief (*Īmān*) in Allah and Belief (*Īmān*) in the Prophets

First of all, since prophets alone of people were provided access to true knowledge, and also because they were granted that enlightenment of vision which does not normally come to ordinary mortals, the only true creed with regards to God can only be the one that has been propounded by a prophet. If people form a dogma on the basis of their own intellectual efforts or the teachings of some intellectuals and wise men, not only would this belief about God be wanting of truth, but they would also be unable to provide any true knowledge about other metaphysical issues relating to ordinary themes of the *dīn* (the Islamic way of life). This is because such issues are beyond the capability of normal human intellect. In short, the strength of the complete set of beliefs and tenets of faith is totally dependent upon 'belief in the prophets'. It is not at all possible for any human being to connect with and integrate true knowledge with his intellect without associating with this essential link. It is for this reason that the Qur'ān emphasizes the need to acknowledge belief in the Prophets:

How many towns rebelled against the commandment of their Lord and His Messengers. Then We called them to a stern accounting, and subjected them to a harrowing chastisement. So they tasted the evil fruit of their deeds; and the fruit of their deeds was utter loss.

[al-Ṭalāq 65: 8-9]

There are those who disbelieve in Allah and His Messengers and seek to differentiate between Allah and His Messengers, and say: 'We believe in some and deny others,' and they seek to strike a way between the two. It is they, indeed they, who are, beyond all doubt, unbelievers; and for the unbelievers We have prepared a humiliating chastisement. For those who believe in Allah and His Messengers, and do not differentiate between them, We shall certainly give them their reward. Allah is All-Forgiving, All-Compassionate.

[al-Nisā' 4: 150-2]

As for him who sets himself against the Messenger and follows a path other than that of the believers even after true guidance had become clear to him We will let him go to the way he has turned to, and We will cast him into Hell – an evil destination.

[al-Nisā' 4: 115]

There are numerous similar verses in which it is made very clear that the link between belief in Allah and belief in the prophets is not subject to any possibility of severance. Thus, a person who rejects the prophets of God and who does not accept their teachings is equally misguided in either case, whether or not he professes belief in God. This is because any creed that is established without being firmly rooted in true knowledge cannot be correct, even if it is belief of tawḥīd (or the unity of Godhead).

The Unifying Declaration

The second important point is that it is only belief in prophethood that can assemble humanity on one dogma. In actual fact, ignorance is the basis of disagreement in this regard. Based upon their conjecture, people make various guesses about anything with whose true nature they are not well acquainted and these conflicting speculations naturally lead to a difference of opinion amongst them. This is because, reaching an opinion upon the basis of conjecture is as good as one made while groping in pitch darkness.

Where there is no illumination, a large number of different people will express an equal number of different opinions about their 'findings'. However, after light becomes available, there remains no difference amongst them and those who are able to see invariably agree on one finding. Thus, when the prophets (peace be upon them) have been endowed with the blessing of true knowledge and the light of vision, it is simply not possible that there arises any difference amongst their opinions or any disagreement in their teachings or any divergence in their ways. It is thus that the Qur'ān states that all the prophets are members of one group, their teachings are one, their common *dīn* is one, they are all heralds of the same straight path and that it is essential for the believer to acknowledge belief in all of them. A person who rejects any one prophet shall be treated as being guilty of the rejection of all of them. Such a person shall not have any belief in his heart because the teaching that he is refusing to accept is not merely the teaching of any one prophet, but rather that of all of them:

> Messengers! Partake of the things that are clean, and act righteously. I know well all that you do. This community of yours is one community, and I am your Lord; so hold Me alone in fear. But people later cut up their religion into bits, each group rejoicing in what they have.
>
> [*al-Mu'minūn* 23: 51-53]

> (O Muḥammad), We have revealed to you as We revealed to Noah and the Prophets after him, and We revealed to Abraham, Ishmael, Isaac, Jacob and the offspring of Jacob, and Jesus and Job, and Jonah, and Aaron and Solomon, and We gave to David Psalms. We revealed to the Messengers

We have already told you of, and to the Messengers We
have not told you of; and to Moses Allah spoke directly.

[*al-Nisā'* 4: 163-164]

These and many similar verses manifest the fact that all the prophets
sent to every nation called their people to the same Truthful Way. Of
these some prophets are explicitly mentioned in the Qur'ān by name;
it is essential to unequivocally profess belief in all of them. As for the
prophets and the guides whose names have not been communicated
to us, the correct belief is that all of them were proclaimers of Islam,
but that their nations distorted their teachings and made different
religions out of them after disagreeing with each other. While we
cannot refer to Buddha, Krishna, Zoroaster and Confucius as God's
prophets with certainty, because nothing is clearly stated in the Qur'ān
about them, however, it is our belief that the prophets of Allah were
sent to all countries and regions of the world including India, China,
Japan, Iran, Africa, and Europe and that all of them called people
towards the Islam of the Prophet Muḥammad (peace be upon him).
Thus we Muslims do not reject the religion or religious leader of any
nation, but only refuse to accept their incorrect ways that are now seen
to be divergent from the Straight Path of Islam. This teaching of the
Qur'ān with regard to the prophets is without precedent. No other
religion has such a philosophy. This forthrightness of the Qur'ān is
clear evidence of its truth. For humanity, this paradigm bears within
itself a satisfying message of universal harmony and the unity of the
messengers' mission.

Allegiance and Obedience to the Messenger

An obvious consequence of belief in the institution of prophethood
should be visible by way of the adherents of that faith following the
path that had been pursued by the prophets not only in terms of their
dogma and ritual worship but also in all practical aspects of life. This
is because the prophets knew with certainty the difference between
the right and wrong paths on account of the Knowledge and light of
guidance with which God had endowed them. Thus, whatever they
adopted or abandoned, and whatever they commanded was all from

God. Ordinary human beings are unable to distinguish between the right and the wrong even after years – and in some cases even after ages – of trials and errors. The little success that they are able to achieve is also not based upon the solid foundations of absolute certainty, but is rather founded upon analogical and inductive reasoning wherein the possibility of error always exists.

Contrary to this, the methods adopted by the prophets in dealing with various issues arising in daily life and which they taught to their followers were adopted on the basis of True Knowledge and, therefore, there is no chance of any error in these. It is for this reason that the Qur'ān, time and again, commands submission and allegiance to the prophets. It refers to the course established by them as the *minhāj al-Sharī'ah* (the 'Broad Way') or the straight path. It asserts that people should abandon allegiance to all others and only submit to God's prophets and follow on their path because submission to the prophets very precisely constitutes submission to God; adherence to the prophets is the very adherence to God's writ:

> (And tell them that) We never sent a Messenger but that he should be obeyed by the leave of Allah.
>
> [*al-Nisā'* 4: 64]

> He who obeys the Messenger thereby obeys Allah.
>
> [*al-Nisā'* 4: 80]

> (O Messenger), tell people: 'If you indeed love Allah, follow me, and Allah will love you and will forgive you your sins. Allah is All-Forgiving, All-Compassionate.' Say: 'Obey Allah and obey the Messenger.' If they turn away from this then know that Allah does not love those who refuse to obey Him and His Messenger.
>
> [*Āl 'Imrān* 3: 31-32]

> Believers! Obey Allah and His Messenger and do not turn away from him after you hear his command. And do not be like those who say: 'We hear,' though they do not hearken.

Indeed the worst kind of all beasts in the sight of Allah
are the people who are deaf and dumb and who do not
understand.

[al-Anfāl 8: 20-22]

It does not behove a believer, male or female, that when
Allah and His Messenger have decided an affair they should
exercise their choice. And whoever disobeys Allah and His
Messenger has strayed to manifest error.

[al-Aḥzāb 33: 36]

But if they do not hearken to this, know well that they only
follow their lusts and who is in greater error than he who
follows his lusts without any guidance from Allah?

[al-Qaṣaṣ 28: 50]

These and many other similar verses emphasize allegiance and
submission to the Prophets. A fact that has been made clear in Chapter
33 of the Qur'ān (The Confederates) is that the Prophet Muḥammad's
life is an excellent model for those people who expect forgiveness from
God and success on the Last Day:

Surely there was a good example for you in the Messenger
of Allah, for all those who look forward to Allah and the
Last Day and remember Allah much.

[al-Aḥzāb 33: 21]

The Importance of Faith in Prophethood
Together with these commandments of submission and allegiance, the
belief in prophethood is, in fact, the heart, the spirit, the sustaining
force, and the real basis of the civilization that has been established
by Islam.

In every culture and civilization three elements are crucial: (i) philosophy, (ii) principles, and (iii) civic laws. The philosophy, together
with its formal processes of thought, is derived from the teachings
of those philosophers and people of wisdom who, for one reason or

another, have come to dominate the mindsets of large groups of human beings. These ethical principles flow from those political leaders, reformers and religious guides who enjoyed power over particular nations in various time periods. People who formulate civic laws are those whose expertise is respected in various walks of life. However, the social system that comes into existence by the convergence of these three elements necessarily suffers from three basic shortcomings.

1. With elements being so presented from these three sources, the concoction that results is one whose characteristics become stable only after centuries, and even then many disconnections, over-indulgences and irregularities remain to be addressed. There are numerous philosophers and people of wisdom. Their thought patterns are distinct from each other rather, they are often fundamentally different. Generally these are the people who have never had any contact with the practical problems of life. In fact, most of them are known for their misanthropy. It is from this first source that human beings obtain their processes of thinking.

   The group from which the second element is derived is also one in which there are considerable differences between the concepts, philosophies and mindsets of various individuals. If there is anything common amongst the members of this group at all, then it is the fact that they are people who live in a world of ideas; they are a spirited and emotional lot who have little connection with hard, down-to-earth issues. As for the third element, i.e. civic law, its sources are also mutually differing. The common factor amongst them is an extreme lack of finer emotions. Needless practicality has made them dry, cold-hearted individuals. Quite obviously, it is very difficult to obtain a correct and balanced mixture amongst such inconsistent elements. Their mutual contradictions have not remained at rest and will not remain at rest without manifesting their distinct colours.

2. The three elements that are derived from these sources neither have the power of sustaining themselves nor the qualifications for widespread acceptance. Various nations have been influenced by different philosophers, leaders and jurists. It is because of these

divergent influences that disagreements arise in their thought processes, moral principles and civic laws. In fact, even in the case of one single nation, the influence of a particular set of philosophers, leaders and jurists who were successful in having an effect in earlier times does not remain forever. With the change of times, these influencers and their stimuli keep on changing and evolving. In this way, on the one hand, civilizations take on a national character, and from the disagreements of nations arises that one great disagreement which then turns out to be the bolt of lightning that can burn the harvest of peace to the ground. On the other hand, within each nation itself, the system of culture and civilization ever remains in a state of flux. Rather than developing along a linear path, its growth and development continue to be constantly impacted by fundamental changes, whose direction is sometimes towards evolution and at other times towards revolution.

3. There is not the slightest suspicion of any sacredness with respect to the sources of any of these three elements. The thought processes that a nation obtains from its philosophers, the moral principles that it receives from its leaders and the civic laws that it acquires from the formulators of law are all the result of human effort. Their human followers are fully cognizant of this fact, that is of their being products of human exertion. The necessary result of this fact is that adherence in respect to them is never complete. Even in their highest state of obedience, followers of these philosophical, moral and juridical elements are not fully saturated with a state of belief. They themselves believe that there is a possibility of error in the foundational elements of their civilization, and, hence, a need for improvement. Moreover, experimental processes proceeding through experiential trial and error also prove their shortcomings from time to time and this leads to manifestation of further doubt and anxiety. In this way, no thought process or legal principle has had the opportunity of being fully accepted by a whole nation or has been able to strengthen the cultural system in a homogenous way.

A civilization that is founded upon belief in prophethood, however, is free from all these three defects.

First, all three elements come from the same source. The one and the same person designates the thought process, specifies the moral principles and formulates the principles of civic laws. He is, at the same time, the leader in the world of thought, the moral realm and the domain of action. His purview of the problems of all three areas is concurrent and uniform. This view is based upon a judicious combination of reason, lighter and pleasant emotions, and strategy. Taking a measured and appropriate quantity from each of these three, he puts together the civilizational amalgam in such a way that no constituent element faces any variation, that there is no mutual mismatching or lack of proportionality, and that nature of the compound remains stable. This fact is beyond human capability. It is absolutely impossible to achieve this without the guidance of God, the Creator.

Secondly, none of these elements is either time or space bound. The thought process and the moral and legal principles that are designated by a prophet of God are not based upon spatial national tendencies or time-bound mannerisms but rather on truthfulness and righteousness – and these two facts are beyond the confines of East or West, black or white, old or new: that which is truthful and righteous is equally so in every corner of the world, in every nation and every era. The sun is the sun in Japan as it is in Gibraltar. It was the sun a thousand years ago and it will remain the sun a thousand years from now.

Thus, if any civilization can possibly become a universal and timeless representative of all human race, then it will be the civilization that has been brought into existence by a prophet of God. Only this civilization has the qualification to be appropriate for all nations and for all times without modifying its principles and foundation.

Thirdly, this civilization is adorned with the grandeur of the sacred. Its followers firmly believe that the person who established this civilization was a prophet of God. He was endowed with true knowledge by God, a knowledge without the slightest doubt (*Lā rayba fīh*): 'This is the Book of Allah, there is no doubt in it; it is a guidance for the pious' (*al-Baqarah* 2: 2). Neither conjecture, approximation, nor personal opinion has any place in his teachings. Whatever he presents is from God. There is no possibility of his straying or walking on the wrong path.

> Your companion has neither strayed nor is he deluded; nor does he speak out of his desire. This is nothing but a revelation that is conveyed to him, something that a very powerful one has imparted to him.
>
> [*al-Najm* 53: 2-5]

When this certainty and belief permeate deep into the hearts and souls of believers, they follow and submit to the prophet with a total endorsement of his being. There is not the least doubt or wavering in their hearts. Never does any misgiving about their path not really being the right one, or any other way being at least equally if not more righteous than their own, cause any anxiety in them. Quite obviously, such a civilization will be extremely durable and its following very strong. There will be much greater discipline in such a civilization as compared to worldly counterparts and its thought processes, moral principles and civil laws will demonstrate greater stability.

The prophets of God were the builders of this civilization. For centuries they strove to create the groundwork for this civilization in every part of the world. And when, finally, the foundations were complete, the Prophet Muḥammad (peace be upon him) came to complete this structure.

The Distinguishing Features of the Prophethood of Muḥammad (Peace Be Upon Him)

Whatever has been said so far has dealt with the general mandate of prophethood. Additionally, however, there are certain issues that specifically deal with the Prophethood of Muḥammad (peace be upon him). Undoubtedly, with regard to the basic stature of prophethood *per se*, there is no difference between the Prophet Muḥammad (peace be upon him), and the other prophets of God (peace be upon them). The Qur'ān clearly states that making any distinction between the prophets of God is not permissible.

We make no distinction between any of His Messengers.

[*al-Baqarah* 2: 285]

Thus, principally, all the prophets share the honour of having been ordained by God, all were granted 'Command' and 'True Knowledge', all were heralds towards the same straight path, and all were guides and leaders of humanity; thus, obedience to all of them is mandatory and the lives of them all are models deserving emulation by all the children of Adam. However, effectively God granted the Prophet Muḥammad (peace be upon him) a special position of distinction with respect to other prophets (peace be upon them). This position of privilege is not merely a superficial one in so far as not having any effect whether one keeps this distinction in view or not. In fact, this status of distinction has a very fundamental and central place in the Islamic theological system. In practice, the foundation of all the beliefs and laws of Islam have been placed upon the singular status of the Prophethood of Muḥammad (peace be upon him). Therefore, no belief with regard to prophethood can be correct until a person professes belief in Muḥammad (peace be upon him), specifically keeping in view this singular status.

The Difference between the Prophethood of Muḥammad (pbuh) and Earlier Prophets

In order to gain an understanding of this theme, it is essential to keep in mind certain basic issues:

(i)   From indications in the Qur'ān, well-known traditions, and intellectual inferences, the number of prophets should exceed several thousand. The Qur'ān states: Never has there been a nation but a warner came to it. [*Fāṭir* 35: 24] It is obvious that historiography has been unable – and will continue to be incapable – of making a full record of all the various communities of humanity since the earliest of times. Therefore, even if only one prophet had been sent to every nation, the number of God's messengers would be in the several thousands. Some *aḥādīth*, sayings of the Prophet Muḥammad (peace be upon him) corroborate this statement. The number of prophets has been stated to be as large as 124,000. However, from amongst this immensely large crowd, the number of prophets who are mentioned in the Qur'ān by name can be counted upon the fingers of one's hands.[3] Together with these names, even if we were to include those national spiritual leaders about whose prophethood the Qur'ān makes no specific mention, the figure would not exceed double digits. The total obliteration of the names and efforts of countless prophets and the fading away of their teachings is proof enough that their mission was for specific time periods and for particular nations, and that they possessed no special teaching or characteristic that could have endowed their mission with stability, longevity, or universality.

(ii) Even with regard to the prophets whose names are known to us, their biographies and teachings have been so badly covered with the heavy drapes of fiction or distorted by subsequent amendments that our knowledge about them is not trustworthy. If we were to examine whatever remnants of their teachings that exist now, not from the viewpoint of blind dogma but strictly on the basis of standards of pure historical scholarship, it would have to be accepted that there is hardly anything in them that is credible. We cannot even determine the exact time periods of their life spans. We are even unaware of their correct names. In fact, we cannot even say with certainty whether they actually lived or not. Historians have expressed their doubts about whether as famous personalities as Buddha, Zoroaster and Jesus were actually historical or merely mythological. Whatever information we have about their lives is so vague and sketchy – and replete with subsequent additions – that they cannot be made role models in any walk of life. The same is the case with their teachings. The books or teachings attributed to them cannot be traced back to them through credible records. Moreover, by way of very strong evidences, both internal and external, it is proved that these books or teachings have been subjected to extensive revisions

---

[3] The exact number is 26 – Translator.

and modifications. These issues are sufficient to establish that the prophethood and leadership of all the prophets and religious leaders who existed before the Prophet Muḥammad (peace be upon him) has now come to an end.

(iii) For nearly all the prophets and religious leaders it can be proved that their teachings were (at least originally) for the particular nation to which they were sent. Some of them clarified this fact on their own, while for others it was proved by the events of their times. The teachings of Abraham, Moses, Confucius, Zoroaster and Krishna never reached beyond their nations. The same was the case with the other prophets and priests of the Sumerians and Aryans. While the followers of Buddha and Jesus conveyed their teachings to other nations, the two individuals never attempted this themselves; the fact is that they did not state that their message was for the whole world. In fact, Jesus is quoted in the Bible as having said that he had only come to guide the Children of Israel.

(iv) Among all the prophets and leaders of religious communities, the Prophet Muḥammad (peace be upon him) is the one and only about whose life and teachings we have such correct, authentic and certain information that there is no doubt about its veracity. Without any fear of contradiction, it can be said that with regard to no other historic personality does such true and credible scholarly material exist. So much so that if any doubter were to suspect the authenticity of available material about the Prophet (peace be upon him), he would have to destroy all the historical records of the world. This is because if one were to cast doubt on such an authentic collection, it would be necessary to consider all historical knowledge as being nothing but a pile of falsehood, even one word of which was not credible.

(v) Similarly, of all the prophets and religious leaders, it is only the Prophet Muḥammad (peace be upon him) whose life have been presented to us in such complete detail. Not only amongst the leaders of communities, but amongst all the historic personalities of the world, do we find a personage whose biography has been preserved in the annals of history in such minute detail. If there is any difference between the age of the Prophet Muḥammad (peace be upon him) and our own, it is the fact that in that age the Prophet existed in a bodily state of life, and that, of course, is no longer the fact. However, if the condition of corporeality is not applied, we may metaphorically say that the Prophet is alive today, and shall always remain with us as long as his minutely detailed biography remains extant. Through the books of *ḥadīth* and *sīrah* (the Prophet's sayings and his biography respectively), the world can see his life as clearly as the people of his own age could have seen him. Thus, it would be absolutely correct to say that of all the prophets and religious leaders, if anyone can be followed correctly and completely then it is the Prophet Muḥammad (peace be upon him).

(vi) The same is the case with the teachings of the Prophet Muḥammad (peace be upon him). As has been stated above, of all the prophets and religious leaders, there is not one whose book (i.e. the scripture brought by him) and whose teachings exist in their true form today and could be attributed to its originator in a credible manner. This honour is the exclusive preserve of the Prophet Muḥammad (peace be upon him) that the book brought by him, the Qur'ān, presumes exactly the same words that were revealed to him. In addition to the Qur'ān, the instructions given by this spokesperson of God's revelation are similarly preserved in their true form, and shall, Allah willing, always remain so. Thus, of all the prophets and religious leaders, if anyone's teachings can be followed on a credible basis, then these are the teachings of the Prophet Muḥammad (peace be upon him).

(vii) If we were to view the accumulated collection of the teachings and knowledge of the biographies of the prophets and religious leaders of the periods past that exist today, whatever authentic illustrations that we find with relation to truth and honesty, goodness and virtue, exemplary morals and superior social conduct, we will find them all in the personality of the Prophet Muḥammad (peace be upon him). Similarly, amongst all the leaders of humankind, we do not find any aspect of truth and honesty, virtue and goodness in them that we do not also see in the teachings and personality of the Prophet Muḥammad (peace be upon him). Moreover, in the teachings and life of the Prophet we also find such a treasure of the knowledge of truth, virtuous actions and principles of uprightness that such is not to be seen in the teachings or lives of any religious leader before or after him. On top of all this, there is no correct concept about Divine Knowledge and temporal morality or worldly interaction which can come to man's imagination that is not found in Islam. Thus, it is an undeniable fact that the teachings and life of the Prophet Muḥammad (peace be upon him) comprise the grand composite of all virtue. The Prophet (peace be upon him) revealed to us whatever was true. All that which collectively comprised the Straight Path was illuminated for us by the Prophet (peace be upon him). In the clearest manner, he presented to us all the true principles that could possibly be required for the uprightness of human morality and social interaction throughout the full spectrum of man's individual and collective capacities and to conduct one's worldly life in a correct way. Thus, there is no longer any scope to add these principles.

(viii) Among all prophets and religious leaders, the Prophet Muḥammad (peace be upon him), is the only one who proclaimed that his mission and call were for the whole of humanity. In reality too, this is exactly what happened: within his own lifetime the Prophet sent invitations to the rulers of the then major imperial powers. In time, his *da'wah* (missionary invitation) reached every corner of the world and every human group. Only Muḥammad (peace be upon him) was privileged with this distinctiveness. Some of the earlier prophets and leaders neither claimed the universality of their message, nor did they receive that privilege. While the religions of some others did gain a global following, the leaders themselves neither ever claimed such a wide transnational mission nor did they make any effort in that respect. Other than the Prophet Muḥammad (peace be upon him), there is none who made the claim of a universal mission, made efforts in that regard, and finally also achieved such a widespread appeal.

(ix) There can be only three reasons for the mission of the Divine prophets. Firstly, that they came to guide a nation to which no prophet had previously come; this principle is based on the Qur'ānic verse, 'To every people has its guide' (*al-Raʿd* 13: 7), which required one or more prophets to be sent to every nation. Secondly, a nation had received a prophet in earlier times, but the signs and teachings of his prophethood disappeared, the book he had brought was distorted, the impressions of his life disappeared to such an extent that it was no longer possible for the people to follow the exemplary model. Thirdly, that the teachings and guidance of a previous prophet were incomplete and required further elaboration.

Apart from these three reasons for the advent of the prophets, no fourth rationale exists or is intellectually possible.[4] It is not possible for another prophet to be sent when a prophet has already come to a nation, where his teachings and biography are intact in their original form and where there is otherwise no need to supplement his mission. The ministry of prophethood is not merely an endowment that may be granted as a reward in return for some meritorious act. Instead, it is a special assignment to provide a specific and required service for which someone is appointed. Moreover, this station is not one of such a lowly and insignificant status that it be established merely for inviting attention to the teachings of some past prophet. For this purpose, the true *ʿulamāʾ* (scholars) and reformers are sufficient.

Thus, the intellect demands, with uncompromising absoluteness, that unless any of three above-mentioned reasons exist, no Prophet may appear. From our foregoing discussion, it has been proved that with the Prophethood of Muḥammad (peace be upon him), all these three have come to a final, eternal end.

---

[4] A possible fourth reason could be that a second prophet is sent to assist another Prophet, living at the same time. Some illustrations of this occurrence are found in the Qur'ān. However, here this situation is not under discussion because the mission of the assisting prophet is actually an appendix to the mission of the main prophet, in assistance to whom he was sent as a minister.

The Prophet's call (*da'wah*) was for all humanity, therefore there is no longer any need for separate prophets for different nations. The Book that the Prophet brought and the complete set of evidences of his prophethood are preserved in their correct state, and, hence, there is no need for any new book or new guidance. The Prophet's teachings and guidance are complete and all encompassing, neither has any part of the True Knowledge remained hidden. Nor is there any shortcoming left in the exemplary model for righteous action. Accordingly, there is no need for any person to add to or complement the existing guidance. Since the three causative situations do not exist, and the grounds for the advent of prophets comprise just these three, therefore it must necessarily be accepted that the gateway of prophethood has forever been absolutely closed after the prophethood of the Prophet Muḥammad (peace be upon him). If this gateway had remained open, it would have meant that God also acts in vain – while, in fact, God is totally above and beyond the possibility of committing any useless act.[5]

It is this distinct stature of the prophethood of Muḥammad (peace be upon him) that is presented by the Qur'ān in great detail and clarity.

A General Invitation

(Say, O Muḥammad): 'O people! I am Allah's Messenger to you all – of Him to Whom belongs the dominion of the heavens and the earth. There is no god but He. He grants life and deals death. Have faith, then, in Allah and in His

---

[5] The issue at hand is not just that sending a prophet where one is not needed would comprise a futile act, but that such an action would be contrary to wisdom. After completion of the mission of prophethood, the closure of this gate is essential so that the whole world can unite in submission to one prophet. If this gate were to have remained open then there would have been a redrawing of the dividing line between belief and disbelief (*īmān* and *kufr*) as a result of which believers already assembled would have again started going astray.

Messenger the *ummī* Prophet who believes in Allah and His words; and follow him so that you may be guided aright.'

[*al-A'rāf* 7: 158]

(O Prophet), We have not sent you forth but as a herald of good news and a Warner for all mankind. But most people do not know.

[*Saba'* 34: 28]

O people! Now that the Messenger has come to you bearing the Truth from your Lord, believe in him; it will be good for you. If you reject, know well that to Allah belongs all that is in the heavens and the earth.

[*al-Nisā'* 4: 170]

We have sent you forth as nothing but mercy to people of the whole world.

[*al-Anbiyā'* 21: 107]

Most blessed is He Who sent down this Criterion on His servant, to be a warner to all mankind.

[*al-Furqān* 25: 1]

From the foregoing verses, a few more principles can be derived: one, that the call (*da'wah*) or mission of the Prophet Muḥammad (peace be upon him) is not specific to any nation or country. Instead, he is the guide and leader of all humanity. Secondly, that it is incumbent upon all humanity to profess belief in the Prophet and submit to him. Thirdly, that without professing belief in the Prophet Muḥammad (peace be upon him) and without submitting to him, no guidance can be obtained.

All three themes are part of Islam's belief system because Islam is another name for the global human civilization that bases its globalism upon this dogma. If it is accepted that guidance may be obtained outside the parameters of the *dīn* of the Prophet, then Islam loses its general applicability and its universality comes to an end.

Completion of the *Dīn* (the Way of Islam)

The second distinction of the Prophethood of Muḥammad (peace be upon him), that the Qur'ān presents is as follows:

> He it is Who has sent His Messenger with the guidance and the True Religion that He may make it prevail over all religions, howsoever those who associate others with Allah in His Divinity might detest it.
>
> [*al-Tawbah* 9: 33]

> This day I have perfected for you your religion, and have bestowed upon you My Bounty in full measure, and have been pleased to assign for you Islam as your religion.
>
> [*al-Mā'idah* 5: 3]

From this we see that whatever collection we refer to as guidance and whatever subjects upon which the true way *(dīn)* is applicable have been communicated through the Prophet Muḥammad (peace be upon him), to a perfect degree. The Prophethood of Muḥammad (peace be upon him) has come to dominate totally the essence of the *dīn*. Through the Prophet, the *dīn* has been completed and the guidance that was being previously granted piecemeal through the agency of all the other prophets has now been provided in full. After this, there is nothing further in terms of guidance, the *dīn*, true knowledge that remains to be communicated or that would require the sending of another prophet or messenger. The logical conclusion that may be drawn from the unambiguous words with which the completion of the *dīn* and the full dispensing of God's beneficence has been proclaimed is twofold: that the connection of obedience and submission to previous prophethoods is now to be severed and that the gateway of prophethood is closed for the future. These two subjects, i.e. the supercession of previous religions and the sealing of the institution of prophethood are the distinguishing features of the Prophethood of Muḥammad (peace be upon him); both these aspects are clearly presented in the Qur'ān.

The Abolition of Previous Religious Ways (Adyān)

By the repeal of previous religions we mean that whatever was presented by erstwhile prophets now stands abrogated. While it continues to be essential to acknowledge dogmatically faith in their prophethood and their truthfulness, because all of them called to Islam, and because their affirmation is actually an affirmation of Islam in operative terms, the association of obedience and submission with these prophets has been severed and these issues have now come to be linked with the teachings and exemplary model of the Prophet Muḥammad (peace be upon him).

Therefore, firstly, in principle, there is no longer a need for what is incomplete after having received what is complete.[6] Secondly, whatever remnants of the teachings and lives of the previous prophets that continue to be extant have now been subjected to such extensive changes and loss of credibility that it is no longer practically possible to follow these. It is because of these reasons that wherever the command to obey or submit to the Prophet occurs in the Qur'ān or where the words rasūl (Messenger) or nabī (Prophet) have been used, the reference is strictly to the Prophet Muḥammad (peace be upon him). For instance:

... and obey Allah and the Messenger that mercy be shown to you.

[Āl 'Imrān 3: 132]

Believers! Obey Allah and obey the Messenger, and those invested with authority among you.

[al-Nisā' 4: 59]

He who obeys the Messenger thereby obeys Allah.

[al-Nisā' 4: 80]

---

[6] In modern terms, this is just like replacing older deficient softwares with a perfect new version – Translator.

Again, it is for this reason that the nations and followers of the prophets whose advent was prior to the Prophet Muḥammad (peace be upon him), have been called upon to profess belief in the Prophet's mission and to submit to him. Thus, the Qur'ān states:

> People of the Book! Now Our Messenger has come to you: he makes clear to you a good many things of the Book which you were wont to conceal, and also passes over many things. There has now come to you a Light from Allah, and a Clear Book, through which Allah shows to all who seek to please Him the paths leading to safety. He brings them out, by His leave, from darkness to Light and directs them on to the Straight Way.
>
> [al-Mā'idah 5: 15-16]

> (Today this Mercy is for) those who follow the ummī Prophet, whom they find mentioned in the Torah and the Gospel that they have. He enjoins upon them what is good and forbids them what is evil. He makes the clean things lawful to them and prohibits all corrupt things and removes from them their burdens and the shackles that were upon them. So those who believe in him and assist him, and succour him and follow the Light which has been sent down with him, it is they who shall prosper. (Say, O Muḥammad): 'O people! I am Allah's Messenger to you all – of Him to Whom belongs the dominion of the heavens and the earth. There is no god but He. He grants life and causes death. Have faith, then, in Allah and in His Messenger the ummī Prophet who believes in Allah and His words; and follow him so that you may be guided aright.'
>
> [al-A'rāf 7: 157-58]

In these verses the supercession of previous religions is explained and its meaning stated. The reason for this act is also revealed and the logical results of this are also communicated. It is also stated that from this point onward, guidance and salvation are linked with submission to the Prophet Muḥammad (peace be upon him). And, finally, it is explained that the *dīn* of the Prophet is, in fact, the perfected and completed form of the *dīn* that had previously been sent to the believers of the Torah and Bible and to the other nations of the world.

The Sealing of the Institution of Prophethood

In a similar way, the second consequence of the completion of the *dīn* involving a capping off or sealing of prophethood is also stated very clearly in the Qur'ān:

> Muḥammad is not the father of any of your men, but he is the Messenger of Allah and the seal of the Prophets. Allah has full knowledge of everything.
>
> [*al-Aḥzāb* 33: 40]

This is such an open declaration of the cessation of prophethood that no one can find any possible room for reopening the gateway of prophethood after such a pronouncement, unless there is crookedness in their heart. Whether the 'Seal' is spelled with a capital 'S' or a lower-case 's', in both cases the result is the same: in the Wisdom of God, the gateway of prophethood has forever been closed – and nothing may take place against His Wisdom.

The Essential Ingredients of Muḥammad's Faith

The three dogmas of the absolute completion of the *dīn*, the transmigration of former religions and the conclusion of the prophetic institution are all part of the belief system of Islam and essential ingredients of the dogma of the Prophethood of Muḥammad (peace be upon him). Islam's open invitation to all humanity is established on the foundational premise that through the mission of the Prophet Muḥammad (peace be upon him), God has presented such a complete religion that all the deficiencies of previous missions and calls to faith have been satisfied. In fact, for the future also, no shortcoming has been left that may ever need to be addressed.

This complete *dīn* has forever established such a well-designated and permanent distinction between Islam and *kufr* (disbelief), between truth and falsehood that till the Last Day there shall be no addition to it or subtraction from it. Whatever comprises Islam and the 'Truth' has been presented by the Prophet Muḥammad (peace be upon him). Nothing further in this category will ever come again, lest in some time in the future a person's status as a Muslim and advocate of the truth may be made conditional upon acceptance of that particular addition. Whatever has been declared to be *kufr* (disbelief) and falsehood by the Prophet Muḥammad (peace be upon him), shall always remain so; nothing so declared can ever again be changed or modified to become Islamic or the Truth nor can the distinction between *kufr* and Islam ever be based upon anything other than what he, the Prophet, laid down. This is the solid and unalterable foundation upon which the structure of Islam's global and eternal nationhood and civilization has been raised. It has been so raised in order to unite all the human beings of the world forever and eternally into one community that is unanimous in its submission to one *dīn* and to one civilization. This is a community upon whose perfection and permanence its members should all have full faith. This is a *dīn* that fully prevails over all Truth and all guidance, so much so that there is not the least doubt about any issue of its kind having remained outside its ambit. This is a civilization whose structure should be in no danger of being breached by some new distinction between Islam and *kufr*. It is upon this state of confidence that Islam's invitation is based and it is upon this belief that Islam's stability and perpetuity are founded.

A person who says that even after the advent of Islam submission to former religions is correct actually takes away from Islam its right as the final open invitation. This is because, if guidance were to be possible through other means as well, it would be a needless act to call all nations and all human beings to Islam. A person who states that supercession and alteration, reform and addition to the teachings of the Prophet Muḥammad (peace be upon him) is possible according to the requirements and conditions of every time period actually deprives Islam of its perpetual and eternal character. Obviously, the reason for this is that if a deficient *dīn*, which itself is deserving of deletion, addition or modification, proclaims to be an eternal means of guidance, its claim would be patently false. Then the person who says that there is still room for the advent of other prophets after the Prophet Muḥammad (peace be upon him) is, in fact, striking at the very foundation of Islam. For, if this doorway to prophethood were to remain open, it would mean that Islam would forever be faced with the dangers of distortion and dissension. After the advent of every new prophet, the distinction between Islam and *kufr* would have to be raised anew and at such junctures many of those people who professed belief in God, His Prophet Muḥammad (peace be upon him), and the Qur'ān would risk being expelled from Islam.

Thus, in Islam, a gateway to prophethood that remains open is actually an open gateway to discord. Amongst all the possible sources of the potential eradication of Islam, the most lethal one is the laying claim to prophethood after the Prophet Muḥammad's advent. The whole collective system of the Muslim community was established on the basis that those people who profess belief in the Prophet Muḥammad (peace be upon him) and the Qur'ān are Muslims and believers; they are one community, one nation, brothers unto each other, and partners in pain and pleasure alike.

Now, suppose that someone were to come along and claim that it was not sufficient to profess belief in the Prophet Muḥammad (peace be upon him), and the Qur'ān, but that together with these it was also necessary to profess belief in his own call, and that those who did not do so, in spite of believing in the Prophet and the Qur'ān, were now disbelievers. Now suppose too, that based upon this new distinction between *Islām* and *kufr*, this person began differentiating amongst Muslims, and as a result succeeded in dividing the community that the Prophet Muḥammad (peace be upon him), had made one nation into small pieces, and was also able to sever the relationship of brotherhood that the Qur'ān had proclaimed, sow discord in their ritual prayers setting them apart, dissolve their marital relationships, and go on to the extent of breaking apart their social relationships comprising at the very least of the visiting of each other's sick, participating in funerals and the offering of condolences. Who else could be a greater enemy of Islam, Islamic nationhood, its civilization and collective system?

From the above discussion it may be understood that, together with the Prophethood of the Prophet Muḥammad (peace be upon him), how important the dogmas of completion of the *dīn*, supercession of former religions and the sealing of Prophethood are and why it is essential for Islam's continuity and stability that these be made the most essential aspects of the Islamic belief system.

7 Belief (*Īmān*) in the Heavenly Scripture

In Islamic terminology, 'the Book' means a Book that has been revealed by Allah to His Prophet for the guidance of His followers. By virtue of this meaning, 'the Book' is the formal official version of the message – in Islamic terminology, 'Divine communication'. It is for the dissemination, explanation, interpretation, and practical implementation of this communication that a Messenger is sent to the world.

Given the scope of this book, this is neither an appropriate place for deliberating on the context in which 'The Book' is God's *kalām* or speech nor on discussing the question 'What exactly is the meaning of its being the Speech of Allah (*Kalām Allāh*)'. This is purely a theological or metaphysical debate that has nothing to do with the present theme. We only have to look at it from the perspective of the role that belief in the Book plays in the establishment of the Islamic civilization. For this, it is sufficient to know that the basic principles of knowledge and the essence of issues that are to be transmitted to human beings through the Messenger are communicated to the Prophet's heart through Divine inspiration. Both in terms of the words and the meanings that they convey, there is not the slightest involvement or contribution of the Prophet's thought or intellect, personal discretion or desire in this communication. This is because, the communication is both literally and semantically the Speech of God and not a text authored by the Prophet. The Prophet only transmits this message to the people of God as a trustworthy courier. He then explains the meanings and propositions therein by virtue of the enlightenment granted him by God.

Based upon these Divine principles, the Prophet establishes a system of morals and social order, a culture and a civilization. Through his teaching and sermonizing, and his pure character, he brings about a revolution in the thoughts and attitudes of his target audiences.

He breathes into them a spirit of God-consciousness (*taqwā*) and moral–spiritual cleanliness, a purity of the spirit and a benevolence of action. By way of his training and practical guidance, he organizes them in a way that a new society comes into existence with a new mind-set, fresh thinking, a new formulation of formal procedures, a new constitution and a new set of laws. Finally, he leaves behind amongst his people God's Book and the impact of his teachings as well as his pure character, which always remain with his followers and continue to serve as the guiding light for all generations to come.

The Relationship between Prophethood and the Book

Both the institution of Prophethood and the Book originate from the same God. Both are constituents of a Divine Order and the means to accomplish the same purpose and lead to completion of the mission. The same Divine Knowledge and Wisdom that are in the heart and soul of the Prophet also glorify the pages of the Book. The same Knowledge whose textual version is the Book can be seen in the form of a living role model in the life of the Prophet.

Human nature is such that human beings cannot obtain any extraordinary benefit from bare bookish knowledge. Together with the provision of educational material they also need a human teacher and a guide who can, by way of his tutoring, cause a diffusion of that knowledge into the hearts and minds of the people and who can, by way of becoming a role model, breathe fresh spirit through his deeds. Throughout human history, there is not a single example in which a Book alone has been able to bring about a revolution in the life and mindset of a nation without the coaching and guidance of a human teacher. If leaders who were able to bring about revolutions in the thoughts and actions of nations they led had not become the true working models of their own philosophies (as they did), but had instead had their ideas and principles published in book form, no one having knowledge of human nature would have dared to declare that the revolutions that unfolded as a result of the practical education imparted by those leaders would still have taken place merely by way of the impact of their books.

On the other hand, it is also human nature that together with a human guide it also desires an authoritative and credible text of their teachings, whether it is in written form or preserved through oral tradition. If the principles upon which a leader bases the thoughts and actions, the character and culture of a group are not preserved in their original form, by and by, over time, the imprint of his education fades away. Further, as the imprint fades away, the foundations of the individual character and the group organization are progressively weakened. So much so that at the end this group only possesses old legends and tales, which do not have the capability to hold and protect a powerful cultural system. It is for this reason that the followers of those leaders whose teachings have not been preserved have degenerated into transgression. Their communities have become entangled in every kind of dogmatic, philosophical, practical, moral and cultural depravity. Nothing of their leaders' original philosophy is left from which those original and true principles may now be ascertained and on the basis of which the community first came into existence.

Being fully aware of the nature of his creations, when the 'Maker of the Cosmos' undertook the task of guiding humanity, He introduced the twin institutions of Prophethood and Revelation at the same time. On the one hand, he approved as leaders, those possessing the best characters for guiding human beings, and on the other hand He also revealed His 'speech' so that these two mechanisms could fulfill the two respective human demands. If those leaders had come without their Books (Divine messages) or if the Books had come without the prophets, the purpose of Divine Wisdom would not have been accomplished.

The Qur'ānic Illustration of the Lamp and the Guide

The Qur'ān describes the relationship between Prophethood and the Book in an axiomatic way. At numerous instances, it uses the rhetorical expression of a guide for the Prophet, a person whose vocation is to lead people on the Straight Path. For instance, see the following verses:

And We made them into leaders to guide people in accordance with Our command.

[*al-Anbiyā'* 21: 73]

And every people has its guide.

[*al-Ra'd* 13: 7]

So follow me that I may guide you to a Straight Way.

[*Maryam* 19: 43]

That I may direct you to your Lord and then you hold Him in awe?

[*al-Nāzi'āt* 79: 19]

On the other hand, He describes the Qur'ān by the names of *Nūr, Furqān, Ḍiyā', Burhān, Munīr* and *Mubīn* for example:

And follow the Light (*Nūr*) which has been sent down with him, it is they who shall prosper.

[*al-A'rāf* 7: 157]

Surely We had granted to Moses and Aaron the Criterion (*al-Furqān*) (between right and wrong), and Light (*Ḍiyā'*).

[*al-Anbiyā'* 21: 48]

O people! A proof (*Burhān*) has come to you from your Lord.

[*al-Nisā'* 4: 174]

Messenger when they came to them with Clear Proofs, with Scriptures, and with the Illuminating Book (*al-Kitāb al-Munīr*)

[*Fāṭir* 35: 25]

There has now come to you a Light from Allah, and a Clear Book (*Kitābun Mubīn*).

[*al-Mā'idah* 5:15]

164

These references are not merely rhetorical or metaphorical, but actually point towards an important fact. Through these, it is intended to communicate that ordinary human beings cannot derive sufficient light and guidance by way of their natural intellect nor gain sufficient knowledge to enable them to follow the Straight Path of truth and righteousness.

To reach this hitherto unknown destination that is shrouded in darkness, human beings need an exceptional leader who, in addition to being well acquainted with the destination, also has the Light with which to lead his followers to it. It is this Light that enables the leader to point out places where there are pitfalls and where the path is slippery, where there are thorny bushes and also forks from where the crooked, wrong paths emerge. Indeed, with the help of the Light, any one walking behind the leader would, after seeing the pointers on the path, recognizing the signs of the Straight Path, and familiarizing himself with the many turns and corners, start following him on account of his innate insight. The relationship that exists between a guide and a light on a pitch-dark night is precisely the same as exists between a Prophet and the Book. If we were to snatch away the light from the guide and proceed on our own, we would come to many intersections and forks where we would either become bewildered and anxious to stop or we would go off on a wrong path in spite of still being aided by the light. This is because the mere presence of a light does not preclude the need for a guide.

Similarly, if our leader did not have a guiding light, and we were to follow him blindly by holding on to his mantle, in the absence of a light neither we nor our leader would have the vision with which to distinguish the wrong, crooked paths from the straight one. We would not be able to discern those tricky places where there is a likeliness of stumbling or slipping. Thus, just as we need an escort who is well acquainted with our destination when we are travelling on unfamiliar roads in the darkness of the night, we also need a light with which both our guide and we ourselves can see the road ahead. We cannot dispense with either of these requirements.

Likewise, when travelling towards an unfamiliar destination in the real world, where the light of our intellect is not sufficient in itself, we need both the Prophet and the Book equally. We cannot find the Straight Path by dispensing with our dire need to follow both of these 'beacons' – the real and the metaphorical.

The Prophet is a guide who by virtue of the vision granted him by God knows the Straight Path of salvation perfectly. He is as well acquainted with the details of this road, just as a guide who has travelled on a particular path hundreds of times is aware of the ups and downs along every step of the way. This vision is also called 'Judgement', 'knowledge', 'and 'the opening of the heart' (sharḥ al-ṣadr), 'Divine instruction' and 'Godly guidance'. Time and time again, the Qur'ān mentions the bestowal of these elements of 'vision' upon the prophets:

> (O Prophet), did We not lay open your breast
> [al-Inshirāḥ 94: 1]

> Allah revealed to you the Book and Wisdom, and He taught you what you knew not.
> [al-Nisā' 4: 113]

> We had granted each of them judgement and knowledge.
> [al-Anbiyā' 21: 79]

> Follow those who do not ask any recompense from you and are rightly-guided.
> [Yā Sīn 36: 21]

The Book is the bright light with which the Prophet not only leads his followers on the Straight Path, but which he also employs to enrich them with the same illumination of knowledge, radiance of thought, and sublime truth that has been endowed to him in a higher degree. By his educating and training efforts, the Prophet enables his followers to not only receive guidance themselves but also to become guides and leaders for others – as long as they follow in his footsteps and hold in their hands the light given by him:

This is a Book which We have revealed to you that you may bring forth mankind from every kind of darkness into light.

[*Ibrāhīm* 14: 1]

We have now sent down this Reminder upon you that you may elucidate to people the teaching that has been sent down for them, and that the people may themselves reflect.

[*al-Naḥl* 16: 44]

In a very eloquent way the Qur'ān also states that the interchange-ability that may exist between the light and the guide in the material physical sense does not exist between the Prophet and the Book. In fact, there is a close partnership between them. Thus, the very same object that is likened to the Book at one point is metaphorically associated with the Prophet at another point. And, on the contrary, in the following set of verses the Prophet is represented as a lamp while the Book is referred to as a guide:

O Prophet, We have sent you forth as a witness, a bearer of good tidings, and a warner, as one who calls people to Allah by His leave, and as a bright, shining lamp.

[*al-Aḥzāb* 33: 45-46]

Verily this Qur'ān guides to the Way that is the Straight-most.

[*Banī Isrā'īl* 17: 9]

From this we see that the relationship between the Prophet and the Book is one that cannot be severed. Human beings need both of these equally. For the establishment of a system of thought and action and a culture and civilization that human beings desire, as well as for their sustainability, strengthening, and eternally retaining the true (original) shape, it is essential that they perpetually maintain this relationship with the Prophet and the Book. It is on account of this absolute necessity that both the Prophethood and the Book are declared separate belief elements. Man is constantly reminded of the need to profess belief in both of these elements. If such a reiteration had not been clearly intended, there would otherwise have been no need to underscore the separate status of these two belief elements because the veracity of the Prophet is inclusive of the veracity of the Book that he has brought and similarly the truthfulness of the Book is attested to by the truthfulness of its Prophet.

Belief (*Īmān*) in All the Heavenly Books

As far as belief is concerned, Islam commands its followers to profess belief in all the Books that have been revealed by God to His prophets. Just as it is essential to acknowledge belief in all the prophets and messengers to become and remain a Muslim, so it is also necessary to profess belief in all God's Books. The Qur'ān repeatedly mentions this requirement:

> Who believe in what has been revealed to you and what was revealed before you, and have firm faith in the Hereafter.
>
> [*al-Baqarah* 2: 4]

> Each of them believes in Allah, and in His angels, and in His Books, and in His Messengers.
>
> [*al-Baqarah* 2: 285]

> He has revealed this Book to you, setting forth the Truth and confirming the earlier Books, and He revealed the Torah and the Gospel.
>
> [*Āl ʿImrān* 3: 3]

> Say: 'We believe in Allah and what was revealed to us and what was revealed to Abraham and Ishmael and to Isaac and Jacob and his descendants, and the teachings which Allah gave to Moses and Jesus and to other Prophets. We make no distinction between any of them; and to Him do we submit.'
>
> [*Āl ʿImrān* 3: 84]

Those who gave the lie to this Book and all the Books which
We had sent with Our Messengers shall soon come to know
the Truth, when fetters and chains shall be on their necks,
and they shall be dragged into boiling water, and cast into
the Fire.

[al-Mu'min 40: 70-72]

Indeed We sent Our Messengers with Clear Signs, and sent
down with them the Book and the Balance that people may
uphold justice.

[al-Ḥadīd 57: 25]

After these general statements of principle, the requirement to profess
belief in certain particular scriptures is also specifically commanded.
These Books are also praised and extolled; for instance the Torah is
variously called 'guidance and light' [al-Mā'idah 5: 44; al-Qaṣaṣ 28:
43], the criterion (standard by which truth may be discerned from the
false) and illumination (al-Anbiyā' 21: 48), 'guide (imām) and a sign
of God's grace' (al-Aḥqāf 46: 12) respectively. Similarly, the Injīl (the
Islamic term for the Bible which is no longer extant) is also referred to
as guidance, light, and an admonition (al-Mā'idah 5: 46). Thus, it is
one of the principles of Islam that belief must generally be professed
in all the Books of Allah and explicitly on those that are mentioned
by name in the Qur'ān. By Islamic dogma there is no nation in the
world to which Allah's Prophets did not take His Books. All the books
that have been revealed to various regions and nations of the world
are streams emanating from the same fountainhead and rays from
the same sun. All have come with the same truth and uprightness, the
same guidance and light that is termed 'Islam'. Therefore, the 'Muslim'
(literally, one who, submits) professes belief in all of them. The person
who rejects any one of them, repudiates them all, and is, in fact, guilty
of renouncing the real Source of them all.

Exclusive Submission to the Qur'ān

However, after professing belief in all the revealed Books, the point
from where actual submission begins by way of deed, it is also necessary

to sever the connection with all these other books and only establish and retain one's relationship with the Qur'ān. There are many reasons for this:

First, many of the heavenly books are no longer extant. Of those that are still found, none except the Qur'ān is preserved both in its original literal text as well as in its meaning. Texts of human authorship have now come to be mixed together with Divine speech, both literally and semantically, in all the originally revealed texts except the Qur'ān. In these books, guidance has been blended with depravity that is the certain outcome of submitting to carnal desires. It is now difficult to ascertain the extent of (original) truth and subsequently inserted falsehood in these books. The same is the case with those other books on which various nations base their religions, and which may at least be surmised to have been of heavenly origin. Of these, some are totally devoid of any concept of having been Divinely revealed. With regard to some others, we can neither determine the names of the prophets to whom these were revealed, nor the period of their revelation, that is if they came at all from God. Certain books exist in languages that are now dead and as such it is difficult to establish their correct meanings. In some, there is an unmistakable mixing of human desires and false mythological concepts. A few contain references to teachings of *shirk* (polytheism), worship of deities other than Allah and other similar false beliefs that cannot be considered to be the Truth in any way. Books which are in such states of deterioration cannot provide the right knowledge and true light to human beings. After submitting to these books, their followers cannot be safe from degeneracy or corruption.

Secondly, all the books other than the Qur'ān, whether they are known to have been revealed or those which are suspected to be of such Divine origin, either manifest a strong influence of limited ethnic nationalism in their teachings and commandments or indicate an overwhelming exigency of certain time-specific conditions. They have neither been a means of salvation and guidance for all of humanity in every historical period nor do they have the capability to achieve the same.

Thirdly, there is no doubt that each one of these books has teachings that are true and righteous, and that present in them are certain admirable principles and good laws for the reformation of human morals and social transactions. However, none of these books is a comprehensive compendium of all the virtues, or one that totally manifests the complete truth, or which alone can provide the correct guidance for all walks of human life.

The Qur'ān alone is free from all these defects; consider the following truths:

(i)   The Qur'ān is preserved in exactly the same words in which it was presented to the Prophet Muḥammad (peace be upon him). From day one to the present age, in every time period and every region, millions of people have memorized it word for word. Tens of millions of people recite it every day. Its volumes have been produced in written form from the earliest days of its existence and not the least difference has been found in any of them.[1] Therefore, there is absolutely no doubt in the fact that the same Qur'ān which was recited by the Prophet Muḥammad (peace be upon him) is still extant today and shall always so remain. Not a word has been changed in this text, nor can it ever be.

(ii)   The Qur'ān was revealed in the Arabic, which remains a living language. There are hundreds of millions of people who speak and understand Arabic today. The standard idiom and classical literature of Arabic is the same today as the one that existed at the time of the Qur'ān's revelation. The process of ascertaining the meanings and propositions of the Qur'ān does not entail the problems that are faced in studying books of dead or non-extant languages (in which many ancient sacred texts are found).

(iii) The Qur'ān is the Absolute Truth. From the beginning to the end, the Qur'ān comprises Divine teachings. Nowhere does the Qur'ān have in its passages the least doubt of human emotions, carnal desires, national or group self-interest or uninformed depravities. There is not even the very slightest mixing of Divine speech with words of human origin in its contents.

---

[1] Many false texts ascribed as being earlier 'Qur'ānic versions' have been produced by Islam's opponents along with fabricated stories of their 'discovery', yet all of these have been rejected after scholarly scrutiny – Translator.

(iv) The Qur'ān addresses the entire human race. It presents such beliefs, moral principles and laws governing deeds that are neither specific to any particular country or nation nor are restricted to any given time period. Its teachings are universal and eternal.

(v) The Qur'ān brings together all the facts and knowledge of righteousness and virtue that were stated in the earlier revealed texts. There is no truth or moral theme of any religious text that can be shown to be missing from the Qur'ān. Naturally, in the presence of such an all-encompassing Book, man is freed from all other revealed books.

(vi) The Qur'ān is the latest edition of heavenly guidance and Divine teaching. Some of the guidance revealed in earlier Books – under specific circumstances – was removed from it. Similarly, many teachings that were not present in earlier Books have been added in the Qur'ān. Thus, it is incumbent upon a person who is not a believer of his ancestors' ways but truly a follower of Divine guidance to accept and abide by this last and latest edition of heavenly revelation and not its earlier versions.

These are the reasons on the basis of which Islam has severed the relationship of believers with all other Books and has declared only the Qur'ān to be worthy of being followed and submitted to. Islam invites the people of the whole world to make the Qur'ān their constitution – collectively as well as individually.

(O Messenger), We have revealed to you this Book with the Truth so that you may judge between people in accordance with what Allah has shown you.

[*al-Nisā'* 4: 105]

So those who believe in him and assist him, and succour him and follow the Light which has been sent down with him, it is they who shall prosper.

[*al-A'rāf* 7: 157]

It is for this reason that those nations that already had their own versions of any revealed Book have also been called upon to profess belief in the Qur'ān and submit their allegiance to it. Accordingly, the Qur'ān constantly reiterates the following message:

> O you who have been granted the Book! Do believe in what We have (now) revealed, which confirms the revelation which you already possess.
>
> [*al-Nisā'* 4: 47]

> People of the Book! Now Our Messenger has come to you: he makes clear to you a good many things of the Book which you were wont to conceal, and also passes over many things. There has now come to you a Light from Allah, and a Clear Book, through which Allah shows to all who seek to please Him the paths leading to safety. He brings them out, by His leave, from darkness to Light and directs them on to the Straight Way.
>
> [*al-Mā'idah* 5: 15-16]

> We surely sent down to you clear verses that elucidate the Truth, (verses) which only the transgressors reject as false.
>
> [*al-Baqarah* 2: 99]

Comprehensive Details of Faith in the Qur'ān

A Book which has been declared to be the true and correct guidance for human thought and belief, and one that has been designated as the enforceable law for our daily lives cannot be followed emphatically and truly until humankind is assured of its being correct, true and free from error. The reason for this is simple: if any kind of doubt about its health were to find its way into an individual's heart (or the collective consciousness of a group), this would lead to a loss of its total endorsement after which it would no longer be possible to truly respect or abide by the Book. On account of this necessity, the following essential elements of belief in the Qur'ān have been stated by the Qur'ān itself:

(i)   The Qur'ān is preserved in exactly the same text in which it was revealed. There has been no addition to or subtraction from it. The following verses attest to this fact:

> Surely it is for Us to have you commit it to memory and to recite it. And so when We recite it, follow its recitation attentively; then it will be for Us to explain it.
>
> [al-Qiyāmah 75: 17-19]

> We shall make you recite and then you will not forget, except what Allah should wish.
>
> [al-A'lā 87: 6-7]

> As for the Admonition, indeed it is We Who have revealed it and it is indeed We Who are its guardians.
>
> [al-Ḥijr 15: 9]

> (O Prophet), recite to them from the Book of your Lord what has been revealed to you for none may change His words.
>
> [al-Kahf 18: 27]

(ii)   There is not the slightest involvement of any Satanic force in the process of Qur'ānic revelation:

> The satans did not bring down this (Clear Book), nor does it behove them, nor does it lie in their power. Indeed they are debarred from even hearing it.
>
> [al-Shu'arā' 26: 210-12]

(iii)   Even the Prophet Muḥammad's wishes have no place in the Qur'ān:

> Nor does he speak out of his desire. This is nothing but a revelation that is conveyed to him ...
>
> [al-Najm 53: 3-4]

(iv)   Falsehood does not find its way into the Qur'ān:

> It is certainly a Mighty Book. Falsehood may not enter
> it from the front or from the rear. It is a revelation that
> has been sent down from the Most Wise, the Immensely
> Praiseworthy.
>
> [*Fuṣṣilat* 41: 41-42]

(v)   The Qur'ān is the absolute truth that has been revealed on the
basis of Knowledge, and not speculation or guesswork. There
is neither any deficiency nor any crookedness in it; it shows the
Straight Path very clearly:

> (O Prophet), those who have knowledge see clearly that
> what has been revealed to you from your Lord is the
> Truth and directs to the Way of the Most Mighty, the
> Immensely Praiseworthy Lord.
>
> [*Saba'* 34: 6]

> Certainly it is a Truth of absolute certainty.
>
> [*al-Ḥāqqah* 69: 51]

> Surely We have brought them a Book which We ex-
> pounded with knowledge; a guidance and a mercy to
> those who believe.
>
> [*al-Aʿrāf* 7: 52]

> Say to them (O Muḥammad): 'It is He Who knows the
> secrets of the heavens and the earth Who has sent down
> this Book.'
>
> [*al-Furqān* 25: 6]

> This is the Book of Allah, there is no doubt in it.
>
> [*al-Baqarah* 2: 2]

Praise be to Allah Who has revealed to His servant the
Book devoid of all crookedness; an unerringly Straight
Book.

[*al-Kahf* 18: 1-2]

Verily this Qur'ān guides to the Way that is the Straight-
most.

[*Banī Isrā'īl* 17: 9]

(vi) No one – not even the Prophet – has any authority to make any
amendments in the Qur'ān:

Tell them, (O Muḥammad): 'It is not for me to change
it of my accord. I only follow what is revealed to me.
Were I to disobey my Lord, I fear the chastisement of an
Awesome Day.'

[*Yūnus* 10: 15]

(vii) Anything that stands opposed to the Qur'ān is not at all worthy
of being followed:

(O people), follow what has been revealed to you from
your Lord and follow no masters other than Him.

[*al-A'rāf* 7: 3]

The above is Islam's detailed dogma about the Qur'ān. It is essential
to profess belief in every constituent element of this creed. Anyone
whose belief is deficient with regard to any of these elements will find
themselves unable to fully and truly abide by the Qur'ān and will then
stray from that straight path that is called 'Islam'.

The Foundation Stone of Islamic Universality

Belief in one Book and one Prophet, submission to the Message
and the Messenger, the setting of minds in the mould cast by these
submissions, the linking of all beliefs and rituals, morals and social

norms and all civic laws with this source, the linking of all followers of Islam in this wholesome relationship of belief, reverence and submission makes Islam a permanent civilization and the Muslims a single nation. This in spite of the numerous ethnic and linguistic, racial and regional differences amongst them.

It is possible that by way of varying erudition and intellectual capacities, research and *ijtihād*, viewpoints and natural temperaments, there may arise differences in the deduction of opinions about Islamic issues from the Qur'ān and the *Sunnah*, or that disagreements crop up in understanding their meaning and intent. But such differences and disagreements are only partial and superficial and neither make such jurisprudential schools separate *adyān* nor their followers distinct nations. The real foundation, on the basis of which the Muslim nation is established, is the acceptance of the Prophet Muḥammad (peace be upon him), as the sole leader on account of his being God's Messenger, the acknowledgment of the Qur'ān as the sole constitutional text in view of its status as the Divine Testament and the declaration of this fountainhead as the source of all beliefs and laws. All those who subscribe to this essence comprise one nation, in spite of whatever divergence and dissimilarity may exist between them on non-substantive issues. All those who fail to agree on this essential minimum agenda are, in Islam's view, a single distinct and different nation, notwithstanding the fact of their being broken up into whatever number of national groups.

The Qur'ān is, in fact, a compendium of all those issues upon which the foundations of Islam are established. Anyone who professes belief in the Qur'ān has in effect also acknowledged belief in God, His angels, His Books, His Prophets and the Last Day. This is because all these belief elements are described in detail in the Qur'ān. The certain reward of a sincere and true belief in the Qur'ān is the achievement of completion of belief. Similarly, all the principles and fundamental laws of the Islamic *Sharī'ah* are stated in the Qur'ān. These have been further elucidated and exemplified by the Prophet Muḥammad (peace be upon him) through his words and actions.

Therefore, a person who, together with the correct *īmān*, makes the Qur'ān and the Prophet's *Sunnah* a law that must be followed in all matters of his life is most certainly a Muslim by way of both belief and action. The summation of this belief and adherence is termed Islam. Where these two essentials are found, Islam will also be found and where these two are missing, Islam too will be absent.

8 Belief (*Īmān*) in the Last Day

In the Islamic context, the term 'Last Day' means the second life after death (or more precisely its starting point). It is for this reason that it is also called the life of the Hereafter (*ḥayāt al-ākhirah*) or the abode of the next world (*dār al-Ākhirah*). There is hardly a page of the Qur'ān that does not make mention of this second and eternal life. In numerous ways, the Qur'ān attempts to register this phenomenon in the minds of its audience. Arguments are established in favour of its truth and its detailed description is presented. Its importance is impressed upon very strongly. People are called to profess belief in it and it is clearly stated that a person who does not believe in the life of the Hereafter will find all his (apparently good) worldly deeds put to waste.

> Vain are the deeds of those who reject Our signs as false and to the meeting of the Hereafter as false.
>
> [*al-Aʿrāf* 7: 147]

> Those who consider it a lie that they will have to meet Allah are indeed the losers.
>
> [*al-Anʿām* 6: 31]

The dogma of the Next Life that is presented by Islam with such forceful emphasis is the answer to many questions that arise naturally in the human mind.

Some Natural Questions
Human beings are more likely to feel sadness than happiness and experience more discontent than tranquillity. It is but natural that the greater the effect anything has on human sentiment, the greater is the

force with which it affects and sets into motion his faculty of thought. Is it not a common experience that whenever we have achieved something special and are blessed with the pleasure of the moment, we do not indulge in the inconvenience of thinking about the source of our happiness by asking questions like 'Where has it come from? How has it come and how long will it last?'

However, no sooner have we lost a specially fond or valuable possession, than the unhappiness coming in its wake whips up a train of thought and we begin to wonder why it was lost? Numerous questions agitate our minds: Where has it gone? Where is it at this moment? Will we ever be able to find it again?

It is for this reason that questions about life and its beginning are not of as much importance to us as are questions relating to its end and death. This is in spite of the fact that upon seeing our own fleeting existence in this temporal glasshouse, the question 'Why all this ado?' must surely arise deep inside us. There are also questions such as: 'How did it all begin? Who launched it all?'

But all these are matters to be considered at leisure in the ease of our disposable time. It is, thus, that apart from the elitist few who possess the faculty of deeper reflection, not many commoners can afford to get bogged down by such questions. On the other hand, everyone has to, inevitably, get involved in the anguish of death. In everyone's life, there are many occasions when one sees relatives, friends and dear ones pass away. The weak and the powerless pass away, just as the powerful and the domineering ones do. There are woeful and sorrow-stricken deaths and there are admonitory, example-setting deaths. In the end, all of us become convinced of the inevitability of walking on the path over which all have walked before.

Viewing such scenes, there is hardly a person in the world in whose heart the question of death has not raised an agonizing challenge, and who has not contemplated upon the question, 'What is death?' Moreover, there are thoughts such as, 'Where do human beings go after passing through this doorway?' And, 'What lies beyond this doorway – if indeed there is anything or not?'

These, of course, are ordinary questions that have been contemplated by all, the commoners and the elite alike. All humans from peasants to philosophers have been confounded with these perennial questions. However, in this regard, there are some other questions that may also engage the hearts of the thoughtful. Many sorrowful events in life must also make this presence ever more disturbing. This brief period of life with which each of us has been endowed is fully utilized with virtually every minute being spent in some work or task, some effort or movement that we consider essential at the time of its unfolding. Even the periods we consider to be restful are motions of another kind. That which we deem to be uselessness is also an occupation. Each of these actions has a reaction, each action has its reverberations, every attempt has a reward and, as we all know, every undertaking must have an end.

It is but natural that we believe that good be rewarded with benevolence and evil with malevolence. We believe it to be essential that a noble effort should have a good end and an ignoble effort should have the bad end that it deserves. But, then, the question arises as to whether we will see the results of all our attempts, the fruits of all our efforts, the answers to all our actions within this lifetime of ours?

A wicked person who indulges in evil throughout his life will certainly have earned the fruits of at least some of his machinations. One of his excesses may have led to an illness, a scam may have caused some personal difficulty or anxiety, but certainly many a malicious act perpetrated by him must have remained unsettled without its full consequences being manifested. Some of his nastiness will have remained hidden from public view and, thus, he will not even have suffered any loss of reputation in this respect; and even if his name may have suffered a reversal, what about the victims against whom he was unjust and who suffered the consequences of his actions? Were their losses compensated for? Will the injustices of this malevolent person and the fortitude of his victims remain in eternal suspension without any conclusion? Will no result of these acts ever be forthcoming?

On the other hand, as we know from experience, many good people who remain busy in acting benevolently throughout their lives do not receive the full recompense for their efforts in the world. In fact, on the contrary, some of their munificent acts may even have caused them to suffer a loss of name and disgrace. Some of their goodwill may have led to personal torments and they may even have been punished or victimized for some of their benevolence by the unscrupulous who took advantage of them or on account of some misunderstandings. For one reason or the other, some of their charitable acts never come to be known to the world. Should it then be assumed, that all or some of their benevolence was wasted? Was the finding of personal self-contentment and gaining a satisfied conscience in their lifetimes enough reward for all their hard work and endeavours?

While the questions posed above only relate to human beings, there is another set of questions that deals with the final end of other living beings, plants and animals, and, indeed, every part of this whole universe. We see that human beings die and that in their place new ones are born. Plants and animals disappear and in their wake come others of their kinds. The question is whether this succession of life and death will continue in this way endlessly? Or will it end after reaching some point? Are all these materials including water and air, and forces like light and heat just natural processes operating within a specific imperishable mechanism? Is there no life span designated for them? Will there never be any transformation in their organization and discipline?

Islam has answered all these questions. In fact, belief in the life of the Hereafter is an answer to all these questions. However, before presenting the answer, and discussing its truth, as well as any moral and cultural outcomes, we must first see how successful human beings have otherwise been in their efforts to resolve these questions?

Denial of the Life in the Hereafter

One group of human beings says: 'Whatever life is or may be, it is limited to this temporal world and death means total annihilation after which there is neither life nor consciousness, neither feeling nor any result.'

> Indeed these people say: 'This is our first and only death, and we shall never be raised again.'
>
> [al-Dukhān 44: 34-35]

They say: 'There is no life other than our present worldly life: herein we live and we die, and it is only (the passage of) time that destroys us.'

[al-Jāthiyah 45: 24]

Such people also believe that the manner in which this cosmic workplace is operating, will eternally go on existing in this way. There is such permanence in this system that it will never be destroyed.

The people who believe and say this do so not on the basis of having acquired such knowledge by some special means or having successfully conducted research proving that there is no life after death, and that this cosmic workshop is beyond any degeneration. Instead, they have merely relied upon their senses and have come to hold this opinion because they have not felt or seen or otherwise perceived by means of their senses a state after death. Neither have they seen any signs of the disintegration of the cosmic system. However, the question is whether our inability to gain awareness about a thing or phenomenon by means of our senses is sufficient evidence or argument for our rejection of that phenomenon? Are our senses and feelings the real proof for the existence of anything and the lack of our ability to 'sense' the proof of its non-existence? If this is true, then it can be said that things only come into existence when one is able to discern them through the senses and likewise when they disappear from the bounds of sensual perception, they actually self-destruct into nothingness.

Continuing this line of argument, the river that I saw flowing was actually created just when I saw it, and when it disappeared from my view, it ceased to exist. Will any person of sound mind accept this statement? If not, then how can a person of reason accept the statement that, 'Since the post-mortal state has not been observed or experienced by us, therefore there is no state of existence after death?'

Just as it is wrong to pass a verdict about death and post-mortal annihilation merely on the basis of our senses, a judgement about life and its continuation based upon information flowing from the senses cannot be credible. If it is correct to pass a judgement about the cosmic workhouse being eternal and indestructible merely on the basis of the statement that we have not seen its disintegration, after seeing a strong building I too can say that it shall last forever, because I have never seen it falling, nor have I observed any weakness or fault-lines that may foretell its fall. Would this line of argument be accepted in any intellectual gathering?

The Impact of Rejecting the Hereafter on Morality

Philosophers are now all but unanimous in their belief that this cosmic system will one day, most certainly, fall apart and collapse. Perhaps, there is no longer anyone amongst such scholars would still hold on to the ancient philosophic concept of the cosmos being eternal. However, there are still many who consider death to be a final act of elimination – and the basis of this belief is the same that has been described above. Notwithstanding the fallacy of this belief, the fact remains that human beings will never gain full satisfaction from it.

There are many other questions that arise from observing the various facets of life but which remain unanswered from this line of argumentation about death being a terminal act). Moreover, if a person's morals and his character development were to be based upon this belief he would not be without two resultant states: first, when the conditions of his life are adverse, this belief would cause such an extreme feeling of dejection and low-spiritedness in him that he would see no result of his righteousness manifesting itself in this world, and so his spirit would naturally cool and zeal would burnout. Secondly, when upon being subjected to injustice he found no way out of his tormented state, his heart would break. When he sees the mischievous, the evildoers, and the unjust prospering in the world, he would think that it is only evil that thrives in this realm and that virtue is destined to be overcome.

On the contrary, when conditions are favourable, the same person would, under the influence of this belief, become a self-seeking, pleasure-loving animal. He would consider ample whatever number of days he is able to pass in self-indulgence and luxury. He would imagine that there would be no other life in which to make up for any sensual pleasure or gratification that remains unfulfilled in this world. Thus, he would act unjustly by usurping other people's rights. For his own gain and the fulfilment of his carnal desires he would not be held back from perpetrating the worst of malevolences. For such a person, the greatest virtue and state of uprightness that could occur would only be one which, once manifested, would bring him good repute, fame, respectability or any other kind of worldly benefit. In this way, he would only consider such crimes unlawful, and only those vices sinful, which were likely to lead to some temporal punishment, bodily harm, or material loss. As for those virtues that are not likely to manifest themselves in the form of some worldly gain, he would consider these nothing less than stupidity. And, any vices that are not likely to lead to any temporal loss would be considered by him to be quite rewarding.

If the whole moral system of a society were to be established upon such a belief and mentality, the complete set of moral conceptualization would be turned upon its head. Indeed, such a moral system would then be built upon selfishness and carnality. Righteousness would only be synonymous with worldly benefit and wickedness would be equated to temporal loss. Falsehood would be a sin only if it were to cause some loss in this world; and if it were to be beneficial, it would become a virtue. If truth were to be a source of gain, it would be righteous; otherwise in case of loss there would be no greater evil. In terms of pleasure and sensuality, unlawful sexual indulgence would be quite a commendable act; if, in any way, there were to arise some implication of wrongdoing in this, it would be limited to the adverse effect it may have on one's health or worldly reputation. In short, when there is no hope or fear of any good or bad result arising from worldly life, people only keep in view those actions whose results become apparent – or are likely to become apparent – in this life. The transformation in the moral values governing human actions that proceed from this mindset are those that cannot be advantageous for any 'civilized' human society. Rather, it would be more appropriate to say that with such moral standards, no human group would be able to avoid falling to a level even worse than that of animals.

Arguably, one could say that material and bodily gains or losses in this world are not the only determinants of reward and punishment, but that there is another force which is active in this regard, deep inside human beings – namely, the conscience. The chastisement and restlessness of the conscience is enough punishment for wrongdoing in this world – and its fulfilment is enough reward for human goodness. However, I would counter by saying that, first of all, there are many sins whose material advantages prompt the conscience into accepting a certain reproof and that for many virtues human beings have to make so many sacrifices that the mere contentment of the conscience cannot be their full return.

Secondly, if one were to reflect upon the reality of the conscience, one would come to recognize that its function is not to generate moral conceptions, but to support those moral notions that have come to be firmly implanted in the human mind by way of a particular type of teaching and training. It is for this reason that a Muslim's conscience does not chide him upon the things that to a Hindu's conscience appear reproachable, for instance-eating beef. Thus, if a society's moral concepts change and its standards of right and wrong are transformed, the direction of its group conscience also changes. The conscience would then stop censuring acts that the society has now ceased to consider sinful, and would similarly no longer feel satisfied with those actions that society no longer deems righteous.

The Theory of Transmigration
A second group of people who reject the life of the Hereafter is the one that has presented the 'Theory of Transmigration'. Very briefly, this theory states that death does not mean annihilation but only a transformation of the corporeal form. At death, the soul or spirit departs from one body, which is merely a container, and adopts a different body or form. This new form is dependent upon certain qualifying criteria – like point scores in a game – which a person has accumulated and provided through his actions and attitudes in his first or earlier life. If his actions have been bad and under the influence of which he has developed evil qualifications in his soul, then the soul descends to a lower animal or plant stratum. However, if his deeds were virtuous and provided good qualifications, the soul ascends and travels to a higher strata. In short, by virtue of this theory, whatever rewards or punishments exist with regard to human and other life are only to be found in this world in its corporeal structures. The soul

keeps coming back to this world in different forms and bodies so that it is able to enjoy or suffer the consequences of past actions.

This theory was very popular at one time. Several centuries before Christ, in ancient Greece, intellectuals like Pythagoras and Empedocles were its proponents. It was also popular in pre-Christian Rome. Its traces are found in ancient Egyptian history also. By way of external influences, the dogma of transmigration also entered Judaism. However, today this belief is either found in religions of Indian origin (Brahmanism, Buddhism, Jainism, etc.) or in the aboriginal religions of pre-civilized and stone-age tribal nations of West and South Africa, Madagascar, Central Australia, Indonesia, Oceania and the Americas. All other civilized nations have rejected this theory because whatever awareness has been made possible by the intellectual and scientific progress of mankind contradicts the ideas upon which the theory of transmigration is based.

Even amongst those religions of Indian origin, when we examine the history of this theory we find that this concept was totally absent from ancient Vedic India. It was only amongst the Aryans of the time that the concept of a second life after death – which was pure contentment for the virtuous and pure affliction for the wicked – existed. Immediately thereafter, there was a sudden transformation in this theory. In the Indian literature of this later period, the theory of transmigration is found in the form of a philosophical dogma. However, we do not know the cause behind this transformation. Some researchers believe that this concept came to the Aryans from the Dravidians while others say that it was present among the lower echelons of the Aryans themselves and from whom the Brahmin philosophers adopted it and then went on to construct a whole structure of conceptualisations and speculations out of it.

Similarly, Buddhism was also initially free of the detailed scheme of transmigration that is found in later Buddhist literature. As far as ancient literature is concerned, the initial Buddhist view was that existence is like a river that is flowing gloriously in constant transformation and revolution. Later, this concept took the modified form in which it came to be held that the whole world comprises just one soul and that there is just one existence that keeps on taking different shapes and forms. From this arises a clear indication that the Indian nations obtained an initial knowledge from the fountainhead of Divine revelation and inspiration, but which was later changed by them. In its place, they invented a philosophic religious creed that was totally of their own creation.

Intellectual Criticism on the Theory of Transmigration
Although, at this point, there is no room for a detailed analysis of the doctrine of transmigration and its related problems, in order to establish its fallacy it is enough to point out that this dogma is based upon concepts that are clearly against reason and contradict all the scientific knowledge that human beings have gained by studying our world and the life therein. Those who believe in transmigration believe that everyone obtains the result of his actions in this world by way of either ascending to higher strata on account of good deeds or descending into lower levels due to bad actions. For instance, if a person committed bad actions in this life, he would slide down towards the animal and plant strata and if an animal was good in its life, it would progress towards human levels. This would accordingly mean that animal and plant life is the result of depraved human actions and that human life is the result of nobility amidst animal and plant life. In other words, human beings who exist today are human because their forerunning animal and plant counterparts performed virtuous acts and the presently existing animals and plants are what they are because their human forbears committed wicked acts in their lives. In order to accept this theory, it is essential to believe in a number of other facts, all of which run against knowledge and intellect, including for instance:

(i)   This cycle of transmigration is one that has no starting point. For a person to be human, it is necessary that one ought to have been a plant or animal, and for a plant or animal to be what it is at present, it is necessary for it to have been a human at some earlier point. This is a cyclical fallacy that is intellectually impossible.

(ii)   If the cycle of transmigration were eternal – lasting from ages primordial to the apocalyptical – then it would have to be accepted that not only the souls that constantly change their forms or resident bodies, but also the bodies that provide abodes for the souls must be eternal. Similarly, this earth, the solar system and the cosmos and the forces therein must also be eternal. However, reason claims – and scientific knowledge confirms – that our cosmos has neither existed from the beginning of time nor will it last indefinitely.

(iii) It would also have to be accepted that all the distinguishing features of plants, animals and human beings are actually the characteristics of their bodies and not of their souls. This is because the soul that is in a human body was endowed with the faculties of reason and reflection but became totally irrational upon reaching animal form and further (down the spiritual road) in a plant body the poor thing even lost the power of voluntary movement.

(iv) The attribute of being good or bad is applicable only to those actions that are undertaken rationally and deliberately. In this way, while human actions may be good or bad – and thus could lead to reward or punishment – it would neither be fair to pass a verdict of probity or improbity on the acts of plants and animals nor is there any good reason for reward or punishment to accrue on such acts. In order to be able to pass such a judgement it would also have to be accepted that plants and animals also have the power to act consciously and deliberately.

(v) If the life of a later period is the fruit of the actions of the present birth-cycle, it should be obvious that the consequences of bad actions should naturally be bad. However, it is not clear how it is possible that good deeds grow out of this bad fruit (as recipients of this bitter fruit have an even chance to ascend or descend) in the next life cycle. Without doubt, such bitter fruit must be the source of even worse actions and obviously, the fruit of this second cycle should be even bitterer in the third life cycle. In this way, the soul of a wicked human being, caught in the cycle of transmigration, would forever keep on falling towards lower strata and it could not be expected to rise upwards again. This would mean that while it would be possible for a human being to become an animal the opposite would not be the case. Now, the question is: From where have the 'living entities' that are presently human arisen and as a response to which good actions on the part of lower entities?[1]

The Impact of Transmigration on Culture

In addition to the above, there are many other reasons why the theory of transmigration is intellectually flawed and, hence, unacceptable. It is for this reason that the dogma of transmigration increasingly came to be regarded as unsound and ineffectual, concurrent with the progress of human intellect and knowledge, so much so that it is now generally restricted to those groups that lag behind in terms of intellectual and educational progress.

Together with this, it is also a fact that the dogma of transmigration is one that downgrades aspirations and kills off spiritual progress. From this dogma has arisen the doctrine of 'Ahimsa' that is extremely fatal both to the individual and communal lives of human beings. A nation that becomes committed to this doctrine loses its fighting spirit. Its physical energy wanes and its prowess deteriorates. It is deprived of the nourishing foods that strengthen the body's physique. Its constituent individuals not only become physically weak but also grow mentally infirm. The result of this double enfeeblement is that such a nation remains subdued and politically subjugated and is eventually either annihilated by conquest or assimilated into other more powerful nations.

The second impairment caused by the dogma of transmigration is the adverse effect that it has on the development of culture and civilization. As an adversary of civilization, transmigration leads human beings towards asceticism and renunciation of the temporal milieu. Believers of transmigration hold that the one thing that defiles the soul is 'desire'. It is because of this source of corruption that the soul has to constantly suffer the consequences of its actions by reincarnating in various bodily forms. If human beings were to totally decimate

---

[1] For further criticism of the theory of transmigration, please see *Towards Understanding the Qur'ān*, Volume III, 1990, pp. 23-29.

desire and remove themselves from worldly transactions, their souls would be delivered from the cycles of reincarnation.[2] This is the only means of release and salvation. Because it is impossible for human beings to escape desires and their attendant linkages (requirements and results) after being caught up in the affairs of worldly life, the inescapable consequence of this would be that those people who seek salvation would necessarily be forced to take up asceticism and retreat from civilization into the wilderness. And those who do not follow this path should give up all hope of salvation and prepare themselves to enter the ranks of animals and plants. Can this concept be helpful in any way in the progress of cultures and civilizations? And can any nation possessing this dogma progress in the world?

Without doubt, the dogma of transmigration is at least better than believing death to be the final end and absolute nothingness. The natural desire that we humans hold for immortality and continuity finds satisfaction to a certain extent in transmigration. At the same time, however, transmigration contains a concept of reward and punishment with respect to good and bad deeds – a concept that can become the rearguard for a strong moral law.

All the same, firstly, it is an undeniable fact, and one which has been pointed out many times earlier, that a dogma which is contrary to knowledge and an impediment in the path of cultural and civilizational progress can never have a strong enough command over the human mind and heart for it to sustain itself with equal vigour at every stage of educational and intellectual evolution and every step of cultural and civilizational development. Moreover, when such a belief cannot maintain its hold, then its mere existence as a philosophic concept cannot be of any benefit for the sustainability and strengthening of the moral system because it would only be valuable when people have full faith in it and when it resides in their hearts and not just in books.

Secondly, with a view to its final outcome, this dogma loses all its moral value when a person is convinced that the system of reincarnation is operating totally mechanically, and that every preordained result of

---

[2] The so-called 'nirvana'.

every action will certainly manifest itself, come what may – and that no amount of prayer or penitence will alter the consequence of the said act. In this way, a person committing a sin once will always be trapped in the unending cycle of sin. Such a person will reason that if it is his destiny to become an animal or a plant, then why should full advantage of this human station (in the transmigration cycle) not be availed by completely indulging in all its pleasures.

Faith in the Life of the Hereafter

Having seen the opinions of two major religious traditions on the issue of the end of the world and humanity, you will now be clear that these two religious beliefs are neither intellectually correct, nor do to they provide fully satisfying answers to those natural questions that arise in the mind after seeing indications of decline and destruction in the world. Furthermore, these two conceptualizations do not have the capability of becoming the bulwark for a true and strong moral system. Now, let us consider a third religion and see what it has to say in this regard.

(i)   Just as everything in the world has, in its individual capacity, a certain life span, at the expiry of which it suffers degeneration, the whole cosmic system also has a life span upon the termination of which this whole workplace shall cease operations and be disbanded. At this point, some other system will take its place whose physical laws will be different from the physical laws of the present system.

(ii) Upon destruction of this system, Allah will establish a Court of Justice in which everyone will be held accountable. That day, every human being will gain a new corporeal life. They will all be assembled before their God. All their individual actions that they performed in the first life shall be judged very accurately and weighed. Every case shall be decided with full Righteousness and Justice. Good deeds will receive good recompense and bad deeds accordingly will receive due punishment.

(iii) The present human life in this world is actually a preface to that life of the Hereafter. This life is temporary and the one to come will be permanent. This one is flawed and that one will be complete. Not all the results of human actions reveal themselves in this provisional lifetime. Every seed that is sown here does not fructify to the extent of its potential with all its natural fruits in this imperfect lifetime. The imperfection of this life will be removed by completion in the next; whatever has remained without a conclusive result here will manifest itself with its true results and fruits there. Accordingly, human beings should not only view merely those incomplete – and occasionally deceptive – outcomes of their actions that arise in this temporal life, but should rather establish value parameters that govern their actions with a view to this compilation of the final results.

This is the religion that has been presented by the Prophets of God. The Qur'ān is a vociferous advocate of this religion. However, before we take up a discussion of its moral outcomes and its status and importance in the Islamic civilization that it creates, we should take a look at the line of reasoning and propositions of this religion vis-à-vis the dogma of life in the Hereafter. Also it is to be seen how far the intellect accepts these arguments.

The Correct Approach to Intellectual Research

The question whether there is any life after death belongs to the category of themes that are beyond the bounds of our senses and sensual experience. Whatever we see and feel is restricted to the observation that a person who was breathing and moving by virtue of his own voluntary accord has now been dispossessed of all attributes of life. The thing that had provided this rigid, nameless, and immobile matter with the power of growth and movement has disappeared. Now the question remains as to where that thing has gone? Does it still exist after being separated from its corporeal body or has it ceased to exist? Moreover, will it again be associated with its original body or another similar corpus?

As far as our senses and our experiential knowledge is concerned, we can neither answer this question in the negative nor the affirmative, as we have neither experienced that particular 'thing' in the past nor are we able to do so at this point in time. On this account, we should understand that this question has nothing to do with science, i.e. the corpus of our experiential knowledge and any practical wisdom. If the practitioners of science cannot pass an affirmative judgement on this issue, then they have no right to pass a verdict in its denial. All that any of them can say is: 'I am unaware as to what happens after death.' However, if such argumentation moves from the point of unawareness and ignorance to a position of, 'Since I do not know what happens after death, therefore I know that nothing happens,' this would certainly exceed the bounds of reasonableness.

After the senses, the second source of our knowledge is 'thought'. Our species has always refused to be confined within the bounds of our sensual perceptiveness. An essential imperative of this human instinct has always been that we have investigated all those hidden realties that are beyond sensual experience by employing faculties of thought and analysis. This philosophical exploration is called the 'thought process' and it may be undertaken in two ways:

First, that we close our eyes to the world and also to the signs and proofs afforded by our own self, or become detached to a great extent, and then start deriving results from purely intellectual arguments and then continue galloping in that direction. This would be the exclusive domain of speculative philosophy and the racing track of all misguided deeds and transgressions. This is the dark road from which have arisen those philosophic religions entangled in whose webs human beings have wandered in the vales of (speculative) imagination. It is from here that those different and contradictory dogmas about God, angels, the cosmic system, and life after death have sprung; all of these are the result of groping in the dark and treading the path of imagination, speculation, and human inference.

The second mode of thought involves keeping our eyes open and observing the signs existing within the cosmos – and also those that are within our own selves; these are the torchbearers on the way to the true destination. Then, bearing these lights, and helped along with a sound intellect and correct thought, we should explore those realities that lie hidden in these signs. In this second mode, both science and philosophy walk together. Although this too is not a certain means of reaching the real truth, apart from heavenly guidance it is nonetheless the only method for approaching the truth available to human beings. Through this method it is possible to reach the truth, or at least get close to it, provided that the explorers' observation is keen, their perceptive powers are penetrating and delicate, and that they possess ample capability for analysis and thought.

In the domain of conceptual wisdom, the pivot of human progress rests on the combination of this observation and thought. None of the concepts upon which the foundations of wisdom have been laid nor any of the principles upon which scientists must profess belief in order to move even one step forward is merely based upon experience and observation. Every concept and every principle is founded upon intellectual deduction for which observation and experience are used as the inferential raw material. The laws of nature generally and the law of gravity, the processes of cause and effect, the theory of relativity, the theories of development and evolution, the theory of natural selection, specifically – and principles upon which all leading people of wisdom have professed their belief – are all the result of analysis, reflection and intellectual inference upon the observations of natural phenomena and their resultant manifestations. Otherwise, no one has ever directly observed these laws and principles.

Moreover, the wise are as confident of the conclusions that they draw from their observations and inferences, as commoners are sure about the sensual perception of something. In spite of this, even the wisest of the wise cannot force a denier or a rejecter to accept such conclusions because, until a person views the signs and manifestations with that particular perspective with which wise people have observed them and does not employ the same analysis and thought which the wise have used, they will never be able to reach the same conclusions. Thus, for common folk the only means of stepping into and progressing in the realm of wisdom is to consent to blind faith in the conclusions drawn by whichever wise person they may trust, unless they are able to reach the same conclusions by way of their individual observation, study and deliberation.

Please commit to heart this line of reasoning, as this internalization is essential for understanding the Qur'ān's exposition and argumentation. A lack of understanding of the Qur'ānic thesis leads to many misinterpretations.

Now we turn to the Qur'ān and its account of life after death.

The Objections to the Life in the Hereafter
The criticism levelled by unbelievers against the life in the Hereafter at the time the Qur'ān was presented is the same that the unbelievers make today. In fact, this is the one and only point of disapproval that is possible – that the phenomenon of coming back to life after death is an act beyond reason and contemplation. In other words, how can we accept that dead corpses, which have lain rotting in the soil, whose elements have been united with the earth or whose parts have been scattered into the earth, water and air, will once again be granted life?

> They say: 'Shall we be created afresh after we have become lost in the earth?'
>
> [al-Sajdah 32: 10]

> They say: 'When we are turned to bones and particles (of dust), shall we truly be raised up as a new creation?'
>
> [Banī Isrā'īl 17: 49]

> 'What? When we are dead and reduced to mere dust, (shall we be raised to life)? Such a return is far-fetched.'
>
> [Qāf 50: 3]

> Who will quicken the bones when they have decayed?
>
> [Yā Sīn 36: 78]

The Qur'ānic Argument
Placed against this doubt is the Qur'ānic argumentation whereby it, first of all, invites all to observe the manifestations of God's power and contemplate thereupon. The Qur'ān states:

Soon shall We show them Our Signs on the horizons and in their own beings until it becomes clear to them that it is the Truth.

[*Fuṣṣilat* 41: 53]

Have they not observed the kingdom of the heavens and the earth.

[*al-A'rāf* 7: 185]

How many are the signs in the heavens and the earth which people pass by without giving any heed!

[Yūsuf 12: 105]

These verses point to the fact that human beings have neither been granted the capability to discern that which is hidden from their senses nor the ability to empirically determine the true reality of such phenomena. However, if they were to really observe these phenomena – the day and night which unfold before their eyes, the management of the earth and heavens, and the very fact of their own creation – and attempt to arrive at their true reality by way of thought and contemplation based upon the experiential and perceptional processes, they will surely realize that whatever has been said in the Qur'ān is correct.

The Possibility of Life in the Hereafter

The Qur'ān presents from amongst the indications and manifestations of God's handiwork those that are the most self-evident. From these it argues that the phenomena which some human beings consider beyond reason or reflection is not impossible, howsoever distant it may seem from anyone's intellectual prowess:

It is Allah Who has raised the heavens without any supports that you could see, and then He established Himself on the Throne (of Dominion). And He it is Who has made the sun and the moon subservient (to a law), each running its course till an appointed term. He governs the entire order

of the universe and clearly explains the signs that you may
be firmly convinced about meeting your Lord.

[al-Ra'd 13: 2]

Is it harder to create you or the heaven? But Allah built
it…

[al-Nāzi'āt 79: 27]

From the evidence presented by the heavenly bodies, the Qur'ān
argues how unintelligent it is to think of a God Who has created such
a vast cosmic system, and Who has held back these huge heavenly
bodies in the restraint of His law, Whose power enables these enormous
bodies to move with such precise management that none of them
moves a hair's breadth from their orbits, nor becomes unsynchronised
for a second, and whose Supreme Control has established the cosmos
on such invisible and imperceptible support, that He does not have
the capability to bring back to life, after having put it to death, such an
insignificant creature as a human being:

Have they not perceived that Allah, Who has created the
heavens and the earth, has the power to create the like of
them?

[Banī Isrā'īl 17: 99]

Say: 'Go about the earth and see how He created for the
first time, and then Allah will recreate life.' Surely, Allah has
power over everything.

[al-'Ankabūt 29: 20]

Let the dead earth be a Sign for them. We gave it life and
produced from it grain whereof they eat.

[Yā Sīn 36: 33]

See, then, the tokens of Allah's Mercy: how He revives the
earth after it is dead. Verily He is the One Who will revive
the dead. He has power over everything.

[al-Rūm 30: 50]

And of His Signs is that you see the earth withered, then
We send down water upon it, and lo! it quivers and swells.
Surely He Who gives life to the dead earth will also give life
to the dead. Surely He has power over everything.

[*Fuṣṣilat* 41: 39]

It is Allah Who sends forth winds which then set the clouds
in motion, which We drive to some dead land giving a
fresh life to earth after it had become dead. Such will be the
resurrection of the dead.

[*Fāṭir* 35: 9]

After this the Qur'ān exhorts us to reflect upon our own souls, for
within our own selves lies the proof of God's ability to revive us from
death.

Was there a period of time when man was not even worthy
of a mention.

[*al-Dahr* 76: 1]

How can you be ungrateful to Allah Who bestowed life
upon you when you were lifeless, then He will cause you to
die and will again bring you back to life so that you will be
returned to Him.

[*al-Baqarah* 2: 28]

O mankind! If you have any doubt concerning Resurrection, then know that it is surely We Who created you from
dust.

[*al-Ḥajj* 22: 5]

He says: 'Who will quicken the bones when they have
decayed?' Say: 'He Who first brought them into being will
quicken them.'

[*Yā Sīn* 36: 78-9]

Tell them: '(You will be raised afresh even if) you turn to stone or iron, or any other form of creation you deem hardest of all (to recreate from).' They will certainly ask: 'Who will bring us back (to life)?' Say: 'He Who created you in the first instance.'

[*Banī Isrā'īl* 17: 50-51]

We created man out of the extract of clay, then We made him into a drop of life-germ, then We placed it in a safe depository, then We made this drop into a clot, then We made the clot into a lump, then We made the lump into bones, then We clothed the bones with flesh, and then We caused it to grow into another creation.[3] Thus Most Blessed is Allah, the Best of all those that create. Thereafter you are destined to die, and then on the Day of Resurrection you shall certainly be raised up.

[*al-Mu'minūn* 23: 12-16]

Was he not a drop of ejaculated semen, then he became a clot, and then Allah made it into a living body and proportioned its parts, and then He made of him a pair, male and female? Does He, then, not have the power to bring back the dead to life?

[*al-Qiyāmah* 75: 37-40]

After having presented these unambiguous and definite proofs that are very close to our own observation and perception, the Qur'ān presents such a clear argument that totally relates to common sense. It asks whether it is more difficult to create things from a state of nothingness than to reconstruct them from their post-destruction residue? Thus, it raises the question as to why a power that did not shy away from performing a more difficult task be incapable

---

[3] Though all this happens in the creation of animals as well, by this process of creation God has shaped man into a special creature different from the animals – Translator.)

of accomplishing an easier undertaking? If a person is capable of inventing an automobile from scratch and has already done so, does it make sense to state that he is incapable of merely reassembling the parts after having taken them apart? Based upon this analogy, the Creator of the cosmos Who brought us into existence from non-existence is certainly capable of recreating us after death:

> Have they never observed how Allah creates for the first time and then repeats it? Indeed (to repeat the creation of a thing) is even easier for Allah (than creating it for the first time).
>
> [*al-'Ankabūt* 29: 19]

> It is He Who creates in the first instance and it is He Who will repeat the creation, and that is easier for Him.
>
> [*al-Rūm* 30: 27]

> Did We, then, become worn out by the first creation? Not at all; but they are in doubt about a fresh creation.
>
> [*Qāf* 50: 15]

Now the only lingering doubt that remains is with regard to how those dead corpses whose parts have long ceased to exist are again endowed with the same body? Some may have drowned and their bodies would have become food for marine animals; some may have burnt to death and virtually all of their bodies would have converted into ash and carbon dioxide, still others may have been buried and their bodies would have combined with the soil. So, how is it possible that an old body is returned and once again united with the same soul? Some Qur'ān commentators have tried to brush this doubt aside by stating that in order to provide a soul with a corporeal existence, it is not essential for it to be reunited with the same body, i.e. the one that it occupied earlier. It is also possible that the soul remains the same and that it is granted another body similar to its previous one.

However, in this regard, the Qur'ān states that God with all His authority and power can endow again the same old body with its soul.

The ingredients of the earlier body have not ceased to exist. Instead, even in their dispersed form, each of the constituent elements exists somewhere or the other – be it in the air, water, soil or in some plant or animal body or in a mineral deposit.[4] God's knowledge is so Overwhelming and so Unparalleled that He alone knows the resting place of every atom and His Capability is so Supreme that He can bring all these scattered parts together to recreate the original appearance:

> (Thus do they imagine, although) We know well what the earth takes away from them. With Us is a Record that preserves everything.
>
> [*Qāf* 50: 4]

> He has the keys to the realm of the Unseen which none knows but He. And He knows what is on the land and in the sea; there is not a leaf which falls that He does not know about and there is not a grain in the darkness of the earth or anything green or dry which has not been recorded in a Clear Book.
>
> [*al-Anʿām* 6: 59]

The purpose of whatever has been stated above is to bridge the knowledge gap on the basis of which people dismiss the concept of life in the Hereafter. The reason for this renouncement is not that the rejecters have come to know with certainty and on the basis of some experience, observation, or definite knowledge or through some other means that there is no life after death. In fact, the rejection is only based on the actuality that such a coming back of an entity to life after its death does not fit into their existing experience and reasoning. They have never seen such a phenomenon. They are accustomed to the dead not returning to life. Therefore, when it is said to them that those who are dead will return to life once again, they consider this statement to be against their experience, beyond reason and conjecture, and therefore impossible.

---

[4] Q.v. The law of the conservation of matter – Translator.

However, when we move ahead on the path of contemplation and analysis, this gap disappears and that which appeared impossible begins to seem very much possible. The reason that we consider certain phenomena to be possible, or actual fact, is because we have become used to seeing their existence. Processes like a small seed germinating in the soil and then going on to become a towering tree, a drop settling in the womb and finally emerging as a human being, the formation of water by the combination of two gases, the transformation of this water into vapour and back to water, the movement of millions of ball-like heavenly bodies in orbits stretched across the immense vastness of the cosmos and being suspended in space without any material linkages in a way that not the very slightest difference occurs in their movements and mutual organizations, all seem to be quite ordinary because we are accustomed to seeing and knowing them. If these things had not been familiar to us, and instead we had been accustomed to some other system, we would have considered all of these phenomena to be beyond reason, and would have refuted their possibility with some vigour.

Consider, for instance, a situation in which we found intelligent life on Mars but at the same time found that there were no plants. If those people were told that a minute amount of matter called a seed when placed in the soil grew millions of times its original size and became a tree, and then that one tree led to thousands of the same kind, this fact would be as astonishing and dumbfounding for the Martians as the tale of coming back to life again after death. The Martians would say that this thing called a tree would not be possible in the way described. Obviously, this pronouncement of impossibility would have been made not on the basis of knowledge, but rather the absence thereof – ignorance, to be precise – and the lack of access to any other reason but the one with which they were familiar.

Precisely the same is the case with the human knowledge gap. If a person or a group were to understand the actuality of their scepticism or distance from the truth, they would come to know that the state of something being beyond the bounds of their knowledge, reason or contemplation is no rationale for the impossibility or improbability of the existence of that thing or phenomenon. The things that we are inventing today were beyond the reason, contemplation and imagination of other human beings a hundred years ago – if not less. Events have proved that these things were not impossible. Similarly the things that we consider impossibly distant today may well come into existence by our own hands in a hundred or two hundred years, if not sooner. Events would then prove that these too were not impossible. When the true state of human reason – and also that of things being close or distant from this supposedly infallible reason – is such, nothing can be declared to be impossible merely on the basis of the fact that its possibility does not fit into the limited capacity of human reason or imagination.

The first step on the road towards proving the existence of a thing that is either hidden or beyond the bounds of the senses is to establish the possibility of its existence. Thus, in order to remove any doubts about life in the Hereafter, the Qur'ān has proved its possibility. Now the second step is to prove the necessity of its existence so that the intellect acknowledges that such a phenomenon should exist and that its existence is better than its absence.

The Cosmic System is a Perfect System

The affirmation of life in the Hereafter actually depends upon a resolution to the question of 'whether this cosmos is the action of a Wise Being or whether it has come into being without any wisdom, all of its own accord?'

Present-day scientists – or at least a good number of them – say that this system was not brought into existence by a Wise Creator and that it came into being by itself. Moreover, it is functioning like an automatic machine together with all its constituent parts which include human beings. The day that this mutual interaction of matter and energy ends, will be the day when this system self-destructs.

Quite obviously, it is futile to search for any purposefulness or prudence in a system that is being operated by a blind nature without any knowledge, intellect, understanding, resolve and wisdom. It is for this reason that materialistically inclined scientists have not only expelled the teleological causation of natural phenomena from their precincts, but have actually termed this philosophical process as being futile and meaningless. With absolute certainty, numerous scientists have declared that there is no purpose in any component of the cosmos or its actions. The eyes have not been endowed for seeing, but the act of seeing is actually the result of that specific organization of matter that is found in the eyes. The brain does not exist to serve as the site of reasoning, thought and understanding, but rather ideas come out of the cerebral matter in a manner that is akin to the production of bile from the liver. It is a mere fallacy to consider the natural actions of things as their 'purpose' just as is the attempt to discover some wisdom or reason in their existence.

If this hypothesis is accepted, there remains no good reason for recognizing the need of any life after the present temporal one. This is because the status of a cosmic system that is operating in the hands of some blind nature without reason or understanding and without any purpose or end-point cannot be anything more than a plaything. It would follow that this system and everything therein is frivolous, that it was created in vain, and that it shall one day end in absurd destruction. It would be fallacious to believe that such an unintelligent nature is endowed with the attribute of justice and equity or to expect it to hold people to judicious accountability.

If for the sake of argument, it is assumed that this nature is imparted with a sense of justice, even then the recognition of a need for a second life seems implausible in a situation in which human beings who are playing in its hands like powerless toys, and who let alone doing anything of their own volition do not even have any free will or determination. Accordingly, it would be only fair not to hold such creatures accountable for their good or bad deeds, just as no responsibility can be placed on an automobile for either staying on its course or deviating from it. Furthermore, once the question of accountability is removed, the whole issue of equity and justice, reward and punishment becomes redundant.

However, this hypothesis is totally against reason. Moreover, no intellectual or scholastic evidence has been presented by way of which its truth may be proved and authenticated. Whatever has been said in its support may be summarized as, 'We neither see any creator or operator of the cosmos nor do we understand any purpose in its creation. We see it operating without any creator. Neither is it possible for us to investigate the reason for its operation, nor do we find any need for inquiring about this.'

Not knowing or not having the ability to know the material cause for the existence or operation of something is not a proof of the fact that such material cause does not exist at all. Consider a situation in which a child sees a printing press in operation. He does not understand the reason for the operation of this machine. Because of this lack of understanding he assumes that it is a mere plaything that is running without any rhyme or reason. He sees the many parts in motion, the vibrating floor, and the sheets of printed paper coming out of the machine and hears its sounds. On account of this he declares that just as all the actions are the results of the operation of the machine, the production of printed papers is also a natural result of the machine's movement. He does not understand that of all these actions that are taking place, only one, that is the printing of the paper sheets, is the purpose for the invention of this whole machine. The other actions are the natural consequences of the machine's operation. His childish and undeveloped power of observation does not have the capacity to perceive the sequential order, proportion and organization in the movement of the parts or to understand that the manner in which every part has been designed and the place where it has been installed is precisely the shape and place that is appropriate for it. He does not understand that in order for the machine to perform its function, every part has to precisely conform to the dimensions of the space where it is found and that such parts have to be placed at precisely the points where these have been mounted.

On account of his own inability to understand the functioning of the machine, the still mentally immature child thinks that this machine has come into existence all by itself merely by the coming together of some pieces of metal and other materials. His faculties of reasoning are still not so well-developed that by looking at the construction and actions of the machine he is able to infer that the machine had an inventor who must have been a wise person as he was able to make a machine of such an excellent design that no part of it is useless, inappropriate, out of sync, or without function.

Neither can he deduce that an object that has been brought into being with such knowledge and forethought cannot, most certainly, be without purpose or without some significance. Based upon his flawed observation of a printing press in action, and his defective analysis and thinking process, if the child does come up with the hypothesis that there is no material cause for the machine's existence and its operation and also that no intelligence has gone into its construction nor is there any purpose for its functioning, will an intelligent adult accept the outcome that the child has reached as a correct conclusion about the real status of the machine?

If this argument is not true with respect to a printing press, how can it be correct about a cosmic system, every speck of which is witness to the knowledge, determination, wisdom, and vision of its Creator? Whatever the child may say, will a person of reason who has seen this cosmos and its implications, even for a moment, doubt that such a strong, well-founded, organized, proportionate system in which nothing is either useless or in vain, in which nothing is either more or less than its requirement, in which each part is placed precisely at its requisite site, and in whose operative code there is no imperfection could have been created or be operated without some wisdom, knowledge or determination?

A Perfect System cannot be Aimless and Worthless

The line of reasoning and arguments established by the Qur'ān on the need for life in the Hereafter are all based upon the basic concept that the Creator of the cosmos is a *Ḥakīm* – a Wise Being – none of Whose actions are without wisdom. Nothing that runs contrary to reason and prudence can be attributed to this Wise Being. After strengthening this foundation, the Qur'ān states:

> 'Did you imagine that We created you without any purpose, and that you will not be brought back to Us?' So, exalted be Allah, the True King! There is no god but He, the Lord of the Great Throne.
>
> [*al-Mu'minūn* 23: 115-16]

Does man think that he will be left alone, unquestioned?

[al-Qiyāmah 75: 36]

It was not in idle sport that We created the heavens and the earth and all that is between them. We did not create them except in Truth. But most of them do not know. The Day of Final Decision is the appointed time for all...

[al-Dukhān 44: 38-40]

Do they not reflect on themselves? Allah created the heavens and the earth and whatever lies between them in Truth and for an appointed term. Yet many people deny that they will meet their Lord.

[al-Rūm 30: 8]

All these verses point to the premise that if this whole cosmic workplace, comprising the earth and 'heavens', has been created to operate for a specific period and thereupon go into disuse without any result or further plan, it would be a futile and meaningless act, a mere sport. Such an act cannot be the work of a Wise Being. If you acknowledge that this cosmos has been created by God, and if you consider this God to be a Wise Being, then, by employing your reason, you should understand that nothing in the whole stupendous range of material existence ever came into being without a purpose, and that nothing will ever fade away without any result. This is especially true of the human species, the highest point of this created cosmos, a rational being that is the culmination of a stage-wise evolution, and one which has been created with great wisdom, and then endowed with vision, authority and decisiveness. The purpose of this creation cannot be so meaningless that it spends a limited period busy in its work – like a machine – and then passes away into eternal disuse.

Rational End of this Perfect System

Now that we appreciate that this cosmos is not a frivolity or a mere sport, and that nothing associated with it is pointless or futile, a second question arises: 'What act in this cosmos, except absolute annihilation, is fully and precisely in conformity with the requirements of wisdom?'

A detailed answer to this question can be found in the verses of the Qur'ān. After reading or hearing this argument, reason is fully satisfied. However, before considering this answer, it is once again essential to internalize some themes:

(i)   All existing material evidence as well as remnants of the material world are witness to the fact that all the entities and variables of the cosmic system point towards evolution. The purpose of all transformations is to raise the flawed towards the heights of perfection and grant ever more perfect countenances and shapes to things by effacing their imperfect states.

(ii) Since all the actions leading from the law of evolution proceed on the path of change, it is essential that for every creation there be an equal destruction. The very coming into existence of a new form demands that the earlier form be invalidated. The passing away of a flawed form is the preface to the appearance of the more perfect form. Although these transformations keep on taking place all the time, not many of them are significant enough to be noticed. However, after so many minor changes there comes about a major and very visible transformation, as a consequence of which there is a very manifest and obvious eradication. This annihilation is commonly referred to as death or operational cessation. From the time that a form comes into existence to the time of its death or absolute elimination, there is an intervening period that we call a life span.

(iii) Every created form requires a specific environment that is appropriate for its existence. No entity can live and survive in an environment that is not appropriate for its existence. For instance an animal body is inappropriate for a botanical life form. Similarly, the human life form requires the particular body and specific physiological system that has been specially made for it. If any entity is to be given a more advanced form or shape, then it is essential that the environment which had been created for the lower form is obliterated and a new, appropriate environment be created for this new form.

(iv) A person who has clearly understood the comprehensiveness of the law of evolution with respect to all the worldly ingredients would not find the possibility of this law governing the total temporal system surprising. There are an existing temporal system that is before us today. We cannot say with certainty as to how many such systems have come and gone since the process of the first and original creation was begun. Who knows how many such systems would have passed after completing their systemic life spans and giving way to other more developed systems? In this way, the process of creation and existence has reached our present stage after passing through the many gradual stages of evolution. However, it goes without saying that in keeping with this practice, the present system is also not the final system. Whenever this present system reaches the pinnacle of the perfection designed into it, and there remains no further capacity for it to incorporate any further stages of superior development, then it too will be annihilated. In its place will be instituted a new system governed by a different set of laws, a system that will have the capability to accept and incorporate even more perfectly developed stages of existence.

(v) After analysing the existing temporal system, we can clearly feel and recognize that this is a defective system; it is one that is in need of a further upgrading on its way to a conclusion. In this system, the true characters of things are so badly polluted with material impurities that facts have traded place with myths and the material coverings of the true cores have assumed the status of realness. The more delicate and subtle an object, the freer it is of material pollutants and it is even more hidden from view and distant from the reach of intellect and reason in this temporal system. Here, only solid material bodies have weight and subtle entities have no substance. Here, wood and stone can be measured and weighed, but temporal law has no mechanism for measuring and weighing intellect and reason, ideas and opinions, intention and determination, emotions and ecstasies. Here, agricultural produce may be weighed but there is no scale for measuring love and hate. Here, cloth can be measured but there is no scale for measuring malice and envy. Here, money can be assigned worth but it is impossible to assign a value to that passion which becomes a stimulus for generosity or miserliness.

These are the defects of this temporal system. The intellect desires that there be another more developed system in which true reality is no longer in need of superficial covering and can be presented without any veil, a system in which the subtlety can overcome the grossness, and whatever is now hidden can be revealed and made obvious.

Similarly, another flaw of this world is that here material laws have supremacy; consequently, only those actions become discernible that conform to the stipulations of these material laws. On the contrary, results that are consistent with the imperatives of reason and wisdom fail to manifest themselves. Here, if we set fire to things, all inflammable materials turn to ash and if we douse things with water, all permeable items are soaked, yet when we do a righteous deed, its benevolent result that should appear on the basis of true reason does not occasionally manifest itself. Instead, its embodiment is in a form that is possible under present material laws, even if the result of a good deed is exactly the opposite, i.e. a malevolent outcome. After seeing such shortcomings, the intellect demands that another more mature and developed system take the place of the presently existing system in which rational laws should replace material laws so that those true results of actions that do not become apparent here, on account of the dominance of material laws in this system, then become clear and obvious.

The End of the Cosmic System

After understanding the above arguments, let us now take a look at the scenario that the Qur'ān presents with regard to the apocalypse and the rebirth that will take place in the Hereafter and see how the various questions in this regard are answered. The Qur'ān states:

We have created the heavens and the earth and all that is between them in Truth and for an appointed term.

[*al-Aḥqāf* 46: 3]

And He it is Who has made the sun and the moon subservient (to a law), each running its course till an appointed term.

[*al-Raʿd* 13: 2]

When the heaven is split asunder, when the stars are scattered, when the seas are made to burst forth, and when graves are laid open ...

[*al-Infiṭār* 82: 1-4]

When the sun shall be folded up, when the stars shall scatter away, when the mountains shall be set in motion...

[*al-Takwīr* 81: 1-3]

So when the stars are extinguished, and the sky is rent asunder, and the mountains are blown away ...

[*al-Mursalāt* 77: 8-10]

When the sight is dazed, and the moon is eclipsed, and the sun and the moon are joined together.

[*al-Qiyāmah* 75: 7-9]

and the earth and the mountains are carried aloft and are crushed to bits at one stroke ...

[*al-Ḥāqqah* 69: 14]

(Do warn them of the) Day when the heavens and the earth shall be altogether changed; when all will appear fully exposed before Allah, the One, the Irresistible!

[*Ibrāhīm* 14: 48]

All these pointers indicate that the present temporal system has a designated life span. This is not an eternal system. When the system reaches the end of its life span, it will be decimated. The sun, earth, moon, this solar system and all the other cosmic systems that comprise this material world will be dispersed, they will collide with each other and this temporary milieu will be rent asunder. However, this does not mean that the realm of existence will end or that the processes of fresh or transforming creation will be closed. Instead, the meaning implied here is that the particular manner of existence that we see in this system will be changed and that a new system will be established in the realm of existence which has been indicated in the Qur'ānic verse [*Ibrāhīm* 14: 48].

What will be the System of Life in the Hereafter?

What will be the system of life in the Hereafter? From what has been described in the Qur'ān, it is clear that the Hereafter will be a perfectly refined end point of this defective temporal system. It will be the final stage of evolution of the present and will be exactly what the intellect desires – that there be weights and measures, accounting and all, and not just for material things, but for delicate, simple and abstract realities as well. There, good and evil, belief and disbelief (*īmān* and *kufr*), morals and principles will also have weights. Intentions and aspirations will also be measured. 'Actions' of the heart and soul will be weighed and measured. In the system of the Hereafter, no account will be kept of the weight of a piece of bread nor of the money given to the destitute, but only of the intention (*niyyah*)[5] that became a stimulus for the act of charity, because the laws of the Hereafter will not be material but intellectual:

> Surely the hearing, the sight, the heart – each of these shall be called to account.
>
> [*Banī Isrā'īl* 17: 36]

---

[5] For instance a poor person may only give a very small amount in charity by way of a genuine intention while a rich person may contribute a large sum, more for public recognition of his act than genuine intent; there the former alone will be recognized and rewarded – Translator.

We shall set up just scales on the Day of Resurrection so that none will be wronged in the least. (We shall bring forth the acts of everyone), even if it be the weight of a grain of mustard seed. We shall suffice as Reckoners.

[*al-Anbiyā'* 21: 47]

The weighing on that Day will be the true weighing: those whose scales are heavy will prosper, and those whose scales are light will be the losers.

[*al-Aʿrāf* 7: 8-9]

On that Day people will go forth in varying states so that they be shown their deeds. So, whoever does an atom's weight of good shall see it; and whoever does an atom's weight of evil shall see it.

[*al-Zilzāl* 99: 6-8]

In that different system, all those things will become evident which remained invisible in this material world on account of the constraints of material laws. There, all hidden and covered realities will be unveiled before us and the genuine, true nature of everything will be revealed.

You were heedless of this. Now We have removed your veil and so your vision today is sharp.

[*Qāf* 50: 22]

That will be the Day when you shall be brought forth (before Allah) and no secret of yours shall remain hidden.

[*al-Ḥāqqah* 69: 18]

There, in the new system, those true results of actions will arise that will be in consonance with the dictates of intellect and wisdom, fair play and justice. The material laws of the present system and the material causes and resources under the influence of which true and intellectually sound results of actions cannot manifest themselves will not be enforced there. Therefore, all those things that obstruct equity and justice here, and do not allow true results to take place, will become totally powerless there. For instance, here the abundance of wealth and material resources, the influence of friends and allies, efforts, intercession, family influences and one's own cunningness and shrewdness, and other similar factors protect and save people from many of the natural consequences of their actions. However, in the system to come all such impacts of the material world's resources will be rendered null and void and every action will only lead to that outcome as should have resulted on the basis of truth and fair play:

> Thereupon everyone shall taste the recompense of his past deeds.
>
> [*Yūnus* 10: 30]

> And when every human being shall be paid in full for what he has done, and none shall be wronged?
>
> [*Āl ʿImrān* 3: 25]

> The Day is approaching when every soul shall find itself confronted with whatever good it has done and whatever evil it has wrought.
>
> [*Āl ʿImrān* 3: 30]

> Fear the Day when no one shall avail another, when no intercession will be accepted, when no one will be ransomed, and no criminal will receive any help.
>
> [*al-Baqarah* 2: 48]

> And then no sooner the Trumpet is blown than there will remain no kinship among them that Day, nor will they ask one another.... those whose scales are heavy, they alone will attain success; and those whose scales are light, those will be the ones who will have courted loss.
>
> [*al-Muʾminūn* 23: 101-103]

The Day when nothing will avail, neither wealth nor off-spring, but only he that brings to Allah a sound heart will (attain to success).

[al-Shuʿarāʾ 26: 88-89]

(And Allah will say): 'Now you have come to Us all alone even as We had created you in the first instance, and you have left behind all that We had bestowed upon you in the world. We do not see with you your intercessors whom you imagined to have a share with Allah in your affairs. You have now been cut off from one another and all those whom you imagined (to be Allah's associates in your affairs) have vanished from you.'

[al-Anʿām 6: 94]

On the Day of Resurrection neither your blood-kindred nor your own offspring will avail you. (On that Day) He will separate you. Allah sees all that you do.

[al-Mumtaḥinah 60: 3]

On the Day when each man shall flee from his brother, and his mother and his father; and his consort and his children; on that Day each will be occupied with his own business, making him oblivious of all save himself.

[ʿAbasa 80: 34-37]

The defect of the present system is that the distribution of nature's rewards is not based upon a person's actions and talents. Instead, these are based upon causes of which personal actions and intrinsic abilities comprise just one source; often, other more powerful causes weaken, and occasionally totally nullify, the impact of merit. It is for this reason that personal right has little or no place in the distribution of rewards. Here, a person can very well enjoy prosperity and worldly blessings in spite of a long life spent perpetrating injustice and immorality while another person can face destitution and all manner of worldly afflictions in spite of having spent a whole lifetime in the pursuit of fair play, trustworthiness, piety and self-control. This defective system is in need of a conclusion. Wisdom demands that the present system progresses and transforms into one in which the distribution of rewards and retributions is equitable and in which everyone receives that which he deserves on the basis of his goodness or badness. The Qur'ān states that the system of the Hereafter shall be like this:

Shall We then treat alike those that believe and act right-eously and those that create mischief on earth? Or treat alike the God-fearing and the wicked?

[*Ṣād* 38: 28]

Do the evil-doers imagine that We shall make them equal to those who believe and do good, making their lives and deaths alike? How vile is their judgement!

[*al-Jāthiyah* 45: 21]

Everyone is assigned a degree according to his deed.

[*al-An'ām* 6: 132]

(On that Day) the Garden will be brought near to the God-fearing, and the Fire will be uncovered for those who strayed…

[*al-Shu'arā'* 26: 90-91]

The above is a sketch of that other world that the religion of Muḥammad (peace be upon him), and the faiths of all other Prophets of God (peace be upon them), propose. People who consider this world and all its activity to be a mere game, a sand castle, a purposeless and result-free demonstration, a meaningless existence that began in senselessness and may end in negligence, will find nothing in this proposal – and all its evidences – worth accepting. However, people who consider the world to be created by God, and believe God to be the Supremely Wise Being will, after analysing these arguments, certainly be forced to concede that there has to arise another world of a description made above after the end of the present one. Moreover, when it has been proved that a second life after temporal death is possible, proving the need for the realization of this possibility is enough for professing belief in the fact that God, the Wise will certainly cause this possibility to become a reality.

From this analysis, it is clear that the life of the Hereafter in respect of which Islam demands a profession of belief is not beyond the bounds of reason, as is often thought. In fact, it precisely conforms to the requirements of reason and wisdom. No progress of knowledge or reason is sufficient to cause any breakdown of this belief, provided that progress is true and genuine, and not superficial or artificial.[6]

The Need for Belief in the Last Day

From whatever has been said so far, it is clear that the vision of another life coming into existence after the end of the present system of temporal life, is not only possible but conforms to the dictates of wisdom. Both reason (provided it is correct) and knowledge (provided it is true) do not stop us from professing belief in the concept of life in the Hereafter that has been presented by the Qur'ān; in fact, they support this act. However, the questions that remain include: 'What need is there for believing in the concept of life in the Hereafter?' Why has this been incorporated into the Islamic belief system? Why has such emphasis been placed upon this element, so much so that belief in the Last Day is essential for a person to be a Muslim and that a person cannot be a Muslim without this belief? Why has it been given so much importance that after renouncing this belief, even the beliefs in God and His Prophets and books are of no avail, and not only that, but that good deeds of a lifetime are also laid waste without this belief?

A person can very well say that this concept of a life in the Hereafter is just another metaphysical concept like others of its kind. It may be

---

[6] For further and detailed arguments of the Hereafter, please see the author's *magnum opus, Tafhīm al-Qur'ān*, translated into English, *Towards Understanding the Qur'ān*. Leicester, Islamic Foundation, 1988-. Nine volumes published so far. Entry under *Ākhirah* (Hereafter). However, the article 'Life after Death' appears as an Appendix to this work – Translator.

further said: 'While we accept that this concept has been exceptionally strengthened by way of arguments and proofs, evidence and reasoning, and that there are plenty of reasons for its acceptance, nonetheless the proving of a metaphysical proposition by way of reasoning does not mean that belief in it be made compulsory, that it be made the criterion for acceptance of Islam or its rejection.' After all, there are other metaphysical concepts like life in the Hereafter in whose support there also exist strong arguments. Why have these not been so included by Islam in its belief system?

If the status of life in the Hereafter had been that of merely another metaphysical proposition, such criticism would have been very valid. In that case, there would have been no good reason for incorporating the proposition of life in the Hereafter into Islam's core belief system because if a proposition is truly metaphysical then this status, in itself, proves that the said proposition has no connection with our daily lives. Thus, even if we were ignorant of a particular metaphysical concept, or refused to accept its existence and validity, this would not have any effect on our morals and actions.

However, by analysing the proposition of life in the Hereafter we see that this is not merely a philosophical matter. Rather, it has a deep relationship with human morals and daily lives. By accepting the truth of this proposition, the human viewpoint and perspective about temporal life and its various sub-issues changes in a very fundamental way. An acceptance of this dogma means that human beings consider themselves to be responsible and accountable beings, that every act they undertake in life is commenced and continued on a clear understanding of accepting responsibility for its outcomes, that they have to answer for all their actions in the next life, and that any blessedness or wretchedness of the future is dependent upon their own good and evil.

Conversely, rejection of this dogma means that human beings consider themselves to be irresponsible and unaccountable creatures who plan the agendas of their lives on the basis of the premise that they are not answerable for their actions in this life in another, a second life, and that no outcome, good or bad, will follow from their actions in this life. The unavoidable result of either being devoid of or in denial of this belief in the Last Day is that the human outlook, both individually and collectively, would be restricted to only those results that arise in this temporal life. Based upon this view, people would then form opinions about actions that are beneficial for them and those that are detrimental. While people would certainly refrain from taking poison and avoid putting their hands in a fire, this would only stem from their certain awareness that they would experience the unpleasant effects of both these actions within this lifetime. However, since the full range of adverse effects arising from actions like the mistreatment of others, corruption, injustice, adultery, lying, backbiting or gossiping, dishonesty, and other similar immoral actions do not appear in this temporal life, therefore they abstain from them only in so far as avoiding the possibility of any undesirable outcome in this world. On the contrary, where no adverse outcome is apparent or where there is an expectation of some benefit accruing from such (evil) acts, they do not hesitate in committing them. In short, acting in consonance with this concept, there is then no specific moral value associated with any act. Instead, any good or bad consequences of an action depend not upon any absolute moral standard but rather on the pleasantness or unpleasantness of the result that arises in this world.

As opposed to this, people who believe in the Last Day have in their purview not only the outcomes of their actions that are formed in this life, but also those results that will only become discernible in a second life. Accordingly, they then decide upon the advantageousness or harmfulness of their actions in view of the results that will arise from them. Just as they would be certain about the injuriousness of poison and fire, they would also be sure about the deleteriousness of dishonesty and insincerity. Similarly, just as they would consider bread and water to be beneficial, they would also consider justice, trustworthiness, chastity and decency to be similarly advantageous. They would also believe in a prescribed and certain outcome of their every action, whether or not that result manifests itself at all in this life, or even if it appears in a manner contrary to their expectations. They possess well-established moral values with respect to temporal actions – based on values that do not change in view of any worldly benefits or deficits. In this moral system, truthfulness, justice, and trustworthiness, in any and every case and event, remain the symbols of excellence and virtue, whether or not any benefit accrues from them in this world, or even if these lead to total loss and ruin. Similarly, falsehood, injustice and infidelity, whatever the circumstance, remain sinful and malevolent, whether or not any loss arises from them, or even if unmitigated benefit accrues as their outcome.

Thus, the fact of either being ignorant of the dogma of life in the Hereafter not only means that individuals or groups are unaware of or reject a metaphysical concept, but that they are negligent of the high status of responsibility and accountability placed upon human beings. It also means that they have come to consider themselves as plenipotentiary and above all answerability, that they have become falsely convinced with the apparent and incomplete – and often deceptive – outcomes of this world and its outwardly visible life, that they have come to believe in the apparent, temporary and doubtful gains and losses while being forgetful of the final account of profit and loss and, finally, that the values which they assigned to their actions are deceptive and changeable.

In this way humanity has been deprived of a true and permanent moral code that can only be formulated by way of a sense of responsibility, an examination of final results, and established moral values. Moreover, this also means that human beings are spending their entire lives being constantly deceived by the superficial and faulty manifestations of worldly life, and on the basis of a flawed and short-lived moral code that has declared real losses as gains, and true benefits as deficits. In this moral code, true benevolence has become ignominiousness, the truly discreditable has been declared commendable, sin has become virtue, and true piety has been declared transgression.

These are the outcomes of not professing belief in the Last Day that have been described in the Qur'ān in great detail. An analysis of the Qur'ānic verses on this theme reveals all those shortcomings that make their way into human morals and actions with rejection of belief in the Last Day.

(i)   Human beings consider themselves to be ungoverned, absolutely powerful, and not responsible to any higher authority. Overall, they deem this life to be without any end result. Generally, they act under the mistaken belief that no one is supervising their action, and nor will anyone ever take an account thereof.

'Did you imagine that We created you without any purpose, and that you will not be brought back to Us?'

[al-Mu'minūn 23: 115]

Does man think that he will be left alone, unquestioned?

[al-Qiyāmah 75: 36]

Does he think that no one can overpower him? He says: 'I have squandered enormous wealth.' Does he believe that none has seen him?

[al-Balad 90: 5-7]

(ii) People who have their eyes focused only on the apparent manifestations of the world, and who consider superficial outcomes to be the final and true results, are deceived by them and, thus, come to form false opinions:

People simply know the outward aspect of the worldly life but are utterly heedless of the Hereafter.

[al-Rūm 30: 7]

Surely those who do not expect to meet Us, who are gratified with the life of the world and are well-pleased with it.

[Yūnus 10: 7]

Nay, the truth is that you love ardently (the good of this world) that can be obtained hastily, and are oblivious of the Hereafter.

[al-Qiyāmah 75: 20-21]

No, but you prefer the present life, whereas the Hereafter is better and more enduring.

[*al-Aʿlā* 87: 16-17]

And who were beguiled by the life of the world.

[*al-Aʿrāf* 7: 51]

(iii) As a result of this superficial view, the standard upon which humanity bases its moral values is totally reversed. The issues and actions that are truly detrimental in terms of their final outcomes are now considered as beneficial in view of their immediate gains, and the actions that are virtuous when viewed in terms of their final outcomes come to be considered unbeneficial by way of their temporary effects. As a consequence of this, temporal efforts deviate from the right path and are finally lost:

Once Korah went forth among his people in full glitter. … 'But none except those who are patient shall attain to this.'

[*al-Qaṣaṣ* 28: 79-80]

As for those who do not believe in the Hereafter, We have made their deeds seem attractive to them so they stumble around in perplexity.

[*al-Naml* 27: 4]

Do they fancy that Our continuing to give them wealth and children (means) that, We are busy lavishing on them all kinds of good? Nay, they do not perceive the reality of the matter.

[*al-Muʾminūn* 23: 55-56]

Say, (O Muḥammad): 'Shall We tell you who will be the greatest losers in respect of their works? It will be those whose effort went astray in the life of the world and who believe nevertheless that they are doing good. Those are the ones who refused to believe in the revelations of their Lord and that they are bound to meet Him. Hence, all their deeds have come to naught.'

[*al-Kahf* 18: 103-105]

(iv) Such people can never accept the True Faith (*Dīn*). Whenever ways and means for bringing about good morals, righteous deeds and virtuousness are presented to them, they reject these and when proposals contrary to these, i.e. ways and means contrary to virtue and righteousness, are presented, they readily adopt the same. This is because all the ways advocated by the True Faith demand the sacrifice of numerous benefits and pleasures of temporal life, given the underlying principle that sacrifice of such fleeting advantages is required for gaining the superior and permanent benefits of the Hereafter. However, the rejecters of the Hereafter only consider the gains of this world to be their reward. They are neither ready to make any such sacrifice that detracts from their temporal benefits, nor willing to adopt those righteous ways that require sacrifices of their self-interest. Accordingly, the rejection of the Hereafter and adherence to the True Faith stand mutually opposed to each other. Whosoever is a rejecter of the Hereafter can never be a follower of the true way of life:

> I shall turn away from My Signs those who, without any right, behaved haughtily in the earth. Even if they may witness each and every Sign, they shall not believe therein. And even if they see the Right Path, they shall still not follow it; but if they see the path of error, they shall choose it for their path. This is because they rejected Our signs and were heedless to them. Vain are the deeds of those who reject Our signs as false and to the meeting of the Hereafter as false. Shall they be recompensed, except according to their deeds?

[*al-A'rāf* 7: 146-147]

(v) By rejecting the Hereafter, the complete moral and practical life of human beings is affected; they become haughty and rebellious:

> But the hearts of those who do not believe in the Hereafter are steeped in rejection of the Truth, and they are given to arrogance.
>
> [*al-Naḥl* 16: 22]

> And he and his hosts waxed arrogant in the land without any right, believing that they will never have to return to Us!
>
> [*al-Qaṣaṣ* 28: 39]

a. Their affairs take a downturn,

> Woe to the stinters; those who, when they take from others by measure, take their full share; but who, when they measure or weigh for others, they give less than their due. Do they not realise that they will be raised to life on a Great Day ...
>
> [*al-Muṭaffifīn* 83: 1-5]

b. They become cold-hearted, mean, narrow-minded, deceitful, selfish and neglectful in their worship of God,

> Did you see him who gives the lie to the Reward and Punishment of the Hereafter? Such is the one who repulses the orphans away, and urges not the feeding of the needy. Woe, then, to those who pray, but are heedless in their Prayers, those who do good (in order) to be seen, and deny people the articles of common necessity.
>
> [*al-Māʿūn* 107: 1-7]

c. In short, transgressing from the Truth and being caught in sin is the unavoidable result of rejecting the Hereafter,

Yet none gives the lie to it except the transgressor immersed in sin ...

[*al-Muṭaffifīn* 83: 12]

These logical outcomes of either being devoid or recalcitrant of belief in the Last Day are such that no prudent individual can deny them. This is specially so when we have seen with our own eyes the fruits of a culture that, being totally devoted to the pursuit of the very perceptible worldly life, is only founded upon a temporal and materialist paradigm and is totally wanting of any belief about life in the Hereafter. Thus, there is no longer any possibility of denying the fact that it is absolutely impossible to establish Godliness, religiosity, and a higher morality concomitant with a renouncement of the Hereafter.

Now consider the fact that when Islam seeks to establish all these objectives, it invites humanity towards righteous principles and virtuous deeds, which, in turn, require the sacrifice of numerous material pleasures and gains in this world. When it persuades human beings to make efforts towards the worship of God and purification of the soul, no apparent worldly gain seems to accrue. On the contrary, when Islam establishes a standard for discriminating between the lawful and the forbidden in all matters of our worldly life, especially while continuing to benefit from material resources and means[7], this causes them to face many a struggle, not only with the outside world but also internally by way of both their bodies and psyches.

The same is true when the true faith occasionally demands of us the sacrifice of our personal vested interests, affectionate relationships and proclivities, and sometimes even our wealth and lives, or when it desires to regulate human life under a moral code in which a certain ethical value has been assigned to every act notwithstanding any temporal benefit or loss that may ensue from it. Given this background, is it at all possible that Islam could have succeeded in establishing such a *Dīn* and *Sharīʿah* without a belief in life in the Hereafter? Would it

---

[7] I.e., while remaining within the folds of society and not renouncing human interactions and taking up an ascetic vocation – Translator.

have been possible for any man or woman to accept Islamic teachings while either being ignorant of or in denial of belief in the Last Day?

If the answer to these questions is in the negative – and it certainly is in the negative – then we will have to accept that in order to establish this kind of a religious system and moral code, it is indispensable to firmly implant the belief of life in the Hereafter first. It is for this reason that Islam has incorporated this dogma in its belief system and has placed an emphasis on it that is second only to belief in Allah.

Let us now see the manner in which Islam has presented this dogma and the effects that develop upon human morals and actions as a result of it.

Preference for the Hereafter over this World

The first feature that the Qur'ān has attempted to firmly implant in the human mind is that this world is only a temporary abode for humanity. This temporal life is not the only life, but that there is another life after the present one which is not only more superior and more permanent but whose benefits are far more abundant than the benefits available here, and whose detriments are much worse than the detriments of this life. People who, deceived by worldly appearances, continuously pursue the pleasures and gains of this world through such means that preclude their securing the pleasures and benefits of that second life make a very bad bargain. Indeed, this trade-off is one in which there is nothing but loss.

Similarly, those who only consider the loss of this world as the true loss and then undertake such efforts to preclude this loss that warrant their becoming recipients of a certain loss in that second life also commit a grave stupidity. In no way can such acts of theirs be worthy of prudence. This theme finds such frequent mention in the Qur'ān that a complete listing of it is not possible here. By way of illustration, the following verses may be considered:

> The present life is nothing but sport and amusement. The true life is in the Abode of the Hereafter; if only they knew.
>
> [*al-ʿAnkabūt* 29: 64]

Say to them: 'There is little enjoyment in this world. The World to Come is much better for the God-fearing.'

[al-Nisā' 4: 77]

Do you prefer the worldly life to the Hereafter? Know well that all the enjoyment of this world, in comparison with the Hereafter, is trivial.

[al-Tawbah 9: 38]

No, but you prefer the present life, whereas the Hereafter is better and more enduring.

[al-Aʿlā 87: 16-17]

Everyone is bound to taste death and you shall receive your full reward on the Day of Resurrection. Then, whoever is spared the Fire and is admitted to Paradise has indeed been successful. The life of this world is merely an illusory enjoyment.

[Āl ʿImrān 3: 185]

The wrong-doers kept pursuing the ease and comfort which had been conferred upon them, thus losing themselves in sinfulness.

[Hūd 11: 116]

Say: 'Behold, the real losers shall be those who will have lost their own selves and their kith and kin on the Day of Resurrection. Behold, that is the obvious loss.'

[al-Zumar 39: 15]

Then he who transgressed, and preferred the life of this world, most surely his abode shall be Hell. But he who feared to stand before his Lord, and restrained himself from evil desires, most surely his abode shall be Paradise.

[al-Nāziʿāt 79: 37-41]

Know well that the life of this world is merely sport and diversion and adornment and an object of your boasting with one another, and a rivalry in the multiplication of riches and children. Its likeness is that of rain: when it produces vegetation it delights the tillers. But then it withers and you see it turn yellow, and then it crumbles away. In the Hereafter there is (either) grievous chastisement (or) forgiveness from Allah and (His) good pleasure. The life of this world is nothing but delusion.

[al-Ḥadīd 57: 20]

People arc naturally tempted by the lure of women, children, treasures of gold and silver, horses of mark, cattle and plantations. These are the enjoyments in the life of this world; but with Allah lies a goodly abode to return to. Say: 'Shall I tell you of things better than these? For the Godfearing there are, with their Lord, Gardens beneath which rivers flow; there they will abide forever, will have spouses of stainless purity as companions, and will enjoy the good pleasure of Allah.'

[Āl 'Imrān 3: 14-15]

It is in this very forceful way that Islam presents its teachings for preferring the Hereafter over this world, for foregoing the fleeting gains of this world in return for the permanent success of the Hereafter, and bearing the temporary losses of this world in order to preclude eternal failure in the Hereafter. It is Islam's intent that any person who has professed belief in the Prophet Muḥammad (peace be upon him), should do so not on account of any pressure or under duress, but should perform with total personal volition every act that the Book and the Prophet have stated to be the means of success in the Hereafter and abstain from every act which both of these have declared to be the cause of detriment in the Hereafter, irrespective of how beneficial or detrimental these may be in this world.

The Record of Temporal Actions and Justice

The second feature that the Qur'ān has attempted to deeply implant in human hearts and minds is the fact that an accurate record of every action that every human being undertakes in this temporal life, no matter how secretively he may attempt to act, is being preserved. On the Day of Judgement, this record will be presented in God's Court of Justice. The smallest atom that has in any way been connected with a human being's actions will give its testimony with regard to those deeds. So much so that a person's own body organs will also be present in the witness box. The meticulously kept record of actions will be considered and weighed precisely. In one pan of the scale of justice shall be placed a person's good deeds and in the other pan, the bad deeds. If the pan of goodness tilts downwards, success in the Hereafter will welcome him and, thereafter, Paradise will become his place of residence. However, if the scale of wickedness weighs down then a clear loss will be the outcome and the worst of all places – called Hell – will be recommended for that person. In that court of justice everyone will be present all alone, and nothing by way of temporal resources will be of use here – neither genealogical privilege nor efforts for putting in a favourable word, neither material wealth nor power and influence.

This theme is also stated in the Qur'ān in great detail and in a very effective way. By way of example, a few verses are presented here:

1. The Status of the Record of Actions:

> It is all the same for Him whether any of you says a thing secretly, or says it loudly, and whether one hides oneself in the darkness of night, or struts about in broad daylight. There are guardians over everyone, both before him and behind him, who guard him by Allah's command.
>
> [al-Ra'd 13: 10-11]

> And then the Record of their deeds shall be placed before them and you will see the guilty full of fear for what it contains, and will say: 'Woe to us! What a Record this is! It

leaves nothing, big or small, but encompasses it.' They will find their deeds confronting them.

[*al-Kahf* 18: 49]

2. The Testimony of Body Parts and Man's Self-confession:

(Let them not be heedless of) the Day when their own tongues, their hands, and their feet shall all bear witness against them as to what they have been doing.

[*al-Nūr* 24: 24]

And when all have arrived, their ears, their eyes, and their skins shall bear witness against them, stating all that they had done in the life of the world. They will ask their skins: 'Why did you bear witness against us?' The skins will reply: 'Allah gave us speech, as He gave speech to all others. ... When you used to conceal yourselves (while committing misdeeds) you never thought that your ears or your eyes or your skins would ever bear witness against you; you rather fancied that Allah does not know a great deal of what you do.'

[*Fuṣṣilat* 41: 20-22]

And they will bear witness against themselves that they had disbelieved.

[*al-An'ām* 6: 130]

3. Standing helpless and alone – He shall then present himself in God's court of justice with his record of actions and his witnesses. What will his state then be? He will stand alone and helpless:

(And Allah will say): 'Now you have come to Us all alone even as We had created you in the first instance, and you have left behind all that We had bestowed upon you in the world.'

[*al-An'ām* 6: 94]

231

4. Everyone to present his own record:

> We have fastened every man's omen to his neck.[8] On the
> Day of Resurrection We shall produce for him his scroll in
> the shape of a wide open book, (saying): 'Read your scroll;
> this Day you suffice to take account of yourself.'
> <div align="right">[<i>Banī Isrā'īl</i> 17: 13-14]</div>

5. Family (and other) connections are of no use:

> On the Day of Resurrection neither your blood-kindred
> nor your own offspring will avail you.
> <div align="right">[<i>al-Mumtaḥinah</i> 60: 3]</div>

6. Intercession is of no use:

> And the wrong-doers shall neither have any sincere friend
> nor intercessor whose word will be heeded.
> <div align="right">[<i>al-Mu'min</i> 40: 18]</div>

7. When material belongings will not work:

> The Day when nothing will avail, neither wealth nor
> offspring. [<i>al-Shuʿarā'</i> 26: 88]

8. Actions will be weighed and every little bit shall be held accountable:

> We shall set up just scales on the Day of Resurrection so
> that none will be wronged in the least. (We shall bring forth
> the acts of everyone), even if it be the weight of a grain of
> mustard seed. We shall suffice as Reckoners.
> <div align="right">[<i>al-Anbiyā'</i> 21: 47]</div>

---

[8] The causes that lead a man to his ultimate salvation or perdition, to his
perpetual happiness or unending misery, lie within himself – Translator.

Today you shall be requited for your deeds.

[*al-Jāthiyah* 45: 28]

Everyone is assigned a degree according to his deeds.

[*al-Anʿām* 6: 132]

It is this police and court of justice whose fear has been implanted in human beings by Islam. This is not the worldly police whose scrutiny people may evade, neither is this a worldly court (of law) from whose jurisdiction a person may go scot-free on account of insufficient evidence, false testimony, or unlawful influences. Rather, this is a police that keeps a constant watch over every individual and this is court in which none may escape the testimony of witnesses, which already has in its custody a detailed record of every thought and action of every human being and whose decisions are so just that no one will escape punishment for evil nor be deprived of the reward for good deeds.

The Benefit of Belief in the Last Day

In this way, Islam has made the dogma of the Last Day an immense bulwark to safeguard its moral code and *Sharīʿah* legal system. In this dogma there is, on the one hand, a rational motivation for acting virtuously and avoiding immorality and on the other hand, this belief incorporates a certain reward for uprightness and a fear of definite punishment for transgression. For their existence and stability, this moral code and the attendant legal system are not dependent upon any material force or any authoritarian regime.

Instead, it is by way of a belief in the Last Day that Islam inculcates and implants a powerful conscience in human beings, which instinctively attracts them – without any external temptation or fear – towards those virtues that Islam has declared to be virtues with respect to their final consequences. Similarly it underscores the need to steer clear of those acts that it has declared to be sins with respect to their ultimate outcomes.

Readers will see that on numerous occasions the Qurʾān uses this belief to teach ethics. Wherever there is a commandment for adopting *taqwā* (God-consciousness) and abstemiousness, there is also the mention – rather the caution – of remembering that every human being has to appear before God:

> Avoid incurring the wrath of Allah. Know well that one
> Day you shall face Him.
>
> [*al-Baqarah* 2: 223]

When believers are persuaded to act courageously, by way of participating in armed struggle, there is a simultaneous assurance that even if they are slain in such a struggle, they will not be killed – as is generally thought – but that they will instead gain eternal life (as martyrs in God's cause):

> And do not say of those who are killed in the way of Allah
> that they are dead; they are alive even though you have no
> knowledge of their life.
>
> [*al-Baqarah* 2: 154]

When the virtue of patience in the face of adversity is inculcated, it is concurrently stated that for those who practise forbearance, there is reward and mercy from God. This truth is explained in the following way:

> Upon them will be the blessings and mercy of their Lord.
>
> [*al-Baqarah* 2: 157]

> But those who believed that they were bound to meet their
> Lord said: 'How often has a small party prevailed against a
> large party by the leave of Allah.'
>
> [*al-Baqarah* 2: 249]

The power to persevere in the face of the worst trial and tribulation is raised by mentioning how Hellfire is far worse than temporal heat:

The Hell is far fiercer in heat.

[al-Tawbah 9: 81]

The spending of wealth in good causes in inculcated by way of the following:

So, whatever you spend in charity will be repaid to you in full and you shall not be wronged.

[al-Baqarah 2: 272]

Those who are niggardly about what Allah has granted them out of His bounty think that niggardliness is good for them; rather, it is bad for them. What they were niggardly about will turn into a halter round their necks on the Day of Resurrection.

[Āl ʿImrān 3: 180]

People are asked to give up all transactions involving usury, telling them:

And have fear of the Day when you shall return to Allah.

[al-Baqarah 2: 281]

The philosophy of developing a total freedom from desire to possess worldly treasures – almost bordering on disdain – and of not looking intently towards the prosperity of others with covetousness is presented thus:

(O Messenger), do not let the strutting about of the unbelievers in the land deceive you. This is but a trifling and fleeting enjoyment; then their destination is Hell – what an evil resting place! But those who fear their Lord: theirs shall be the Gardens beneath which rivers flow and therein they will live forever: a hospitality from Allah. And Allah's reward is best for the truly pious.

[Āl ʿImrān 3: 196-198]

9 The Importance of Belief (*Īmān*) in Islamic Civilization

Salient Features

All the five constituent elements of *īmān* – the Islamic belief system – have been examined in great depth in the above chapters. We have examined the detailed Islamic doctrine with regard to each of them, their correct intellectual status and influence on the development of human character and their role in the establishment and formulation of Islamic civilization. Now, as we draw towards the conclusion of this book, it will be useful to once again take a look at all of them in an all-embracing manner, especially with a view to determining the kind of civilization which these elements of the Islamic belief system, when combined as a whole, give rise to.

In the early chapters of the book it was stated that the foundation stone of Islamic civilization is the concept in which human beings' position in this transitory worldly milieu is not like that of other physical constituents of the natural world. Instead, in this concept they are here to act as vicegerents of God. Following from this basic concept – as a logical intellectual outcome – is the Islamic objective and purpose of human life: seeking the pleasure of our Creator and Lord. To accomplish this objective and purpose, it is essential that we:

- firstly, seek the correct knowledge about God;
- secondly, consider God alone to be the Sovereign, the only One deserving obedience, and submit all our power and authority unto Him;
- thirdly, seek to learn those ways and means by which God's pleasure may be obtained, and when that knowledge has been acquired to spend all our lives according to these ways and means, and

- fourthly, to learn about the fruits of God's pleasure and the consequences of His wrath, so that we are not deceived by the notion that the rewards and punishments of this world are complete and final.

The five belief elements whose details we have discussed at length fulfill this need.

The purpose of whatever has been mentioned about God's essence and attributes in the Qur'ān is to provide us with the correct knowledge about the Being Who has appointed all members of humanity as His vicegerents and the seeking of Whose pleasure is the very objective of life.

Whatever has been said about the angels is to preclude any chance of us considering the subordinate forces of the cosmos as being self-operative, and then from subsequently considering some of these to be Allah's partners in His autonomous actions.

The act of acquiring this correct belief, and professing *īmān* in Allah, means that we acknowledge Allah's sovereignty in the voluntary aspects of our lives just as we believe that God governs the whole cosmos, including the involuntary aspects of human life. Thus, in every matter, we should consider God to be the only Lawgiver and ourselves to be solely at the receiving end of His Law. We should restrict all our freedoms and authorities within the boundaries that God has established. It is this *īmān* that has within itself the force that persuades humanity to voluntarily and happily submit their bowed heads before the Sovereignty of God. Together with this, there arises in believers a special type of conscience that leads to the development of a special kind of personality, both of which are essential for following the laws of God and remaining within His boundaries, not by way of compliant surrender to an obligatory enforcement but by way of voluntary submission.

The belief in Prophethood and the Book fulfill the third need. It is by way of these two that we learn in detail about those laws and means which God has assigned for us. As a result we come to recognize those boundaries within which God has restricted human authority. Considering the knowledge given by the Prophet as God's knowledge, and regarding the book presented by the Prophet as God's Book is the essence of belief in Prophethood and belief in the Book. With this belief, we are able to gain the ability to abide – with full faith and confidence – by those laws, ways and means and boundaries that God has revealed to His Prophet through His Book.

In order to fulfill this last requirement, we have knowledge of the resurrection and the Day of Judgement. This sharpens our vision in a way that we are able to see another world behind the apparent façade of temporal life. We come to know that the prosperity or adversity of this life, its gains and losses, are not the measures of God's pleasure or displeasure, and also that God's reward or retribution for actions of this life does not end here. Instead, the final judgement will take place in another world. That decision alone will be worthy of credence. And the only sure way for success in obtaining a favourable decision in the final judgement is to fully abide by God's law in this world and to observe His bounds completely. Absolute belief in this creed is called belief in the Final Day. After belief in God, this is the second overwhelming force that encourages human beings to follow Islamic law. The force of this doctrine plays a great role in mentally preparing human beings for the establishment of an Islamic civilization.

From this account, it should be clear that these foundational creeds have helped establish and develop a civilization on the lines that have been delineated by a particular concept about this temporal life and the specific objective that follows from the concept. The foundational creed that is required for such a civilization can only comprise these five elements. Apart from these, no other belief system or doctrine has this capacity to become the foundation for this particular type of civilization. Indeed, no other creed has any similarity or correlation with this particular concept of life and its objective.

An Outline of Islamic Civilization

By going through the details of Islam's belief system that have been stated earlier, a complete outline of the civilization which the five elements of the Islamic belief system attempt to create emerges. The salient features of this outline are:

(i)   The system of this civilization is like that of a state. The status and role of God in this framework is not merely akin to a deity in the usual religious sense. Instead, from a temporal conceptualization, this deity is an Absolute Ruler. He is, in fact, the Emperor Plenipotentiary of this kingdom. The Prophet is His representative, the Qur'ān is the kingdom's constitution, and every human being who acknowledges God's majesty, submits to His representative and follows His constitution. The meaning of being a Muslim is that one accepts, without any exception or reservation, all the laws that the Majesty has promulgated through His representative and His constitution, whether or not one understands the cause or rationale behind these. Any person who does not accept this unconditional and absolute authority of God and the supremacy of His law over and above any individual or collective opinion, and retains for himself the right to accept or reject any of His commands, has absolutely no place in this kingdom.

(ii) Given the premise that the end goal of this civilization is to prepare human beings for the 'Final Success' (that is, gaining the pleasure of God as expressed through the decision on the Last Day), and that the achievement of such a success is dependent upon right actions in the present life, and also because it is beyond human capacity to know which actions are beneficial and which are detrimental with respect to the final outcome, this civilization demands of human beings that they follow the ways and means prescribed by God for each and every aspect of their lives, and surrender their independence of action in favour of confinement within the bounds of the Divine Law (*Sharīʿah*). Accordingly, this civilization is a combination of this life and the next, the temporal and the spiritual. This creed cannot be called a 'religion' in the ordinary limited meaning of the word because it is such an all-encompassing system that it overrides human beings' thoughts and concepts, their personal character and morals, their individual and familial actions, their social, cultural and political lives. The collective term for all the laws and procedures that have been ordered by God in all these and

239

still other aspects of life is the *Dīn* of Islam or the 'Civilization of Islam'.

(iii)   This civilization is not a national, racial or a state-based civilization, but is, in the right sense of the world, a human civilization. It addresses human beings in their capacity as a member of the human race and takes within its folds all those who have come to believe in *tawḥīd, risālah* (Prophethood), the Book and the Last Day. In this way, this civilization has created a community in which every human being is free to enter without any distinction as to colour, race or language. It has the potential to spread far and wide over the entire globe. It has the capacity to bring together all of humanity in one organized community. Essentially, the real purpose for establishing this universal human community is not to increase the population of its followers, but to enable all human beings to share in the blessings of this correct knowledge and truthful course of action that their God has bestowed for the good of them all. By imposing the restriction of *īmān* as a condition for entry into this grouping, this civilization only aims at choosing all those people who are willing to bow their heads in submission before God's absolute authority and who are willing to accept the rules and bounds that God has imposed through His Messenger and His Book. This is because, only these people (howsoever few in number they may be) can become part of this civilization and only they can establish a correct and strong system. The entry of unbelievers, hypocrites or people of weak *īmān* will not be a source of strength for the system but will instead lead to systemic weaknesses.

(iv)   Together with its comprehensiveness and universalism, another salient feature of this civilization is its immense discipline and its powerful hold with which it obliges its followers to abide by its constitution in both their individual and collective capacities. This is the reason for which this civilization undertakes to have its laws followed and its boundaries respected prior to promulgating these laws and establishing these boundaries. Prior to issuing a command, it makes necessary arrangements to have that command enforced. First of all, it solicits human beings to accept the suzerainty of God, and then it assures them that the commandments that have been given through the Messenger and the Book are God's commandments and that submission to these laws is indeed submission to God. Next, it establishes a law enforcement mechanism deep within human beings which constantly, at all times and in all circumstances, encourages them towards submission, admonishes them over their contraventions and instills in them fear of the Last Day. In this way, it is only after Islam has firmly established this force within the spirit and conscience of its followers and has enabled them to follow the laws, observe the bounds, and practise good deeds of their own free will does it present these laws before them, issues commandments, sets the bounds, proposes the ways for living out their lives, and demands from them – for their own good – the heaviest of sacrifices. There can be no wiser plan of action, other than this one. It is in this way that the Islamic civilization has been able to achieve an immense influence that has not been the good fortune of any other civilization.

(v)   From a worldly point of view, the Islamic civilization aims to create a righteous collective system and a virtuous, upright society. However, it is not possible for such a society to come into existence until its members possess excellent morals and praiseworthy attributes. For this purpose, it is essential to undertake a purification of the inner characters of people so that these do not become the gathering places for corrupt thoughts. It is also necessary to ingrain in them an unblemished and virtuous mindset that leads to a strong character from which righteous deeds spring forth of their own natural accord. Islam has thoroughly maintained this principled plan in its civilization. For the training of individuals, it begins by installing īmān deep within their personalities. This is the only means of creating a strong, high quality character. It is through this īmān that it generates within them, among other character traits, the high attributes of truthfulness, trust-worthiness, and good-heartedness; a sense of accountability, righteousness, self-discipline, organization, generosity, broad-mindedness, self-reliance, humility, ambitiousness, boldness, and high-mindedness; and a spirit of sacrifice, dutifulness, patience and fortitude, courage, contentedness, submission to authority and being law-abiding. It enables individuals to rise to a high moral standard so that a most excellent society can emerge from their collective association.

(vi) The belief system of the Islamic civilization possesses, on the one hand, all those forces that create in human beings excellent morals and perfect accomplishments and then ensure their growth and protection, and, on the other hand, the power to lead human beings towards worldly progress. These forces and elements enable human beings to make the best use of worldly resources and to use all the powers granted them by God with moderation. Moreover, these belief elements also generate all those superior attributes that are essential for true progress in this world. They also have the power to organize the forces of human action and spur them on in an orderly manner, possessing as they do the power to restrain the resulting actions within certain bounds and paths, deviation from which would be a cause of ruin. In this way, these belief elements have within them all those merits that are found individually and separately in other religious and temporal belief systems; simultaneously, they are totally free from all those demerits that are found in various religious and worldly belief systems.

The Importance of Belief (*Īmān*) in Islamic Civilization

This is a brief outline of the civilization established by Islam. If we were to look at this by way of an analogy and consider this civilization to be a building, then we may say that this is a building that has been strengthened by way of an extremely deep foundation, for which every building block has been carefully selected and which have then been joined with the best mortar. This building has been raised in a manner that it rises high into the sky and spreads far and wide beyond the horizons. Despite its loftiness and vastness, however, there is not the slightest stress in its elements, so much so that its walls and pillars continue to stand with the strength of a rocky cliff. The doorways and windows of this building have been designed in such a way that they allow all the light and clean air to enter and freely illuminate and ventilate the structure, and yet deny entry to all unwanted dusts and pollutants, and rain and stormy winds. All these qualities are made possible in this building because of one basic element – and that is *īmān*.

It is this core that makes possible proper foundation laying, the selection of the best building materials after discarding the poor and useless, and the production of good blocks and construction of a solid structure from these materials and blocks. It is *īmān* upon which the loftiness and vastness of this structure and its stability is dependant. It is *īmān* that enables it to expand and rise, that strengthens it, protects it from external problems and only allows wholesome things to enter into it. Thus, *īmān* is the heart and soul of this structure. If it were not for *īmān*, what to speak of its continuation, its very existence would not have been possible. If the *īmān* is weak, it means that the foundations of the structure are weak, its building blocks are poor, its mortar is inferior, and its structural elements are shaky; and that the amalgamation between the parts and the potential to rise and spread is absent; that it does not have the power to stop externally mediated defects from spreading nor of protecting its internal purity and integrity.

In short, the absence of *īmān* is the absence of Islam; the weakness of *īmān* is Islam's weakness, and the strength of *īmān* is Islam's strength. Moreover, because Islam is not merely a religion, but a civilization, a system of morals, politics, civic life and a culture, the role of *īmān* in this system is not only that of a religious creed but that of a focal point dependent upon which are the morals and characters of people. It is responsible for the correctness of their daily interactions and it is *īmān* that brings them together to form a nation. It guards their nationhood and their civilization. It is also the very precursor of their culture, civic and political life. Without *īmān*, not only would Islam be unable to establish itself as a 'religious entity', but this would also fail to affirm itself as a culture, a political system and a civilization. If the *īmān* is weak, it would not merely spell the weakness of a religious doctrine, but would also mean that the morals of Muslims would degenerate, their characters would deteriorate, their interactions would turn messy, their civic and cultural systems would become disordered, their interrelationships as members of a nation would break down and they would not be able to survive as an independent, respectable and powerful nation.

It is for this reason that Islam makes *īmān* the singular basis for differentiation between Islam and *kufr* (disbelief) and the foremost condition for entry into the Islamic system. *Īmān* is the first aspect of Islam that is to be presented to a human being; acceptance of *īmān* allows entry into the Muslim community whereby the person becomes an equal partner in the Muslim society, culture and politics, and all the commandments of the faith, its boundaries and laws are now applicable to him. However, if he does not accept *īmān*, entry into the Islamic fold is not possible in any capacity, and neither would any Islamic law or commandment be applicable and participation in Muslim communal life would not be possible in any way. Such a person cannot observe the laws and bounds of Islam and is of absolutely no use to this civilization. Such people have no place in its system.

The Danger of Hypocrisy (*Nifāq*)
As for those who openly reject the invitation to accept *īmān*, their status is very clear. The dividing line between *kufr* and *īmān* that exists between them and the Muslims is so clear and prominent that they cannot enter the Islamic realm so as to cause any disruption therein. However, those who are not true believers, but who are still able to penetrate into the Muslim community, either by way of a superficial expression of having accepted *īmān* or those whose hearts are afflicted with the disease of doubt, and also those whose *īmān* is weak – represent a graver danger for the Islamic system. The reason for this is simple: while they are able to enter into the fold of Islam they neither adopt Islamic morals nor develop an Islamic character; they neither submit to Islamic laws nor observe Divine bounds. Instead, they pollute Islamic culture and civilization by their poor morals and actions. By way of the evil that is in their hearts, they dig out the roots of Muslim community and political decorum; they take part in instituting and inflaming every discord that strikes at Islam either from within or without. The Qur'ān calls these people *munāfiqūn* or

the 'hypocrites'; it describes, one by one, all those dangers that arise as a result of their entry into the Islamic community.

> While such hypocrites claim to have accepted *īmān*, in truth they are not believers: There are some who say: 'We believe in Allah and in the Last Day,' while in fact they do not believe.
>
> [*al-Baqarah* 2: 8]

They address the Muslims in their own idiom and when they talk with the *kuffār* (the disbelievers) it is very much as if they were their allies:

> When they meet the believers, they say: 'We believe,' but when they meet their evil companions (in privacy), they say: 'Surely we are with you.'
>
> [*al-Baqarah* 2: 14]

They make fun of Divine verses and express doubts about their veracity:

> When you hear the Signs of Allah being rejected and scoffed at, you will not sit with them.
>
> [*al-Nisā'* 4: 140]

They shirk away from Islamic religious duties, and even when they do perform such duties (like formal worship) it is merely for the apparent consumption of Muslims, otherwise, in reality, their hearts are repelled by submission to Divine commandments:

> When they rise to Prayer, they rise reluctantly, and only to be seen by people. They remember Allah but little. They dangle between the one and the other (that is, faith and unbelief), and belong fully neither to these nor to those.
>
> [*al-Nisā'* 4: 142-143]

And whenever they come to Prayer they do so lazily, and whenever they spend they do so grudgingly.

[*al-Tawbah* 9: 54]

And among the Bedouin Arabs there are such as regard whatever they spend (in the Way of Allah) as a fine.

[*al-Tawbah* 9: 98]

They lay claim to Islam but do not follow Islamic laws. Instead they follow the laws of *kuffār* in their daily transactions:

(O Messenger), have you not seen those who claim to believe in the Book which has been revealed to you and in the Books revealed before you, and yet desire to submit their disputes to the judgement of *Ṭāghūt* (the Satanic authorities who decide independently of the law of Allah), whereas they had been asked to reject it.

[*al-Nisā'* 4: 60]

Not only are their actions immoral and sinful, but they also attempt to corrupt the beliefs and actions of Muslims:

They (The hypocrites) enjoin what is evil, and forbid what is good, and withhold their hands from doing good. They forgot Allah, so Allah also forgot them.

[*al-Tawbah* 9: 67]

They wish that you should disbelieve just as they disbelieved so that you may all be alike.

[*al-Nisā'* 4: 89]

They only remain associated with the Muslims as long as these relationships are in their interests; whenever they see their interests dwindling, they part company with the Muslims:

(O Prophet), some of them find fault with you in the distribution of alms. If they are given something of it they are pleased, and if they are given nothing they are angry.

[al-Tawbah 9: 58]

Whenever Islam and Muslims face a crisis, they refuse to help the community. They do not take part in military action, because, in actual fact, they have no affection for Islam on account of which they are prepared to undertake some sacrifice for it. They neither believe in any reward accruing for their sacrifice. Nor are they certain of Islam's rightfulness that they may be persuaded to put their lives at risk in its support. Through one pretext and subterfuge or another, they attempt to shy away from battle, and even when they are forced to take part in an engagement, it is with great unwillingness. Instead of being a source of power, their participation becomes a cause of weakness for the Muslims. This role of the hypocrites is described in the Qur'ān in detail (in the following *Sūrah*s *Āl 'Imrān* [3: 118-120, 156, 165-168]; *al-Nisā'* [4: 72-73, 81]; *al-Tawbah* [9: 45-52, 73-97] and *al-Aḥzāb* [33: 12-14]).

The most dangerous feature of the hypocrites is that they join hands with the *kuffār* (unbelievers) whenever the Muslims are facing a crisis. They act as spies, offer them support, express delight at the predicament and reversal of the Muslims, accept awards and gain eminence in return for treachery against their own nation. Indeed, they are at the forefront of every dissension that rises against Islam and conspire to create divisions amongst Muslim ranks. All these attributes are described in detail in the Qur'ān (see *Sūrah*s *Āl 'Imrān*, *al-Nisā'*, *al-Tawbah*, *al-Aḥzāb* and *al-Munāfiqūn*).

Thus, it may very be appreciated that a correct and pure *īmān* is indispensable for the establishment, survival and stability of the Islamic system. The weakness of *īmān* makes this system hollow from the inside, right from its roots to the ends of each of its branches. No aspect of the system, from its morals to social life, politics, culture, and indeed the whole civilization can escape from the dangerous influences of weak faith.

Appendix: Life after Death

Is there another life after death or not? If there is such a life, what is it like? Indeed, the answers to these questions are beyond the reach of our knowledge, for we do not have the vision with which to reach beyond the boundaries of death and see what lies there and what does not. We neither have the ears with which to hear the sounds from 'over there' nor do we possess a tool that enables us to say with certainty whether anything exists on the other side or not.

Accordingly, as far as science is concerned, this question is completely out of its bounds. The person who, in the name of science, declares that there is no life after death is giving a totally unscientific statement. On the basis of science, it can neither be said that there is any life after death nor that there is not any such life. At least till the time that we acquire a certain scientific means to comment on the issue, the correct scientific attitude can only be that we neither accept nor reject life after death.

However, the question remains whether, in practical life, we can actually hold and defend this scientific view and attitude successfully. Perhaps not. Rather, certainly not. While it may be intellectually possible to restrain ourselves from giving either a negative or an affirmative response with regard to a thing or an issue about which we do not have the means to acquire knowledge, when the same thing has a connection with our lives then we have no option but to take a position on it – either by rejecting or accepting it.

For instance, there is a person with whom you are neither acquainted nor have had any previous or ongoing transactional relationship. In this case, it is possible for you not to pass judgement about the said person's honesty or dishonesty. However, when you are about to enter into a transaction with them, you will have to make a judgement about them and enter (or not) the transaction depending on whether you consider them to be either honest or dishonest. While, in your mind, you can go on holding to and practising a policy that until their integrity or lack thereof is proved, you will deal with them with an assumption of doubtful integrity (i.e. cautiously), the fact remains that your manner of interacting with them is of the kind that it would have been had you considered them to be dishonest. Therefore, in fact, the state of doubt – a state between rejection and acceptance – can only exist in the mind. Thus, a practical response can never be based upon doubt; for this, an attitude of either acceptance or rejection is inevitable.

The fact that the question of life after death is not merely a philo-sophical proposition, but one that has a deep relationship with our daily lives is clearly and easily understandable for anyone of us after only brief consideration and contemplation. Indeed, our ethical re-sponse is totally dependent upon our response to this question. If it were to be my view that life is whatever exists temporally, and that there is no other life after this, then my ethical response would be of one kind. However, if I think that there is another life after the present one, and it is one in which I shall not only be called to account for my present life but also that the manner of life therein – good or bad – shall be dependent upon my actions in this present life, my ethical course of action will be of a totally different type.

This case can be illustrated thus: consider a person who is travelling to Karachi in the belief that upon reaching Karachi the journey will not only end forever, but that after reaching that city he will be totally beyond the jurisdiction of the police and courts and any other authority which can question him on any account. Conversely, there is another person who believes that the trip to Karachi is just one leg of his journey, after which he will travel overseas to a country where the authorities have a complete record of his past actions and deeds in Pakistan in a secret dossier. This record will be examined in order to reach a decision regarding the status that will be assigned to him with regard to his work and stay in that country.

Any intelligent person can easily guess how different the courses of action of these two people are. The first will naturally only prepare for the trip to Karachi, while the other will also plan for the subsequent stages of the journey. The first will believe that whatever gain or loss he is to encounter will only be operative until he reaches Karachi and not beyond it. The second, who is only transiting through Karachi will think that the real loss or gain is not to be had on the first leg of the journey but rather in the last. While the first person will only have his attention directed towards those events and possibilities that are likely to occur on the trip to Karachi, the second person will also have within his focus those outcomes that will ensue after he reaches his country of final destination. Clearly, the difference in attitudes of these two people will be the result of the outlook that they possess about their respective journeys.

Exactly in the same way, in our own ethical lives, the beliefs that anyone holds about life after death have the same crucial effect. Whatever step any one of us takes in any field of action, its direction will be determined by what he considers this temporal life to be: the first and final phase of life or just a transitory one. In other words, such actions will depend on whether there is in that person's mind a subsequent life and its outcomes. In the first instance, the actions will lead towards one direction, while in the other case the direction will be completely different.

Thus we see that the question of life after death is not only an intellectual and a philosophical one, but one that relates to our practical lives. This being the case, there is no occasion for us to stop at the point of doubt and indecisiveness in this regard. Whatever may be the attitude that we adopt in life, if it is full of doubt it too shall unavoidably be one of rejection. Therefore, in any case, we are forced into determining whether there is life after death or not. If science cannot help us in this regard, then we have recourse to intellectual exercise. The next question that arises is what material or grounds do we have for a valid rational judgement?

First of all, we have before us, the human race itself. Secondly, we have the cosmic system. Placing human beings within this cosmic system, we should examine whether it is possible to cater for all their requirements from within this system, or whether some essential needs remain to be fulfilled for which we may require some other system.

Consider the fact that we have bodies composed of numerous minerals, salts, gases and water. The equivalent counterparts of these materials are also found in the physical universe – for instance, rivers and streams also contain metals, salts, gases and water. All these elements are governed by natural laws that are operative throughout the cosmos. Just as these laws enable mountains, rivers and the winds to perform their roles in the external atmosphere, in a similar way the human body is also enabled to work under the same laws.

Consider also that our bodies are entities which grow by acquiring nourishment from their environment. Similar types of creations comprise trees, plants and grasses that are also found in the universe. The laws that are required for the growth of these entities are also found here.

Moreover, we are living beings who move about by our own volition, acquire food by our own endeavour, provide self-arranged protection for our bodies and arrange for the preservation of our kind. There are many other kinds of similar beings in the cosmos. On land, in water and air there are innumerable living beings. Also operative, in these milieus, are numerous laws that are required for these beings to be able to fully function and for them to prevail over natural processes in their respective areas of activity.

Above these all, human beings occupy a different category of exist-ence, one which we call ethical existence. We have within ourselves the ability and consciousness to do good and evil, the capacity to dis-tinguish between right and wrong, and the power to be righteous and unscrupulous. Our nature demands that the consequence of virtue be good and that of vice be bad. We are able to differentiate between un-fairness and justice, truth and falsehood, right and wrong, mercy and cruelty, gratefulness and thanklessness, generosity and miserliness, trustworthiness and deceitfulness and other similar pairs of ethical and unethical traits. These are not merely imaginary characteristics but are practically found in our life. Indeed, the influences of these traits actually impact upon human cultures to a remarkable degree. Accordingly, the nature with which we have been inherently imbued strongly demands that just as there are physical results emanating from our actions, there should also be moral results from our actions.

Take a deep look at the physical cosmos. Is it possible for the moral consequences of human actions to fully manifest themselves in this system? I can assure you that there is no possibility of this in this present state of existence. This is because, to the best of our knowledge, there is no other living being that exists on a moral plane. The whole cosmic system operates on the basis of physical laws. Moral principles cannot be seen in operation. Here, money has power and value but truthfulness has neither of these. Here, a mango seed always bears a mango plant, but the one who sows the seed of honesty is sometimes greeted with a shower of praise and at other times condemned to suffer disgrace. Here, material elements are governed by specific laws, which always lead to preordained results. Yet there is no law governing moral elements in a way that their interactions may always lead to a predetermined result.

In this milieu governed by the supremacy of physical laws, at times no moral consequences arise, and even when they do take place then only to the extent that is allowed by such physical laws. It often so happens that morality requires a certain result to emerge from a given action, and yet due to the interference of physical laws, the final outcome is exactly opposite to the moral one. Acting through our own cultural and political systems, we have made limited attempts towards obtaining the moral outcomes of human actions according to an established code. However, this attempt has been on an extremely limited scale, and thus has been very deficient. On the one hand, physical laws make the attempt incomplete and imperfect, and, on the other hand, many of our own weaknesses enhance the defects in its management.

I would like to elucidate my argument with a few illustrations. Consider a situation in which one person – who is the enemy of another – sets fire to the home of his opponent; naturally, the house will burn down. This is the physical result of the arsonist's action. The moral result should be that the arsonist is punished to exactly the same extent as he has damaged the said family. However, for that outcome to take place, it is essential that evidence linking the accused to the fire be found, that he be apprehended by the police, that his crime is proved beyond reasonable doubt, that the court is able to fully determine the total extent of damage to the affected family and its future generations, and then acting with full measure of justice award it exactly the same punishment. If any of these conditions were not fulfilled, then the moral outcome would not take place at all or, if and when it does take place, it will only materialize partially.[1] It is also possible that having destroyed his opponent, the arsonist goes scot-free and prospers, on account of the absence of full evidence.

Take another illustration on a much larger scale. A few individuals are able to become so influential in their national spheres that their whole nation starts following their dictates. Taking advantage of their positions, they are able to generate passionate feelings of nationalism and jingoism. Then, declaring war on countries in their region, they cause the deaths of hundreds of thousands, destroy one country after another, and cause tens of millions of people to fall into misery and destitution. So great is the impact of their actions on the course of human history that its effects continue to grow generation after generation over the next several hundred years.[2]

Do you believe that the individuals who were guilty of such immense crimes can ever be awarded just and appropriate punishment in this temporal life? It should be apparent that even if they could be skinned and their bodies cut up into pieces, or burned alive, or given any punishment within the power of human beings, it would still not be possible to penalize them in any way that comes close to the destruction they wreaked upon countless millions and their generations to come.

---

[1] Is it really possible to assess the emotional damage caused by the burning down of one's ancestral home or all the lost possibilities for the family's future prosperity? What if the house burned down at a time when the children were having their examinations; would they not suffer the loss of an academic year forever? How many dear possessions of an emotional value were lost in the fire? Is it possible to recreate an old letter written by one's grandfather or a rare old manuscript? – Translator.

[2] Numerous real life historical events within the last century such as the World Wars, the Vietnam War, the tragedy of Muslims in Palestine, Iraq and Afghanistan have left mind-boggling statistics of death and destitution and destruction – Translator.

Under the existing physical laws on the basis of which the present cosmic system operates, it is simply not possible that they be punished in a way that is commensurate with their crimes.

In the same way, take those virtuous people who have instructed humanity in truth and uprightness, given it the light of proper guidance, and as a consequence of whose benevolence countless generations have benefited and will continue to benefit in the centuries to come. Is it possible to truly and fully reward such people for their services? Can you even imagine that an individual be entirely compensated for actions, the benefits of which have spread out to an incalculable number of people over thousands of years within the bounds of the present physical laws?

As stated above, firstly, the physical laws under which the present cosmic system operates simply do not have the capacity to fully encompass the moral outcomes of human actions. Secondly, the consequences of actions that human beings undertake within the limited period of their temporal lives extends so far and wide, and continue for so long, that to fully obtain and reckon their resultant effects would require a life span of several thousand, if not hundreds of thousands of years. Within existing natural laws, it is impossible for human beings to have such a life span.

From this argument we can understand that while the present physical world and its natural laws may suffice for the temporal, corporeal and animal elements of human existence, these are totally inadequate for the moral elements. For these, we require another cosmic system whose governing code is a moral law under the supremacy of which physical laws merely operate in a facilitating role. Under this system, the life span is not limited, but would rather be infinite, and it would be one in which all the moral outcomes which may not have materialized in this temporal world, or which may have materialized in an adverse manner, will manifest in their proper manner. In such a scheme of things, not gold or silver but virtue and truth will have weight and value. It will be one in which fire will burn only that object which would morally deserve to be set ablaze, where the pious lead luxurious lives and misery is the exclusive domain of the evil.

Our intellect desires, and nature demands, that such a cosmic system should exist.

As far as intellectual reasoning is concerned, it just leads us to a normative 'should be' state. As far as the question about whether any such milieu actually exists, both our intellect and knowledge are unable to ascertain this. Here, the Qur'ān comes to our assistance. It declares that the state of affairs which both our intellect and nature demand, will, indeed, come to pass. There will come a time when the present system of physical laws will be broken asunder, after which another system will be established in which the earth and the heavens and all other things will operate in a different manner. It will be then that Allah will cause the rebirth of all those human beings who were ever born from the beginning of time till its apocalyptic end and assemble them before Himself. At that assembly, the record of every individual, every nation and, indeed, the whole of humanity will be available without any mistake or omission. The complete details of every result caused by every individual action will be available. All those generations that were affected by a certain person's action will stand in the witness box. Every speck and grain upon which human words or actions created any impression will come alive to tell its tale. The very body organs of a human being, hands and feet, eyes and tongues, will give testimony on how they were used by the individual possessing them.

Finally, based upon all this documentation, the Greatest Ruler of all, acting with total justice unknown to human beings in their world-ly life, will decide the reward and punishment that each deserves. Both this reward and punishment will be on such an immense scale that no estimation of its extent is possible with the limited measurements of the existing cosmic system. There, in the system to come, the measurements of time and space will be altogether different. All quantifications will be of a type unknown to us. There, the laws of nature will also be of some other kind. People whose good deeds continued to have an impact upon humanity for thousands of years will be able to obtain their full recompense, without disease, old age or death being able to curtail their lives of luxury. Similarly, human beings whose evil deeds continued to impact on the world for thousands of years will suffer the full punishment for them, without unconsciousness or death being able to rid them of their pain.

I pity the limited intellect of those who consider such a life and such a cosmic system that will certainly come into existence in the future to be impossible. If it is possible for our present cosmic system to have come into existence with the present set of natural laws, why is it impossible for a different cosmic system to come into being with a different set of laws? However, the fact that such a system will surely come into existence can neither be proved by evidence nor by intellectual proof. This only requires a belief in the unseen.

Index

F

Falāḥ (Deliverance, Prosperity, Success), 90, 101
Fāsiq (One who goes beyond the boundaries set by Allah), 65
Fear of Allah, 21, 23, 47, 55, 65, 78, 80, 92, 107, 110–11, 118, 217, 228, 235
Fisq (Wickedness), 79
Fiṭrah (Primary and Instinctive Life), 24–7

G

Greeks, xii, xvii

H

Ḥalāl (Lawful), 64
Ḥarām (Forbidden), 64, 66
Hereafter: belief in, 192–6, 218–27; denial of, 182–6, 196–7; life in, 197–204; preference over temporal life, 227–33; system of life in, 204–18; Qur'ānic argument in favour of, 196–7
Humility, 110–11
Huntingdon, Samuel, xi
Ḥusain ibn 'Alī, 67
Hypocrisy, 240, 244–7

I

Ideal, collective, 37–43, 70
Īmān see Belief
Īmāniyāt see Belief system
India, xi, 42n, 139, 187
Individual responsibility, 22–4
Individualism, 41, 54, 75
Injustice (ẓulm), 1, 11, 90, 119, 184, 216, 220–1
Intellect, 4, 18, 26, 42, 44, 52, 59, 72, 73, 84–7, 97, 104, 121, 125, 136, 151, 165, 188, 190, 193–4, 204, 210–11, 213–4, 255–6
Iqbāl, Muḥammad, ix

Islām ka Niẓām-i-Ḥayāt (by Mawdūdī), xxii
Islam, universality of, 177–8
Islāmī 'Ibādāt par aik Taḥqīqī Naẓar (by Mawdūdī), xxii
Islāmī Tahdhīb awr uske Uṣūl–o–Mabādī (by Mawdūdī), xxii(n)
Islamic civilization: characteristics of, 238–42; danger of hypocrisy in, 244–7; harmony between thought and action in, 52–3; ideal of, 62–7; role of belief in, 236–47; unimportance of historical continuities in Mawdūdī's thought, xii–xiii

J

Jamā'at-i-Islāmī, ix
Jihād, 51
Justice, 13, 169, 205, 251, 253; and the Last Day, 192, 213–8, 220, 230–3, 255

K

Khuṭubāt (by Mawdūdī), xxii
Knowledge, 98–101, 162, 175; experimental, 193–4; prophetic, 134–6
Kufr (Disbelief), 64, 79, 90, 93, 96, 152n, 158–9, 213, 244; Kāfir (Disbeliever), 64, 80–1

L

Last Day: and justice, 192, 213–8, 220, 230–3, 255; and theory of transmigration, 186–92; belief in, 179–235; benefits of belief in, 233–5; necessity of belief in, 218–27; record of temporal actions, 230–3
Law, natural, 26–7, 29
Life, 36–57; concept of, 24–7; ideal of, 36–67; temporal, 1–35, 54,

Trust in Allah, 114–16
Trusteeship, 10–12, 32–3

V
Vicegerency, 7–13
Virtue, 56–8, 98, 149–50, 172, 185,
   221, 224, 251

W
War, 51, 253

Z
Zakāh, 47, 51
Ẓulm (Injustice), 11, 90